WHAT HAS SOCIOLOGY ACHIEVED?

Also by Christopher G. A. Bryant

*POSITIVISM IN SOCIAL THEORY AND RESEARCH
SOCIOLOGY IN ACTION

Also by Henk A. Becker

IMPACT ASSESSMENT TODAY (*editor with A. L. Porter*)
SOCIOLOGIE EN VERZORGINGSSTAAT (*editor with P. Glasbergen*)

*Also published by Macmillan

What Has Sociology Achieved?

Edited by
Christopher G. A. Bryant
University of Salford

and

Henk A. Becker
Rijksuniversiteit te Utrecht

MACMILLAN

First published 1990

Published by
THE MACMILLAN PRESS LTD
Houndmills, Basingstoke, Hampshire RG21 2XS
and London
Companies and representatives
throughout the world

Typeset by Vine & Gorfin Ltd,
Exmouth, Devon
Printed in Hong Kong

British Library Cataloguing in Publication Data
What has sociology achieved?
I. Bryant, Christopher G. A. (Christopher Gordon
Alastair), *1944*– II. Becker, Henk A., *1933*–
301
ISBN 0–333–46045–6 (hardcover)
ISBN 0–333–46046–4 (paperback)

In memory of
Nicholas C. Mullins
1939–88

Contents

Contents

Preface and Acknowledgements

The thinking behind this volume is set out in the Introduction. Briefly, we have been concerned that, in an age when continued financial and other support for teaching and research in sociology cannot be taken for granted, sociologists have often made their predicament worse by their failure to present a clear statement of the achievements of sociology in the western world in the second half of this century. In order to begin to remedy this, we invited a number of sociologists to contribute papers to a symposium at Noordwijk in the Netherlands from 26 to 29 November 1987. We are very grateful to the Netherlands Science Foundation and the University of Utrecht for their financial support for the symposium, and to Lizette Jongen for her help with its organization.

All but two of the chapters of this book are derived from papers presented in person at Noordwijk. One of the exceptions is the chapter on American sociology. Illness prevented Nicholas Mullins from travelling to Noordwijk but he sent his paper for the other participants to discuss in his absence. It was with great sadness that we learned in July 1988 of his death and it is the wish of all the contributors to this volume that it be dedicated to his memory. The other exception is the chapter on French sociology. We failed in our protracted endeavours to get a French sociologist to join us at Noordwijk, but shortly afterwards we made contact with Philippe Bernoux and we were delighted when he agreed to write for us.

Both symposium and book are products of the link between the Department of Sociology and Anthropology of the University of Salford and the Research Group on Planning and Policy of the University of Utrecht. We are grateful to our colleagues for their comments and encouragement and to our Universities for the travel funds which have enabled us to meet, plan and edit in both Salford and Utrecht. We also wish to thank the following for permission to reproduce tables and figures: Professor W. W. Baldamus for Table 3.1; *Sociology*, the journal of the British Sociological Association, for Figure 7.3; and the University of California Press for Figure 13.1. Last, but very definitely not least, we should like to thank Sheila Walker for typing and photocopying with good humour and great patience.

Salford   CHRISTOPHER G. A. BRYANT
Utrecht   HENK A. BECKER

Notes on the Contributors

Peter Abell is Professor of Sociology in the Department of Sociology and Social Policy, University of Surrey, Guildford, Surrey GU2 5XH, England.

Wil A. Arts is a Research Fellow in Sociology in the Department of Economics, Erasmus University of Rotterdam, PO Box 1378, 3000 DR Rotterdam, Netherlands.

Henk A. Becker is Professor of Sociology and the Methodology of Social Research in the Research Group on Planning and Policy, Faculty of Social Sciences, University of Utrecht, PO Box 80.108, 3508 TC Utrecht, Netherlands.

Philippe Bernoux is Director of Research in the Groupe Lyonnais de Sociologie Industrielle (CNRS), University of Lyon II, Maison Rhône-Alpes des Sciences de l'Homme, 14 avenue Berthelot, 69007 Lyon, France.

Christopher G. A. Bryant is Professor of Sociology in the Department of Sociology and Anthropology, University of Salford, Salford M5 4WT, England.

Martin Bulmer is a Reader in the Department of Social Science and Administration, London School of Economics, Houghton Street, London WC2A 2AE, England.

John Eldridge is Professor of Sociology in the Department of Sociology, University of Glasgow, 61 Southpark Avenue, Glasgow G12 8FL, Scotland.

Leo Laeyendecker has now retired but was formerly Professor of Sociology in the Faculty of Social Sciences, University of Leiden, 242 Stationsplein, 2312 AR Leiden, Netherlands.

Stephen Mennell is a Reader in the Department of Sociology, University of Exeter, Amory Building, Rennes Drive, Exeter EX4 4RJ, England.

Nicholas C. Mullins was, until his death in 1988, Professor of Sociology in the Department of Sociology, Virginia Polytechnic Institute and State University, Blacksburg, Virginia, VA 24061, USA.

Ansgar Weymann is Professor of Sociology in Fachbereich 8, University of Bremen, Bibliothekstrasse, 2800 Bremen 33, FRG.

Robin Williams is a Lecturer in the Department of Sociology and Social Policy, University of Durham, Elvet Riverside, New Elvet, Durham DH1 3JT, England.

1 Introduction
Christopher G. A. Bryant and
Henk A. Becker

ACHIEVEMENT IN SOCIOLOGY: THE TWO SIDES TO THE
STORY

What has sociology achieved in the western world since 1950? On the
face of it, it has achieved a very great deal. In North America it has
greatly expanded what was already a considerable presence in
universities and colleges, whilst in the higher education systems of
western Europe it has enjoyed even more spectacular growth if only
because its beginnings were so much smaller. Production of books and
articles has also increased enormously, and most people have now at
least heard of sociology even if they seldom have an accurate idea of
what it is. This, however, is only one side of the story. The other, in
many societies, has to do with growing government, media and
business indifference, suspicion or even downright hostility towards
the discipline. In the 1980s these negative sentiments have proved all
too easily translatable into disproportionately severe cutbacks for
sociology (and other social sciences) in those societies whose governments have made a shibboleth out of reducing public expenditure.

It is not practical here to go into how this has come about in any
detail. No doubt exaggerated expectations of sociology played their
part. In Britain in the 1960s there may have been a belief in some
quarters that the identification of social laws, trends or developments
would somehow guide government and people towards rates of
economic growth comparable to those found in Germany and France.
In America, Converse has given a nice cameo of what may have gone
wrong in the social sciences generally. He contrasts the optimism
which suffused the symposium to mark the twenty-fifth anniversary of
the Social Sciences Building of the University of Chicago in 1954 with
the pessimism that hung over the fiftieth anniversary symposium in
1979:

> In 1954, social scientists saw themselves as being on the brink of two
> major coups; one scientific, one political. The scientific coup, of
> course, was the imminent arrival at the apex of an exact science of

human affairs, reduced to a few crucial mathematical equations. The political coup was that of unerring policy problem solution by a new breed of philosopher-kings. Against such a backdrop, the pessimism suddenly made sense to me. After all, it was a full quarter of a century later, and we still were not there. (Converse, 1986, p. 43).

In addition there may, in the 1960s, have been some who, like Daniel Bell, associated the 'sociologising mode' with the transition to the wine-and-roses of a post-industrial society (Bell, 1973). Then again, on the Continent in the 1960s and 1970s, there may have been those who identified sociology with ever more pervasive state administration and provision, or supervision, of welfare, and others who identified it with Marxist activists, student revolutionaries and other demons of the left. If these suggestions are right, contemporary disillusionment with sociology is easy enough to understand. Britain's relative economic decline relentlessly continued at least until well into the 1980s – no proof of the value of sociology there. In America, the philosopher's kingdom has proved as misconceived as the philosopher's stone, and everywhere the post-industrial dream has faded. De-industrialisation and unemployment are as evident now, and much service sector employment plainly affords neither high pay nor high job satisfaction – how much the product of a brief historical moment the 'sociologising mode' now seems. And on the Continent, the long arm of the state is held by many to have reached too far – sociology seems to have been aligned with social regulation rather than individual freedom; alternatively, the hard left is still felt to threaten – and is believed to draw support from sociologists.

It is worth noting that in all three of these cases, sociology is associated with social intervention and collective action. These are not causes for which today's neo-liberal governments, dévotés of market forces, have much sympathy. Personally we refuse to abandon these causes. At the same time we would emphasise that from Spencer onwards there have always been those who have articulated sociologies consistent with liberal principles. There is no necessary connection between sociology and socialism, social democracy or conservatism.

From examples of the kind just given, it could be concluded that sociology has suffered unjustly from too exclusive an association, in the eyes of its critics, with particular social, economic and political circumstances. If this is correct then the prospects for sociology should improve if its practitioners can continue to do significant work in the very different circumstances of the 1980s and 1990s. There is, however, one crucial respect in which we sociologists have been our own worst enemies – namely our readiness to dramatise debate as a war of the schools and reflection as the crisis of our discipline. Over the last quarter-century, sociology has sustained an extraordinarily intense theoretical debate between representatives of competing modes of sociological inquiry. For the participants, the experience has often been exhilarating. Among lay onlookers, however, the disorderly spectacle has appeared at best an indulgence and at worst an object of contempt. This is a pity because much was learned in the course of the war; the excesses of the past have given way to both more judicious recognition of the limitations, as well as the strengths, of particular modes of inquiry and greater interest in the possibilities of *creative* tensions (Johnson *et al.* 1983) and synthesis (as in the work of Giddens, 1976 and 1984). Also the debates have influenced the design of empirical social research in *all* the social sciences, and prompted interest in multiple methods and triangulation.

TAKING STOCK OF ACHIEVEMENT

It seems to us that this is an opportune time intellectually to take stock of what sociology has achieved in the western world since 1950. We also believe such an exercise can help sociologists to *marshal arguments and supply examples* of successful research which will win continued funding for teaching and research from those who control the necessary moneys or have influence over their disbursement – government, business, the media and our fellow citizens. We have limited ourselves to the western world just to make the task more manageable. We do not doubt that there has been a record of achievement in the eastern bloc (especially in Poland and Hungary) and in the Third World, but we must leave it to others to document it. We have also confined attention to the second half of the century because it is the greatly expanded provision for teaching and research in this period whose wisdom is now sometimes questioned – especially in Europe. Also the Second World War gave sociologists in America new opportunities to show what their researches could do; by 1950 most of those researches had been published and a new era was beginning there too.

Taking stock of so large and varied a body of work is more than we have the competence to do unaided. We therefore decided to proceed by inviting distinguished colleagues to write essays on particular areas of special interest to them, first for a conference in the Netherlands in November 1987 and then for publication by Macmillan. We will comment on the breakdown of these essays in a moment, but we want to comment first on the kind of essays we commissioned. Each is addressed to sociologists in general in the belief that many of us could do with a clearer statement of the case we can make, *based not on promise but on achievement*, for continued support for our discipline. The intended readership includes undergraduates majoring in sociology in the final years of their courses, because their ability to promote the cause of sociology inside and outside academic employment is crucial to its future. For their benefit, as well as that of colleagues who are being asked to consider matters beyond their usual interests, key items for further reading in the references at the end of each essay are starred.

IDENTIFYING ACHIEVEMENT

So far we have spoken of achievement both assertively and coyly. We do not want to labour the notion of achievement. We simply have in mind work of quality that is recognised by friend and foe alike to have been important in the emergence and development of a particular mode of inquiry, methodology or specialty including exemplary empirical researches. In his book *Social Mobility*, Heath refers to studies by Marx, Pareto, Sorokin, Glass, Lipset, Bendix, and Blau and Duncan as 'landmarks' (Heath, 1981, ch. 1). Perhaps the work of the Oxford Social Mobility Group, of which he was a member, could be added to that list. Our idea of achievements is similar. Achievements have a presence which cannot be ignored and they help others to orient their work. They give form to what otherwise might have been amorphous and they point the way where otherwise there might have been aimlessness. Asked to name good researches, and to justify their choices, most sociologists, in our experience, can do so readily. This is what we have asked our contributors to do here.

We have spoken coyly in so far as we have refrained from reference to the growth of sociological knowledge or to progress in sociology. Whether a record of achievement constitutes growth or progress is much more difficult because ideas of growth and progress vary between modes and methodologies. We shall return to this in the

Conclusions after we have considered our colleagues' essays. For the moment let us just note that there is one hypothetical set of circumstances, at least, in which it might be said that sociologists know *less* than they used to. Imagine a rapidly changing world in which sociologists, for whatever reason, lose favour, numbers and money so that they are unable to do research of the same quantity and quality as once they did. Those that remain might be said to know less of their world than their forebears did of theirs. (It happened in the Soviet Union following the fall of Bukharin in the late 1920s.) Wherever growth or progress lies, it does not lie there; and yet it is a fate we risk unless we can present a record of achievement to those who have a say in our funding.

One way of taking stock of achievement is to look at the record, specialty by specialty. We have not done that here because there would be more candidates for inclusion than we could cope with. More pertinently, the debates which have given outsiders the impression that sociology is beset by intolerable disorder recur in most specialties. We therefore proposed that contributors address the following cross-cutting topics, and that in all cases they emphasise the best work, rather than the merely average, and give examples. First we invited separate essays on the three main traditions of sociology: the analytical (or empirical-analytical), the hermeneutic (which includes symbolic interactionism, phenomenology and ethnomethodology), and the historico-institutional. We acknowledged that each tradition contains more than one partial paradigm, to use Wells and Picou's term (1981); that there is no reason to assume that the record of achievement in all traditions and partial paradigms is equally good; that different traditions and partial paradigms often have good reasons for constituting their objects differently and for harbouring different ambitions with respect to explanation, prediction and generalisation; and that assessment of achievement depends, on occasions, not only on criteria peculiar to sociology in particular or social science in general, but also on ideas drawn from what is thought to happen in different natural sciences, the writing of history and studies of language. (There are interesting discussions of some of these issues in Fiske and Shweder (eds), 1986.) In short, we had no wish to impose a false uniformity of character and record upon sociology; but we did believe both that each tradition and partial paradigm could be said to have achievements to its credit, and that none has a monopoly on virtue. Put another way, we suspected both that different traditions and partial paradigms have more in common and more complementarities than their partisans sometimes suppose, and that the diversities which remain are more a strength than a weakness in so far as (different facets of) different problems, conceptualised in different ways, move sociologists to adopt different methodologies with a view to offering different kinds of solution.

Next we sought essays on theory, research methods and applications. The essay on theory deals with work which has contributed to a more sophisticated idea of what social theory is and can be, and considers types and levels of theorising as well as metatheoretical discourses which transcend the three traditions of the first three essays. The essay on methods looks at innovation and refinement in quantitative and qualitative methods, and evidence of increasing understanding of the strengths and limitations of particular methods. The essay on applied sociology counters Scott and Shore's *Why Sociology Does Not Apply* (1979), and considers much more sophisticated ideas of what application consists of.

SOCIOLOGY IN NATIONAL CONTEXTS

The first six essays are predicated on the assumption that a record of achievement can be identified. They are intended to furnish the armoury of sociologists wherever they are engaged in a struggle to win continued support by marshalling arguments and providing examples from research literatures which sustain claims to a record of achievement. With the exception of applied sociology, however, they treat achievement as something internal to sociology which sociologists alone are fit to recognise, but which they have sometimes been remiss in making known outside the academy or even to academics in other disciplines. Achievement unrecognised except by those who claim it can never be satisfactory because it carries no guarantee that support for future work will be forthcoming. Accordingly, we also decided to ask for examinations of achievement in sociology in national contexts in essays covering the United States, Britain, France, Germany and the Netherlands. We asked our authors, where possible, to connect the external environment in which sociology operates – government, business, media and popular support or lack thereof; provision for teaching in universities, colleges and schools; public and private funding of research; and the employment of sociologists in state administration and the private sector as well as in teaching and research – to its character and content. Here the meaning of achievement is different and the record more equivocal, because sociologists have to satisfy not only themselves but also their paymasters and those their paymasters heed; by the same token, reflection on what may be judged an achievement by sociologists themselves, and what has and has not seemingly commanded support outside the academy, is especially valuable because it can prompt thoughts on how we might go about improving our collective lot. Strategies to this end are considered in the penultimate chapter.

There is a case for the teaching of sociology which stresses that it is exceptionally well-placed to produce graduates who are highly literate, numerate and articulate. Indeed where else are such graduates going to come from? Science and engineering courses do not develop skills in the written and oral presentation of evidence and argument, and arts courses are all too often refuges for the innumerate. We would like to see this case made more often and more forcefully. We also note with pride the open-ended intellectual excitement that still attaches to the study and practice of sociology when some other undergraduate programmes, in particular, confine attention to the acquisition of a meal-ticket. But it is the intrinsic value of sociological analysis and research which we have most need to convey. Specifying the record of achievement in sociology, making it known to all sociologists (let alone other academics), and securing recognition for it outside the academy – these are huge tasks. This volume is offered as one small contribution to their realisation.

References

Bell, D. (1973) *The Coming of Post-Industrial Society* (New York: Basic Books).

Fiske, D. W. and Shweder, R. A. (eds) (1986) *Metatheory in Social Science: Pluralisms and Subjectivities* (Chicago: University of Chicago Press).

Converse, P. E. (1986) 'Generalizations and the Social Psychology of "Other Worlds"', in Fiske and Shweder (1986) ch. 2.

Giddens, A. (1976) *New Rules of Sociological Method* (London: Hutchinson).

—— (1984) *The Constitution of Society* (Cambridge: Polity Press).

Heath, A. (1981) *Social Mobility* (Glasgow: Fontana).

Johnson, T., Dandeker, C. and Ashworth, C. (1983) *The Structure of Social Theory* (London: Macmillan).

Scott, R. A. and Shore, A. R. (1979) *Why Sociology Does Not Apply* (NewYork: Elsevier).

Wells, R. H. and Picou, J. S. (1981) *American Sociology: Theoretical and Methodological Structure* (Washington: University Press of America).

2 Achievement in the Analytical Tradition in Sociology
Henk A. Becker

1 INTRODUCTION

When sociology was founded as an academic discipline, the spirit of the time was predominantly positivist. Studying society in those days meant searching for scientific laws that would enable man to predict future events in a reliable and precise way, thereby enhancing human capacity to intervene in social reality at will. The guiding image of this tradition has been aptly formulated by Comte as 'savoir pour prévoir, prévoir afin de pouvoir'. This guiding image implicitly contains criteria for identifying achievement in the early years of the tradition: causal understanding of the phenomena to be manipulated, prediction based upon causal laws, intervention based upon causal understanding and prediction. We are talking about sociologists who wanted knowledge primarily in order to be able to apply it to the solution of practical problems. We are also talking about the mainstream tradition in sociology.[1]

The quest for scientific laws as found in physics is not anymore the primary preoccupation of sociologists who carry on the mainstream tradition. Nowadays biology is the principal frame of reference, as we shall see later on in this chapter.[2] The sociologists concerned have also changed names a number of times. After a while they did not call themselves positivists any more, or neo-positivists. They became the empirico-analytical sociologists. Since the middle of the 1970s they prefer to be referred to as analytical sociologists.

In this chapter I will be looking for answers to four (clusters of) questions. First, what are the main characteristics of analytical sociology and what criteria are used to identify achievement? (see Section 2). Second, what examples can be given of achievement in analytical sociology with regard to theory-related empirical research? (see Sections 3 to 6). Third, what examples can be given of achievement in analytical sociology regarding theory formation? (see Section

8

7). Fourth, to what extent can these examples be seen as instances of achievement in sociology that are of a more than incidental character? (see Section 8).

Examples of achievement in research have been taken from a number of areas in sociology; some of these are well-established, others have only received systematic attention more recently. All, however, demand research into characteristics of social systems as well as individuals in large numbers. The extent to which the areas and examples chosen represent a general overview of sociology will be discussed in Section 8. Some examples of achievement given in other chapters may be seen as instances of achievement in analytical sociology as well. This applies in particular to Chapter 7, 'Successful Applications of Sociology'. In addition, Section 7 on theory formation complements the discussion of theory in Chapter 5.

2 THE ANALYTICAL TRADITION

The guiding image of analytical sociology and its criteria for identifying achievement can be summarised by formulating four questions that are vital to this tradition and by giving preliminary answers to them. The first two questions have been asked since the emergence of positivism – or positivisms, because it never was a homogeneous movement (Bryant, 1985a). The other two questions have become pressing in the second half of this century, but they played some role before as well.

The first question reads: Can the end-result of sociological investigation be formulated as 'laws' or 'law-like' generalisations of the same kind as those established by natural scientists? (Bryant, 1985a, p. 8, citing Giddens).

For a long time the subject of laws in social science has been approached by way of the 'covering law model' as presented by Hempel in 'The Function of General Laws in History' (1942). D'Andrade (1986, p. 19) describes this model as follows:

The covering law model of science seems close to the way people think about science: on the surface, the model seems unexceptional. Its main outline goes as follows: (a) science consists of a search for 'general laws' to explain events; (b) the statement of a general law can have different logical forms, but it typically makes a universal generalization across some domain of events; (c) the main function of general laws is to connect events in patterns, which are usually referred to as 'explanation' and 'prediction'. Major debates about the covering law model have involved whether it corresponds to what historians do, or could do, and whether it can be used more generally in explanation of human behavior. There has also been an extended and inconclusive discussion of the necessary and sufficient characteristics a statement must have to be a general law.

Since the mid-1970s, most social scientists treat the covering law model and the methodological prescription of testing hypotheses by predictions as metaphors only and not as rigorous requirements. Social scientists deal with systems that contain a lot of 'disorder' (also called 'chaos' or 'noise'). As a consequence the best they can do is to search for 'underlying mechanisms' capable of explaining the emergence of phenomena. Any predictions they make will not provide decisive tests of their theories (cf. Outhwaite, 1987, p. 58, on realist philosophies of science).

The most convincing contemporary answer in sociology to the first question comes from Boudon who (with regard to social change) distinguishes relatively closed and relatively open situations in social systems. Open situations show a relatively large degree of 'disorder'. He sees two categories of generalisations, matching these types of situations. In the first place there are laws and theories *stricto sensu* (1984, pp. 202, 217). Laws and theories belonging to this category, which might be falsified according to the requirements formulated by Popper, are rare in sociology, and presumably they will remain rare, because the subject-matter of sociology shows a lot of disorder. Boudon's second category contains formal theories. These theories he sees as 'not in themselves directly applicable to reality, but which offer a mode of discussion or describe ideal examples which may be useful in the analysis of certain process' (1984, p. 219; 1986, p. 207).

Boudon has little faith in the search for general theories *stricto sensu*. But if partial or local theories are aimed for, some situations might be sufficiently 'closed' to make success feasible. He states that 'the only *scientific* theories of social change are *partial* and *local* ones' (1984, p. 220; 1986, p. 208).

Boudon does not say explicitly that 'partial and local scientific theories' are concepts taken from contemporary biology. But in biology the quest for universal laws no longer predominates, because it only yielded vague notions about, for example, 'life'. The degree of disorder found in the subject-matter of biology does make it feasible (and relevant) to formulate laws that are restricted to a limited number of aspects and that are bound in time and space, however. Whenever biologists want to deal with phenomena that show a relatively high degree of disorder, they use models (as heuristic frames of reference). Models like these resemble the formal theories to which Boudon refers (cf. Fiske and Shweder, 1986).

The second question reads: How technical or instrumental can sociological knowledge become, and will there ever emerge a positive polity? (cf. Bryant, 1985a, pp. 8, 11).

Discussing the first question we have already met Boudon's conclusion that general theories *stricto sensu* are not to be expected in sociology. Sometimes partial or local theories *stricto sensu* will be feasible, but in all other cases formal theories will have to be used. This implies that a positive polity will not emerge, because as a rule policy-makers have to act in situations that are relatively open.[3] If sociologists cannot provide policy-makers with instruments for a postitive polity, they can nevertheless be useful in other ways. Sociologists can assist (or criticise) policy-makers by providing 'frames of reference'. Theories in particular can have a very practical usefulness. In the same spirit sociologists can offer 'enlightenment' without pretending to be able to provide kinds of knowledge that would facilitate intervention along strictly predictable lines. A 'low-profile' presentation of sociology in the corridors of power is not easy, however, because many policy-makers still have positivistic expectations of sociology, demanding 'hard' data and reliable and precise forecasts. Time and time again sociologists have to point out that the social systems concerned show varying degrees of disorder.

The third question is: How can continuity and change in scientific disciplines be accounted for and how are they related to achievement (and progress) in science?

Since the late 1960s the discussion about continuity and change in science has been dominated by the ideas about scientific revolutions developed by Kuhn (1962). According to Kuhn, periods of normal science and widely accepted paradigms shift into revolutionary periods with new paradigms. The new paradigms contain 'exemplars' totally different from those dominating the prior period and, if Kuhn is to be believed, norms covering both old and new paradigms do not exist. Rather than summarise this discussion, we shall draw attention to something Kuhn omits, but which is vital to the question we are trying to answer. Virtually all applied parts of scientific disciplines have two interrelated analyses in common.[4] First, they look for an answer to the question: 'How did these practical problems come into existence?'

Second, they ask: 'What will be the effects (and side-effects) of interventions directed at these practical problems?' Together these two analyses constitute a 'metaparadigm' covering all applied parts of natural and social science. The metaparadigm is based upon the assumption that all applied science tries to assist interventions that attempt the mitigation or liquidation of human suffering (injustice, injuries, etc.) or human inefficiency (underdevelopment, waste of resources, etc.). Scientists engaged in the applied part of their discipline have a moral and practical obligation to take this meta-paradigm seriously. With regard to human suffering this is obvious. With regard to human inefficiency we have to consider that each dollar, pound, mark or guilder wasted cannot be used to decrease human suffering. This metaparadigm enables us to formulate criteria for identifying achievement (and progress) in the applied parts of the disciplines concerned. The metaparadigm is powerful enough to affect the relationships between disciplines. The applied parts of natural and social science are forced into more co-operation (compare the emergence of applied systems analysis).

The 'pure' part of the disciplines involved is not submitted to a metaparadigm of this kind. Scientists trying to satisfy their own intellectual curiosity, that of fellow scientists, or that of the public in general, have more freedom in choosing approaches. If a historian engaged in pure research prefers description to explanation, he is free to do as he pleases. He is not obliged to try the covering law model. Of course, pure science is not devoid of rules. Objectivity, for instance, is demanded in pure science as well. Pure science shows paradigmatic shifts with little similarity of 'exemplars' before and after the revolution. With regard to pure science the ideas of Kuhn about absolute paradigm shifts make sense.

The pure part of analytical sociology enjoys the freedom typical of all pure science. The applied part follows the metaparadigm described before. The metaparadigm is responsible for the ongoing process of integration in applied sociology, lowering the barriers between the three traditions (Becker, 1981 and 1986). Pure sociology shows less inclination for integration.

Question four reads: How can achievement be identified in social science?

In this paragraph we will first concentrate our attention on the identification of achievement with regard to one specific type of research: empirical studies producing statements about social reality that are not only descriptive but also try to analyse and explain relationships. They must show reliability, validity and relevance. With regard to reliability, the criterion is consistency within empirical evidence; as a rule, consistency is tested by predictions. Validity requires consistency between empirical statements on the one hand and the concepts and theories utilized on the other hand. Relevance demands usefulness and non-triviality. A statement about social reality is useful if it enlightens (a category of) practical problems. A statement can be useful also if it satisfies intellectual curiosity. Non-triviality implies that the level of generality is not too low and that the statement is not just a repetition of something someone else has already stated. In all cases, the 'cutting point' between achievement or non-achievement is determined by taking prior 'judgements' in the scientific community into account.

Achievement in theory formation (Section 7) can be identified by taking the two types of theory and their preconditions mentioned by Boudon as a frame of reference. If we prefer a more precise assessment, the list of ten criteria developed by Hondrich (1976) might be useful.[5] Regarding the assessment of achievement in theory formation, we must keep in mind also that each of the criteria has to be used in relationship to the 'jurisprudence' developed over the years. Judgements have to be made with discretion. If criteria are applied in an over-ambitious attitude, no achievement will ever be registered. If too permissive an attitude prevails, each attempt at theorising is embraced as an achievement.

The principal aspects of questions 1, 3 and 4 can be summarised by quoting Converse:

> My own view is that science devotes itself to the systematic decoding of observed regularities and the reduction of the regularities to more parsimonious and general principles that account for wide ranges of phenotypic detail. As long as one is engaged in such activity, one is doing science, although there is an implicit pact that if one is doing science, then one is relentlessly attempting to move knowledge up that inclined gradient toward greater generality in time and space. (Converse, 1986, p. 52).

3 RESEARCH ON INDUSTRY AND GOVERNMENT

Analysing social change and organisational structures in industry and in government is one of the oldest research activities in sociology. The

Hawthorne project in the 1930s opened our eyes to the informal structure in industrial enterprises, paralleling the formal structure (Roethlisberger and Dickson, 1939). Blau's observation in two government agencies responsible for the administration of social security demonstrated the marginality of personnel working in contact with the public (Blau, 1963). What examples can be given of achievement since?

Our first case comes from industrial sociology. In the Federal Republic of Germany, Horst Kern and Michael Schumann investigated the 'new' labour force that emerged as a result of technological change. Is this labour force characterised by a relatively high income, education, and professional skill in handling numerically controlled machines? The research findings of Kern and Schumann (1970) show that the labour force is being split into two parts, and that the gap between these parts is widening. Inequality between them is increasing with regard to income, education and skills; in short, between winners and losers as a result of technological change. One group of workers is more and more incorporated into the middle class; the other is threatened by unemployment, or employment under unfavourable conditions. Their research results induced Kern and Schumann to formulate their 'thesis of polarisation' with regard to the new labour force. In the 1980s they carried out a follow-up study (Kern and Schumann, 1984). In the second study the scope of the investigation was broadened, and the researchers now looked also at the substitution of white-collar workers by electronic machines. The thesis of polarisation proved to be valid for the white-collar labour force also. The second report by Kern and Schumann is a fair example of a publication capable of reaching a large audience. Scientists and practitioners alike were able to understand the findings and to draw their own conclusions. The book went through three editions in the first year of publication, and it turned out to be a marked success with regard to the utilisation of research results.[6] The work of Kern and Schumann fits into a research programme being carried out in a number of countries (for earlier contributions, see Braverman, 1974; also Goldthorpe *et al.*, 1969–70; Hörning, 1971; Mallet, 1972); the project by Kern and Schumann is *primus inter pares* not an exceptional achievement. In 1986 Blossfeld showed that polarisation in the labour force is related primarily to a combination of age and education (Blossfeld, 1986).

Our second case is related to governmental organisations. Blau and Schoenherr (1971) were interested in the relationships between organisational size, degree of complexity, and the requirements for managerial manpower. They investigated thirty-three employment security agencies in the United States, their 387 headquarters divisions, and their 1201 local branches (excluding the smallest and simplest). Next they took their empirical findings as a starting-point for constructing a formal theory with regard to the structure of organisations. This formal theory consists of two fundamental generalisations and a number of derived propositions. The formal theory may be summarised in the following way:

Fundamental generalisation 1: increasing size generates structural differentiation in organisations along various dimensions at decelerating rates;

derived proposition 1–1: as the size of organisations increases, its marginal influence on differentiation decreases;

derived proposition 1–2: the larger an organisation is, the larger is the average size of its structural components of all kinds;

derived proposition 1–3: the proportional size of the average structural component, as distinguished from its absolute size, decreases with increases in organisational size;

derived proposition 1–4: the supervisory span of control is wider the larger the organisation is;

derived proposition 1–5: organisations exhibit an economy of scale in management overhead;

derived proposition 1–6: the economy of scale in administrative overhead itself declines with increasing organisational size.

Fundamental generalisation 2: structural differentiation in organisations raises requirements for managerial manpower;

derived proposition 2–1: the large size of an organisation indirectly raises requirements for managerial manpower through the structural differentiation it generates;

derived proposition 2–2: the direct effect of large organisational size, namely production of savings in managerial manpower, exceeds its indirect effect, namely the increase in managerial overhead consequent upon structural complexity;

derived proposition 2–3: the differentiation of large organisations into segments arrests the decline in the economy of scale in managerial manpower with increasing size.

On the one hand the conclusions of Blau and Schoenherr are in harmony with everyday stereotypes; on the other hand they challenge these stereotypes. In short:

> *Ceteris paribus*, a large scale of operations would effect tremendous savings in administrative overhead, but these savings are much reduced by the structural complexity of large organisations. Consistently, however, the economies of scale exceed the costs of complexity, so that large organisations, despite their greater structural complexity, require proportionally less management manpower than small ones. (Blau and Schoenherr, 1971, p. 314)

Blau and Schoenherr examined the hypotheses implied by their theory in a first test in another type of government organisation, namely the major financial departments of 416 state and local governments in the United States. The data on finance departments confirmed the hypotheses implied by the theory and closely replicated the empirical regularities observed in the employment security units and their subunits which served as the foundation for constructing the theory.

The study by Blau and Schoenherr fits into a research programme to which social scientists from different disciplines contribute. For instance Dahl and Tufte, both political scientists, have reported on 'size and democracy' (Dahl and Tufte, 1974).

4 RESEARCH ON SOCIAL MOBILITY

Our third case comes from Britain. John Goldthorpe and his collaborators have studied social mobility and its impact on the class structure in their country. In 1972 they conducted a survey, interviewing 10 309 males between 20 and 64 years old. In 1974 a follow-up survey took place. Goldthorpe takes as his frame of reference the belief in the essential 'openness' of liberal democratic society (Goldthorpe, 1980 p. 3). To what extent does British society in the 1970s reach this ideal or diverge from it?

According to Goldthorpe, the literature on mobility research shows a wide measure of agreement with regard to the generic form assumed by occupational mobility patterns within modern industrial societies. This agreement, known as the 'closure thesis', may be summed up in three interrelated propositions:

(i) mobility is most likely to occur between groupings which are at a similar level within the occupational hierarchy, whether this is conceived of as one of desirability, prestige, or socio-economic status; (ii) mobility will tend thus to be greatest in the intermediate levels of the hierarchy and least towards its extremes – if only because at the intermediate levels the possibility will exist for mobility to occur within its most frequent range both upwards and downwards, whereas, as the extremes are approached, one or other of these possibilities will tend to be precluded; (iii) the least mobility of all will be found towards the peak of the hierarchy, since those who hold the superior positions may be presumed to have not only a strong motivation to retain them, for themselves and for their children, but further the command over resources to enable them to do so, at least in terms of whatever aspects of social advantage and power it is that defines their position as superior in the first place. (Goldthorpe, 1980, p. 42.)

The second theoretical notion, the 'buffer zone thesis', has an obvious connection with the first thesis. It claims:

(i) that while the sons of higher-level, that is to say, skilled manual workers will be significantly more likely than the sons of semi- and unskilled workers to achieve non-manual occupations, such occupations as they do achieve will for the most part be ones at the base of the non-manual hierarchy, and the chances of men of manual origin gaining access to non-manual occupations of superior grade will fall off to the point of being almost negligible; and (ii) that while the sons of lower-level non-manual workers, that is, of clerks, salesmen, supervisors, petty entrepreneurs, etc., will be significantly more likely to be found in manual work than will the sons of men higher in the non-manual scale, such movements will be very largely into skilled manual grades rather than into semi-skilled or labouring jobs. (p. 47)

The third explanation is offered by the 'counterbalance thesis'. Central to this thesis is that the occurrence of work-life advancement is becoming steadily less probable:

This is the result, it is held, of growing 'professionalisation, bureaucratisation and technical complexity in work', which means that access to the middle and higher levels of the occupational hierarchy is made increasingly dependent upon formal educational qualifications, while the importance of experience and in 'training on the job' declines. (p. 54)

Goldthorpe's inquiry leads him to the conclusion that, despite supposedly propitious circumstances like economic growth in Britain in the period studied, no significant reduction in class inequalities has in fact been achieved (p. 252). He sees a serious underestimation of the forces maintaining the situation in which change is sought, relative to the force of the measures through which, it is supposed, change can be implemented. He concludes by arguing that:

if class inequalities are to be significantly modified, this can only be achieved through a process of conflict between classes: that is, through those who are chiefly disadvantaged by the inequalities that prevail compensating for their lack of social power as individuals by acting collectively, and being able, by virtue of their numbers, organisation and solidarity, to mount a successful challenge to the status quo. (p. 253)

The project by Goldthorpe and colleagues is part of a larger research programme in sociology that focused on social mobility and stratification. Goldthorpe positions his book in this programme, one of the most active and productive research programmes in the discipline (Blau and Duncan, 1967; Blalock, 1980; Short, 1981; Bottomore *et al.*, 1982).

5 RESEARCH ON INTERVENTION

In 1983 Rogers published *Diffusion of Innovations*. His main concern was the process by which an innovation is communicated through certain channels over time among the members of a social system (p. 5). Diffusion he sees as part of a larger process which begins with a perceived problem or need, continues with research and development on a possible solution, followed by a decision by a change agent that this innovation should be diffused, and then its diffusion (p. xvi). Rogers analysed 2297 empirical diffusion research reports and tried to formulate generalisations on the basis of these reports. He started by taking a close look at the generation of innovations. How does the innovation-development process take place? Next he dealt with the innovation-decision process. He specified the stages that exist in this process, and summarised his findings in ten generalisations. For instance: 'Earlier knowers of an innovation have more exposure to interpersonal channels of communication' (p. 169). In the third place he looked at the attributes of innovations and their rate of adoption. For instance: 'Earlier adopters have more social participation than late adopters' (p. 169). Ultimately he analysed the consequences of innovations: desirable versus undesirable, direct versus indirect, anticipated versus unanticipated. In total, eighty-four generalisations are formulated, and information is provided with regard to supporting and non-supporting empirical evidence.

At first sight the generalisations of Rogers may look quite obvious. Most of them are close to generalisations that figure in commonsense speculations also. As soon as a closer look is taken, however, the picture changes. Most of Rogers's generalisations also seem plausible if they are stated the other way round. They differ from commonsense statements only because of the large amount of empirical evidence that accompanies them.

Rogers has included in his book an exposé of his methodological preferences. He states:

Meta-research is the synthesis of empirical research results into more general conclusions at a theoretical level. The first step in this approach is to explicate all concepts. A *concept* is a dimension stated in its most basic term. Next, we postulate a relationship between two concepts in the form of a *theoretical hypothesis*. A theoretical hypothesis is tested by a corresponding *empirical hypothesis*, which is the postulated relationship between two operational measures of concepts. An *operation* is the empirical referent of a concept. Empirical hypotheses are often accepted or rejected on the basis of statistical tests of significance, but other criteria may be used. Finally, a theoretical hypothesis is supported or rejected by testing its corresponding empirical hypotheses, resulting eventually in a series of middle range generalisations. We believe that middle range generalisations are the stepping stones to more general theories of human behavior change, once they are abstracted to a yet higher level of generality. (p. 133)

6 RESEARCH ON CONTINUITY AND STRUCTURAL CHANGE IN SOCIETY

About 1970 Gadourek started to study social change in the Netherlands. As a result, in 1982 his *Social Change as Redefinition of*

Roles appeared. In 1975 he questioned a representative sample of the Dutch population, and he interviewed the same people again in 1977. He based his conclusions on surveys of other social scientists, too, and on an analysis of election results. Gadourek finds a lot of continuity in the 1970s, but also a major shift. His data shows an ongoing weakening of role norms up to about 1974 and a slow reversal of this trend after that period (Gadourek, 1982, p. 420). This reversal primarily takes place in role norms related to authority: demands for power-sharing decline after the middle of the decade. In other words, Gadourek has data to document the decline of the Cultural Revolution of the early 1970s that struck the Netherlands like most other Western countries. The reversal of trends is not a universal one, however, because, for example, changes in roles related to sexual life continue even after 1975. The changes in sexual roles are most obvious if we look at active members of orthodox churches in the country. At the beginning of the decade it would not have been accepted for an unmarried couple to live together and still participate in church activities. At the end of the decade a lifestyle like this is largely accepted.

Gadourek explicitly analyses change from an anti-voluntaristic perspective. In *Social Change as Redefinition of Roles* he focuses on ongoing processes of change that are not guided or enacted by government but are enforced by changes in other countries or that evolve more or less spontaneously. His dependent variables are role norms, role expectations and role behaviour. As independent variables he takes structural changes like shifts in the spirit of the time (*Zeitgeist*), in differential cohort socialisation and in life-cycles. Behind these shifts he detects a number of 'prime movers', namely ongoing secularisation and an increase in the level of formal education. The two operate independently of each other, yet induce a third prime mover – the decrease in the average size of families. Gadourek's research fits into a wider programme on changes in value orientations (*inter alia*, Becker, 1988).

The second case in this section brings Peter Blau to the fore again, this time in co-operation with Joseph Schwartz. In *Crosscutting Social Circles* (1984) they developed a macrosociological theory of inter-group relations, and they tested them on empirical data. As a starting-point they took a concept of Simmel's: *Die Kreuzung sozialer Kreise* (literally 'the intersection of social circles' but translated by Bendix as 'the web of group affiliations'). According to this concept, individuals in society are located at the intersection of a multitide of social categories. Individual A may be young, a single male, a Protestant boy scout, living in a small town. Individual B may be young, a single female, a Catholic girl guide, living in the countryside. How large is the chance that the two will ever meet? How large is the chance that they will not only meet but get to know each other well, and ultimately marry? Only in severely segregated countries is the number of crosscutting social circles small (*apartheid*).

Blau and Schwartz start by constructing a theory, specifying four assumptions and twenty-seven theorems. Their first assumption is that 'Social associations are more prevalent between persons in proximate than those in distant social positions' (p. 27). Theorems associated with this assumption include: 'As group size increases, the probable rate of outgroup relations decreases' (p. 31); 'Heterogeneity promotes intergroup relations' (p. 41); and 'The greater the inequality, the greater is the probability of status-distant social relations' (p. 42). To test their theorems, Blau and Schwartz took data on the 125 largest standard metropolitan statistical areas (SMSAs) in the United States in 1970. Measures of heterogeneity (such as racial, industrial, and occupational heterogeneity) were derived. Other concepts were operationalised likewise. A sample of young married couples was selected in every SMSA. The dependent variables for the major tests of the theory are rates of intermarriage (p. 19). No claim is made that marriage patterns are not influenced by any condition other than those specified in the theorems, however (p. 21). The empirical evidence confirms the theory's major theorems for various forms of inter-marriage (p. 203).

Blau and Schwartz include a methodological credo in their book. This statement of their convictions regarding theorising and testing bears similarities with that of Rogers.[7] The books of Gadourek and of Blau and Schwartz are both derived from pure research. Examples of pure research in analytical sociology are rare. Moreover, even when analytical sociologists explicitly try to keep policy aspects out of their research (as Gadourek does) the results may indirectly throw light on practical problems. The distinction between pure and applied research in sociology (as in other social sciences) is a gradual one. This does not make it irrelevant, however, as the discussion of criteria in Section 2 of this chapter has shown.

7 THEORY FORMATION IN ANALYTICAL SOCIOLOGY

Theory formation in analytical sociology has been attempted in two sub-traditions: institutional and utilitarian theory formation.[8] The first approach is closely related to empirical research. The second sub-tradition shows less close ties with research, and relies mainly, but by no means exclusively, on axiomatic reasoning.

Typical followers of the *institutional sub-tradition* are actively engaged in empirical research. They try to find explanations for the (few) regularities they have been able to find in their data. Or they design a theoretical model based on a pilot study in order to test (predictions derived from) hypotheses in the main project. In this sub-tradition the behaviour of individuals is mainly explained on the basis of (a) institutional stimuli, (b) constraints, and (c) resources. Examples of this kind of theorising can be found among the cases described in this chapter. Goldthorpe explains the difference between actual social mobility and the mobility to be expected in an open society by pointing at institutional prescriptions and at the self-interest of those in power, unwilling to give up their privileges. Rogers explains failures in the diffusion of innovations by referring to role behaviour and to resistance to change. Gadourek explains redefinition of roles by referring to structural change. Blau and Schwartz explain rates of intermarriage by pointing at intergroup relations (in particular prescriptions) and distance between residents (constraints). The theory that these explanations have in common lies on a high level of Rogers's taxonomy. Role prescriptions, in particular, are seen as relatively valid and reliable predictors of future individual behaviour.[9]

Because in the institutional sub-tradition theory formation is undertaken mainly to explain empirical relationships, this approach is characterised by strong links between data and theory. Theories are not allowed to contain statements which it is difficult to relate to the data available (compare Bryant in Chapter 4). But this sub-tradition has to pay a price for this close link. Sociologists working in this way often end up with theories that are *ad hoc* and that remain at a relatively low level of abstraction. The institutional theory has been called *Theorie der Forscher* (Sahner, 1982). Menzies (1982, p. 189), in his evaluative overview of sociological theory in use, summarises: 'some of the best theorising in sociology is presented in the first pages of many research articles'. Because structural assumptions are pre-dominant, this approach has also been called 'quantitative structuralism' (Wells and Picou, 1981).[10]

Adherents to the *utilitarian sub-tradition* in analytical theory formation originally got their inspiration from the theory of games and from prisoners' dilemmas.[11] After temporary enthusiasm for learning theory and exchange theory they discovered in the mid-1970s that economists productively apply utility theory to the explanation of individual behaviour. This led to an adoption of utility theory by sociologists belonging to this sub-tradition in analytical theory formation.[12] Utility theory implies the explanation of individual behaviour by looking at (a) utilitarian preferences, and (b) constraints – including resources (Elster, 1986, p. 89). Economists usually assume that a change of behaviour has been induced by the constraints and not by the preferences. They argue that one may usefully treat preferences as stable over time. Sociologists working with utility theory are as a rule willing to accept that both preferences and constraints are relevant factors. They argue that it has to be ascertained by empirical research which factors play a role in specific explanatory problems (Opp, 1985, p. 235). The sociologists involved frequently stress their adherence to the 'principle of methodological individualism' which basically states that social phenomena, particularly macrophenomena, can and should be explained by applying general individualistic propositions. As a rule, sociologists working in the other sub-tradition are also prepared to accept this principle.

Sociologists working with utility theory have elaborated already a large array of models at a high level of abstraction.[13] Applications of these models (after deductions) in empirical research have been successful especially with regard to individual behaviour that is dominated by self-interest. The examples given in this chapter provide illustrations, although the publications involved do not utilise utility theory explicitly. Kern and Schumann explain polarisation within the labour force by pointing to changes in constraints, treating preferences as constants. Also, Blau and Schoenherr, and partly Rogers, use utilitarian preferences as explanations. The boundaries between the two sub-traditions are not too strict.

Utility theory is sometimes called 'rational choice theory' (Elster, 1986). There are two other connotations of the term 'rational choice theory', however (Elster, 1986): first, theory related to all individual (not insane) behaviour; second, normative theory of individual behaviour, providing rules for the selection of optimal alternatives in situations of choice. Theories related to individual behaviour in general lack empirical content. They are relevant only as mental exercises and as heuristics in designing theories on a less high level of abstraction. Normative theories are not at stake in this chapter. In order to avoid misunderstanding I have used the term 'utility theory' and do not speak about 'rational choice theory'.

Utility theory has been presented by a number of its followers (*inter alia*, Lindenberg, 1985b) as 'the' new general sociological theory. In a considerable number of cases utility theory does not provide a convincing explanation of individual behaviour, however. For example: why do people participate in a national election, knowing that their vote will not make much difference? Why are people courteous towards strangers they do not expect ever to meet again? Gadourek (1986, 1988) has stressed that a lot of behaviour is not dominated by utilitarian preferences, and behaviour like that could best be explained by referring to role expectations or other institutional stimuli. In my opinion this implies that analytical sociology is in a stage of *theoretical pluralism*. Popper has pointed out that competition between theories can be highly productive in a scientific discipline. We have to keep in mind, however, that the two theories involved (institutional and utility theory) both lie on a relatively high level of abstraction, and that for that reason a conclusive empirical testing of neither theory is feasible. Testing of deductions can, however, lead to more insight into the conditions under which one of the theories is to be preferred above the other.

Both sub-traditions in analytical sociology (especially in theory formation) show achievements, as the cases illustrate. Prospects for further achievement can also be sketched out. It is to be expected that in the near future handling the two theories as rival explanations in one and the same theory-related research project will be attempted more frequently. Rational choice theory related to individual behaviour in general belongs to what Sahner (1982) has called *Theorie der Theoretiker*. Without specifications to bridge the gap between behaviour in general and behaviour in particular situations, rational choice theory remains empty, useful only as an intellectual exercise.

8 THE IDENTIFICATION OF ACHIEVEMENT IN ANALYTICAL SOCIOLOGY

I claim that the cases of theory-related research presented in this chapter are representative of achievement in analytical sociology. If more cases had been selected from the areas chosen, or if cases had been taken from other areas, no stronger arguments for achievement would have become available. Which conclusions can be drawn from this picture? If the production of 'law-like statements' would be taken as a criterion, little achievement has been found. But in all empirical sciences a different criterion is in operation also. If a scientific discipline can argue that it has searched for 'order' in its subject-matter in a methodologically sound way but that its subject-matter shows a lot of 'disorder' after all, this discipline is considered to have come forward with achievement. This applies to disciplines like meteorology, epidemiology and demography, to give some examples from the natural and social sciences. Analytical sociology can claim achievement primarily on the strength of this argument. If the assumption is accepted that the subject-matter of sociology does contain a lot of relatively 'open' situations, formal theories are an achievement. Acceptance of this assumption also implies that empirical research which finds a lot of disorder and only a little order is an achievement, provided the approach has been methodologically sophisticated.

My conclusions regarding theory formation in analytical sociology are, briefly, that this tradition has succeeded in developing two theories at a high level of abstraction: institutional theory and utility theory, competing in a situation of theoretical pluralism. At lower levels of abstraction we find theoretical hypotheses, empirical hypotheses and statements about empirical observations.[14]

If we look for contributions to the rationalisation of politics, the study by Rogers provides a relevant example. Because there is relatively much disorder in structural developments in society, and also in systematic attempts at innovation, analytical sociologists concentrate on studying large numbers of cases in a comparative way. Rogers's results demonstrate that this approach can yield results relevant to policy-making. Because our understanding of order and disorder is also enhanced, a study like Rogers's is an achievement in basic sociology as well.

The development of analytical sociology is substantially influenced by the 'pull' from those actors in society who request knowledge suitable for practical application. As this chapter and the chapter by Bulmer show, the results of sociology are applied on a wide scale. Sociology is *en vogue*; sociologists themselves, paradoxically, are not.

The identification of achievement in analytical sociology depends heavily upon the willingness of its readership to accept the assumption that the subject-matter of sociology is harassed by relatively much disorder. One has also to accept the assumption that in this kind of discipline the identification of achievement is not in the first place a matter of counting the law-like statements produced. Achievement has been accomplished if statements about the subject-matter have been elaborated (on different levels of abstraction) and if convincing arguments have been produced with regard to the adequacy of the methods used. All empirical disciplines responsible for the analysis of subject-matters characterised by a relatively high degree of disorder are granted this line of argument whenever achievements are evaluated. It is time to grant sociology a fair trial too.

Notes

1. 'Mainstream' signifies that the number of followers of this tradition and the number of articles in scientific journals coming from it (Sahner, 1982) are larger than that of other traditions; neither the term nor the number imply an evaluation of the tradition.
2. Biology taken in a broad sense, including epidemiology; later on in this chapter we will see that economics also has been a source of inspiration to analytical sociologists.
3. In general, a 'positive polity' is as difficult to accomplish as 'scientific management'. Exceptions to this rule exist, but they are small in number and restricted to highly unusual situations. The section on 'interventions' in this chapter provides an overview of achievement regarding planned social change.
4. In this chapter *pure science* is defined as the enhancement of the body of knowledge of a scientific discipline to satisfy intellectual curiosity. *Applied science* is defined as enhancing the body of knowledge of a discipline to elucidate a category of practical problems. *Applications of science* = application of knowledge to elucidate a specific practical problem. (*Application* = proceeding according to the rules of scientific analysis, but without aiming at enhancement of the body of knowledge of the discipline involved.) *Utilisation of science* = the use made by laymen of scientific knowledge to elucidate and assess problematic situations and to improve interventions. *Basic science* is defined as improving methods, concepts and theories in order to strengthen the capabilities of scientists to do their work (Becker, 1981, 1986).
5. The dimensions elaborated by Hondrich could be summarised as (i) range of the theory, (ii) type of interpretation of the problems involved, (iii) type of solution to the problem, (iv) type of knowledge aimed for, (v) logical structure of the theory (aiming at causal, functional, etc., explanation), (vi) structural characteristics of the theory, (vii) relationship towards data gathering, (viii) strategies and priorities incorporated in the theory, (ix) relevance with regard to problem-solving in non-scientific social systems (including relevance with regard to categories of practical problems), (x) relationship towards other systems of knowledge. This summary does not give enough details to provide an overview that could serve as an instrument for assessing achievement in theory formation.
6. See *Soziologische Revue*, 1986.
7. 'The fundamental requirement for constructing a scientific theory is to

formulate a deductive system of propositions in which definitions of primitive terms and postulated assumptions logically imply less general synthetic propositions, which are the theorems and, on a still less general level, empirical predictions of the theory. Propositions are said to be explained by more general ones from which they are deducible, although many scientists do not consider deducibility a sufficient criterion for adequate explanation. Deductive theorising is still quite rare in the social sciences, but there are some cases of it . . . Most theories in the natural sciences take this form, often expressed in mathematical equations. Darwin's theory of natural selection is a beautiful example' (Blau and Schwartz, 1984, p. 5).

8. The sub-traditions involved are known under other names also, for instance 'sociological' and 'economic'.

9. The question, 'What constitutes the best available predictor of future behaviour? is a shorthand indication for 'What constitutes the best explanation of individual behaviour?' Neither raw empiricism nor future research are implied in the shorthand description.

10. Institutional theory formation has been developed, *inter alia*, in policy sciences (Kaufmann *et al.*, 1986; Mintzberg, 1979). The theory involved often uses contextual developments as independent variables (contingency theory). Institutional developments too are frequently taken as independent variables (in structuralist, non-voluntaristic explanation for instance).

11. Both game theory and prisoners' dilemmas have been designed as normative models; their utilisation in empirical research and related theory formation requires reformulation.

12. On rational choice theory, see, *inter alia*: Axelrod, 1984; Elster, 1979, 1983, 1986; Hardin, 1982; Heath, 1976; Lindenberg, 1985a and b; Margolis, 1982; Opp, 1985; Raub, 1984. Rational choice theory has been developed *inter alia* in (new political) economics and in political sciences.

13. If the concept of rational choice is used not with regard to utilitarian choice but with regard to choice in general, the concept becomes rather empty and virtually meaningless (cf. Gadourek, 1986 and 1988).

14. A theory 'explaining' individual behaviour in general belongs to the highest level in Rogers's classification scheme; cf. 'rational choice theory' in Elster, 1983.

References

Andrade, R. d' (1986) 'Three Scientific World Views and the Covering Law Model' in D. W. Fiske and R. A. Shweder (eds), *Metatheory in Social Science* (Chicago: University of Chicago Press) pp. 19–41.

Axelrod, R. (1984) *The Evolution of Cooperation* (New York: Basic Books).

Becker, H. A. (1981) 'Voortgang en Vooruitgang in de Sociologie', in *Mens en Maatschappij*, vol. 2, pp. 118–53. [Achievement and Progress in Sociology]

—— (1986) 'Tegenstellingen en Vooruitgang in de Sociologie', in H. A. Becker and P. Glasbergen (eds), *Sociologie en Verzorgingsstaat* (The Hague: VUGA). [Controversies and Progress in Sociology]

—— (1988) 'Generationen, Handlungsspielraume und Generationspolitik', in A. Weyman (ed.), *Handlungspielraume* (Stuttgart: Enke).

Blalock, H. M. (1980) *Social Theory and Social Research* (Glencoe/Ill: Free Press).

Blau, P. (1963) *The Dynamics of Bureaucracy* (Chicago: University of Chicago Press).

—— and Duncan, O. D. (1967) *The American Occupational Structure* (New York: Wiley).

—— and Schoenherr, P. A. (1971) *The Structure of Organizations* (New York: Basic Books).

—— and Schwartz, J. E. (1984) *Crosscutting Social Circles: Testing a Macrostructural Theory of Intergroup Relations* (Orlando: Academic Press).

Blossfeld, H. P. (1986) 'Career Opportunities in the Federal Republic of Germany: A Dynamic Approach to the Study of Life-Course, Cohort and Period Effects', *European Sociological Review*, vol. 2, pp. 208–25.

Bottomore, T., Nowak, S. and Sokolowska, M. (eds) (1982) *Sociology: The State of the Art* (Beverly Hills: Sage).

*Boudon, R. (1984) *La place du désordre* (Paris: Presses Universitaires de France).

*—— (1986) *Theories of Social Change: A Critical Approach* (Cambridge: Polity Press). [Translation of *La place du désordre*]

Braverman, H. (1974) *Labor and Monopoly Capital* (New York: Monthly Review Press).

Bryant, C. G. A. (1985a) *Positivism in Social Theory and Research* (London: Macmillan).

—— (1985b) *After Postivism?* (Salford: University of Salford).

Coleman, J. S. *et al.* (1986) *Equality of Educational Opportunities* (Washington: Government Printing Office).

Converse, P. E. (1986) 'Generalization and the Social Psychology of "Other Worlds"', in Fiske and Shweder (1986), ch. 2.

Dahl, R. A. and Tufte, E. R. (1974) *Size and Democracy* (London: OUP).

*Deutsch, K., Markovits, A. S. and Platt, J. (eds) (1987) *Advances in the Social Sciences 1900–1980* (Lanham: University Press of America).

Elster, J. (1979) *Ulysses and the Sirens: Studies in Rationality and Irrationality* (Cambridge: CUP).

—— (1983) *Sour Grapes: Studies in the Subversion of Rationality* (Cambridge: CUP).

*—— (ed.) (1986) *Rational Choice* (Oxford: Blackwell).

Fiske, D. W. and Shweder, R. A. (eds) (1986) *Metatheory in Social Science: Pluralisms and Subjectivities* (Chicago: University of Chicago Press).

Gadourek, I. (1982) *Social Change as Redefinition of Roles* (Assen: Van Gorkum).

—— (1986) *De Moeizame Weg naar de Verklaring van de Maatscheppelijke Verschijnselen* (Amsterdam: Noord-Hollandsche Uitgevers

Maatschappij). [The Stony Road Towards Explanation of Social
Phenomena]
—— (1988) *De wederzijdse Verhouding van de voornaamste Gedrags-
en Maatschappijwetenschappen, de veranderende sociologische visie*
(Amsterdam: Noord-Hollandsche Uitgevers Maatschappij). [The
Relationship Between the Principal Behavioural and Social Sciences]
Goldthorpe, J. H. (1980) *Social Mobility and Class Structure in Modern
Britain* (Oxford: OUP).
——, Lockwood, D., Bechhofer, F. and Platt, J. (1969–70) *The Affluent
Worker*, 3 vols (Cambridge: CUP).
Hardin, R. (1982) *Collective Action* (Baltimore: The John Hopkins
University Press).
Heath, A. (1976) *Rational Choice and Social Exchange* (Cambridge:
CUP).
Hempel, C. G. (1942) 'The Function of General Laws in History',
Journal of Philosophy, vol. 39, pp. 35–48.
Hondrich, K. O. (1976) 'Entwicklungslinien und Moglichkeiten des
Theorienvergleichs', in M. R. Lepsius (ed.), *Zwischenbilanz der
Soziologie* (Stuttgart: Enke Verlag) pp. 14–36.
Hörning, K. H. (1971) *Der 'neue' Arbeiter, zum Wandel sozialer
Schichtstrukturen* (Frankfurt: Fischer).
Kaufmann, F. X., Majone, G. and Ostrom, V. (eds) (1986) *Guidance,
Control and Evaluation in the Public Sector* (Berlin: de Gruyter).
Kern, H. and Schumann, M. (1970) *Industriearbeit und Arbeiterbewusst-
sein*, 2 vols (Frankfurt: Verlag C. H. Beck).
—— (1984) *Das Ende der Arbeitsteilung?* (Munich: Beck).
Kuhn, T. S. (1962) *The Structure of Scientific Revolutions* (Chicago:
University of Chicago Press).
Lindenberg, S. (1985a) 'An Assessment of the New Political Economy:
Its Potential for the Social Sciences and for Sociology in Particular',
Sociological Theory, vol. 3, pp. 99–114.
—— (1985b) 'Rational Choice and Sociological Theory', *Journal of
Institutional and Theoretical Economics*, vol 141, pp. 144–55.
Mallet, S. (1972) *Die neue Arbeiterklasse* (Berlin: Neuwied). [La
nouvelle classe ouvrière]
Margolis, H. (1982) *Selfishness, Altruism and Rationality: A Theory of
Social Choice* (Cambridge: CUP).
Menzies, K. (1982) *Sociological Theory in Use* (London: Routledge &
Kegan Paul).
Mintzberg, H. (1979) *The Structuring of Organizations* (Englewood
Cliffs/NJ: Prentice-Hall).
Opp, K. D. (1985) 'Sociology and Economic Man', *Journal of
Institutional and Theoretical Economics*, vol. 141, pp. 213–43.
*Outhwaite, W. (1987) *New Philosophies of Social Science: Realism,
Hermeneutics and Critical Theory* (London: Macmillan).
Raub, W. (1984) 'Rationale Akteure, Institutionelle Regelungen und
Interdependenzen' (unpublished dissertation, University of Utrecht).
Roethlisberger, F. J. and Dickson, W. I. (1939) *Management and the
Worker* (Chicago: University of Chicago Press).
Rogers, E. M. (1983) *Diffusion of Innovations* (Glencoe/Ill: The Free Press).

30   *Achievement in the Analytical Tradition in Sociology*

Sahner, H. (1982) *Theorie und Forschung, zur paradigmatischen Struktur der westdeutschen Soziologie und zu ihrem Einfluss auf die Forschung* (Opladen: Westdeutscher Verlag).

Short, J. F. (ed.) (1981) *The State of Sociology: Problems and Prospects* (Beverly Hills: Sage).

Soziologische Revue (1986) special issue (no. 1) on *Das Ende der Arbeitsteilung?* by Kern and Schumann (1984).

Wells, R. H. and Picou, P. S. (1981) *American Sociology: Theoretical and Methodological Structure* (Washington: University Press of America).

3 From Cognitive Style to Substantive Content: Programmatics and Pragmatics in the Development of Sociological Knowledge
Robin Williams

1 INTRODUCTION

The view that the conduct of professional sociologists is partly to blame for the recent decline of interest in the production and funding of sociological knowledge and research is held by many interested in the nature and development of the human sciences. One aspect of that conduct has been the unseemly eagerness with which we have sought to prosecute internal disciplinary disputes at the expense of the image of the discipline as a whole. The editors of this collection have written of a 'disorderly spectacle' that seemed to outsiders an object of ridicule, and perhaps even contempt. It is, then, in our collective disciplinary interest to do what we can to repair the damage that results from such perceptions, but it would be foolish, if not downright dishonest, to try to do this at the expense of the real issues that divide our profession. We have somehow to regain and retain interest in, and support for, a discipline whose practitioners have yet to establish even provisional agreement on a number of fundamental issues about the nature of the social as an object of study and the professional knowledge that we might legitimately claim to hold of it.

My particular concern in this chapter will be with the contribution made to the development of sociological knowledge by the 'interpretivist' sociology of the post-war period. The rather barbarous term 'interpretivist' is used to refer to that sociology which attempts to understand and explain the nature and organisation of the subjectively

31

meaningful conduct of reflexive social actors. Space and competence exclude consideration of those closely related projects which add to this aim a further, explicitly critical, edge.[1]

2 AN INITIAL CONSIDERATION

In 1966, Wilhelm Baldamus, then Professor of Sociology at Birmingham University, drew attention to the presence of what were then recent developments in sociology. He was careful not to claim that such developments contained any new *substantive* sociological theory; indeed he argued that the very failure of sociologists after Parsons to produce new substantive theory of any significant generality was one of the reasons for the new developments. These developments consisted of claims about 'the philosophical, logical, epistemological, cultural and sociological basis of sociological theory' (Baldamus, 1966, p.1). Searching for a name for what seemed a relatively incoherent and variously influenced set of work, he opted provisionally for 'phenomenological'. Alternative designations for approximately the same group of writers, include 'existential sociologists' (Tiryakian, 1965), 'humanistic sociologists' (Cuzzort, 1969), 'sociologists of everyday life' (Douglas, 1973), 'sociologists of the absurd' (Lyman and Scott, 1976), and 'creative sociologists' (Morris, 1977).

I have chosen to refer to Baldamus's formulation partly because he undertook it so early, and partly because he treated with caution the logical status of the predominatly programmatic statements current at that time. He was forced to make 'cognitive style' the basic issue given the relative absence of substantive research. The features of this 'cognitive style' are best understood in relation to the predominantly positivist alternative programme previously dominant in sociology. Baldamus summarised this contrast with the aid of Table 3.1.

Three points of interest arise from Baldamus's table. First, despite the use of the vague expression 'cognitive style' he was able to display for comparison a remarkably large number of theoretical, methodological and procedural differences on issues central to the conduct of sociological work. Second, the claims made by either side as to the substance and method of sociological theory and research are clearly not observationally refutable; rather, they serve as constitutive presuppositions of work of differing and incompatible cognitive styles. Third, and related to the previous point, the differences reported in the early and mid 1960s contained echoes of the *Methodenstreit* in the late nineteenth and early twentieth centuries, and of the neo-positivist

Table 3.1 Baldamus's two sociological styles

Criteria of comparison	Positivistic style	Phenomenological style
1. Dominant value orientations	Rational Utilitarian Pragmatic	Traditional Artistic Existential
	Objectivity Scientific progress Social (etc.) progress Value-free	Truth: relevance Significance Value-committed
2. Perceived purpose of theory	Explanation Discovery	Verstehen Interpretation Understanding Insight
	Instrumental value; tools for research, causal models, hypothesis testing	Intrinsic value; theory building, systemisation theorising
3. Perceived substance of theory	Causal laws Scientific observations Measurement, prediction operationalisation	Structures and processes of social action centred on subjective meaning, expressive symbols, cultural forms
4. Presentation of work	Cumulative report of formal model building, replicable experiments replicable surveys, etc.	Literary essay of non-replicable conceptualisations, ad hoc interpretations
5. Techniques of work	Formal hypothesis testing based on statistical probability, rules of procedure, causal inference	Informal theorising based on comparative analysis of structured entities; conceptual plausibility.
6. Typical technical vocabulary	Variables (dependent, independent, intervening) prediction, testing operational; data behaviour	Types, systems, classes, sorts of . . .; structured, dilemma, dichotomy, conflict, stability, etc.

Source: W. W. Baldamus, 'Some Recent Developments in Sociological Theory', Working Papers in Sociology, Birmingham, University of Birmingham, 1966, p. 3.

attack on *verstehende* sociology of the 1940s. Indeed, the fact that certain disputes can be seen to recur so often in the history of sociological thought might cause us to speculate on their necessity rather than their irrelevance.[2]

By 1966, it was neo-positivism itself that was subject to the most severe attack. Those who pressed this attack deployed a series of new philosophical and rhetorical resources. These new resources were attractive not only for their novel forms of anti-positivist arguments, but also for their renewed vision of a sociology responsive to the claim that human actions are understandable in a way that natural events are not. Three of these resources deserve particular attention: Schutzian phenomenology, neo-Wittgensteinian analytic philosophy, and Kuhnian history of science.

3 NEW RESOURCES

3.1 Schutz

In his critique of Weber, first published in 1932 (Schutz, 1967), Schutz undertook the provision of a philosophical basis for interpretative sociology by the application of Husserl's phenomenological programme. Arguing that Weber's formulations of the nature of social action were vague and generalised, Schutz sought in this and subsequent works to explicate the basic concepts necessary for the achievement of objective knowledge of a subjectively meaningful social reality. His work consisted of a compelling effort to characterise the forms of knowledge that actors have of the world in which they live, and a further effort to differentiate that knowledge from the knowledge produced by science. Within Schutz's programme, social reality was defined as:

> The sum total of objects and occurrences within the social cultural world as experienced by the commonsense thinking of men living their daily lives among their fellow men, connected with them in manifold relations of interaction. (Schutz, 1962, p. 53)

The selection and interpretation of objects of attention in this social world was made possible by the utilisation of a series of commonsense constructs; these cognitive constructs defined the choice of means and ends oriented to by actors and also provided the determinants of their conduct. The social world at large is assembled from the primary experience of face-to-face relations, and therefore the foundations for knowledge of that world must also be located at that point. Certitude is anchored to the immediacy of our knowledge of others in our presence, and what we know of the remainder of the world rests on that basic certainty.

For Schutz, there was no necessity for the social sciences to undertake empathic manoeuvres of the kind suggested by earlier writers. Subjective interpretation was no longer to be formulated as a special method of the social sciences, but as a constitutive feature of the world known in common to participants and investigators alike. And in addition, our science need have no concern to portray what any particular real individual experiences. Rather, we are to be concerned with typical individuals and their typical motivations and actions. At the same time, however, we are required to ensure the provision of systematic connections between our constructs and the actions of real individuals, and it is the function of Schutz's three postulates (of logical consistency, subjective interpretation and explanatory adequacy) to guarantee these connections.

What was particularly important about Schutz's version of this cognitivist programme is the contrast it offered to those previous sociological programmes which had also claimed an interest in precisely this issue. In place of the standard and explicit contrast between what actors think they know and what is scientifically known, Schutz substituted a radical programme of investigation into the nature of commonsense knowledge, a programme not subject to any such disturbingly ironic contrasts.

3.2 Winch

Among writers who contributed to the neo-Wittgensteinian analytic philosophy of language (including Dray, Anscombe and von Wright), the work of Peter Winch proved most immediately accessible to sociologists, largely as a result of the publication of his monograph *The Idea of a Social Science* (1958). His attempt to exhibit the 'logical grammar' of the concept of the social can be approached, like Schutz's work, through his critique of Weber. Weber had required that sociological explanations be adequate both on the level of meaning and on the level of causation. For Winch, however, insistence on the second of the two requirements introduces a category mistake into the discussion of valid knowledge of the social. Human actions can only be grasped, according to Winch, by reference to the concepts which give them meaning to the actors involved. In undertaking the description of social phenomena we commit ourselves to a consideration of this necessary and sufficient 'internal relatedness' of concept to action. Such relatedness is not only a necessary feature of the act in question, but it also links the act to its context of performance. Internal relationships between actions and the concepts that govern them are not matters of fact, but matters of logic. Accordingly, actions carry with them their own explanations, and thus the pursuit of such explanations (as well as the testing of those that are proposed during the course of an inquiry) can only be carried out by undertaking a conceptual analysis; never by reference to a statistical behavioural regularity. Such analyses are capable only of logical consideration, and where doubts are expressed concerning the validity of an interpretation of an action, these doubts can be resolved only by comparing one interpretation with another. To understand action is to grasp the rules that are being applied to generate its performance, and, since it is the framework of rules common to a collectivity which makes possible the definition and evaluation of actions, to grasp those rules is also to understand a society. The conceptual and linguistic inquiries that are necessitated by the nature of the social are different in kind from those traditionally undertaken within empirical sociology, yet only these former inquiries are capable of handling the basic problems in sociology.

3.3 Kuhn

The third new resource, the new history of science represented by Kuhn's *Structure of Scientific Revolutions*, impacted more indirectly, though with equivalent force. First published in 1962, Kuhn's book offered a radically different history of science from that presupposed by the neo-positivists of the 1940s and 1950s. Prior to Kuhn (and with a few exceptions), the history and sociology of science had been dominated by progressivist assumptions concerning the nature of change in science (current science is better than past science) and by modest humility in the face of the truth claims of science (sociology and/or history could offer explanations for the development of science, but not for the facts of science). Kuhn undertook a more radical historicisation of science. His descriptions of the emergence of paradigms, of the manner in which such paradigms govern the practice of 'normal science', of the nature of the crises that are necessary for the downfall and replacement of paradigms, and most especially of inter-paradigm incommensurability, are all well known, though much contested.

Kuhn's work was of undeniable importance in the development of confidence among many interpretivist sociologists during the 1960s. Both the way in which he posed the problems of accounting for science, and his solutions to these problems, served to emphasise a strongly interpretative view of scientific activity. This view emphasised the necessity of extensive socialisation into the perspectives of the scientific community, the operation of regulative rules to ensure compliance with such perspectives, and the importance of unfalsifiable non-scientific presuppositions in the practice of science. His work was used both to attack the relevance of previously formulated philosophical accounts of science on the grounds that they simply did not accord with the practice of science, and, simultaneously, to make the activity of science itself available as an object of inquiry in ways that had previously seemed impossible to justify.

3.4 New Resources and Old Sociologies

Each of these resources played a part in the developing self-confidence of interpretivist sociology during the period in question. That they were not entirely consistent with one another, and that each of them contained certain internal problems, will not concern me at this point, though I shall return to these issues later. Their deployment led not only to proposals for new kinds of inquiry within sociology, however; they also played a part in the renewal of interest in already well-established forms of sociological thought and inquiry.

The most prominent of these was symbolic interactionism. Despite the vigour of the empirical work of symbolic interactionists, and the several attempts by Herbert Blumer (see Blumer, 1969) to argue for the inability of positivistically oriented sociology to deal adequately with the indisputably meaningful character of social life, symbolic interactionism had not succeeded in fundamentally challenging the predominant structural-functionalist style of sociology. Rock (1979) has argued that this is because of the absence of any imperialist or foundationalist pretensions on the part of interactionists themselves. Not only, he argues, did they remain uninterested in promulgating strong claims of their own concerning the theoretical basis of sociology, but their lack of participation in such debates meant that there was no pressure for the clarification of their own presuppositions.

Despite the principled disdain for certain forms of intellectuality within this style of sociology, interactionist concepts of human nature, human action, social process and the negotiated character of social order, seemed not only to resonate with more formal phenomenological and linguistically informed programmes, but also to benefit from the attention they received from those who were concerned to prosecute them.

The sense of a strong and programmatically promising re-orientation of sociology present in Baldamus's 'phenomenological cognitive style' derived its strength not only from movements outside of the discipline and the renewal of neglected ventures within it, but also from what it saw to be the failure of the alternative positivist programme of sociology to deliver anything resembling the universal or quasi-universal laws of social life that had eluded the searches of its proponents for so long. Such a failure could only lend weight to the claim for the necessity for new foundations for sociological knowledge – for both theory and research. Interpretivists saw themselves as offering, perhaps for the first time, the possibility of firm foundations upon which sociology might rest. In contrast to the methodological monism of positivism, the kind of sociology advocated by such practitioners was to have its methodological and analytical resources and aims defined by reference to the nature of the object under study, rather than by a universal standard for explanations derived from a misrepresentation of scientific practice and then applied to the social world in a way which neglected or distorted its most basic features. The characteristic style of such programmatics can be seen in two books first published during the 1960s; Aaron Cicourel's *Method and Measurement in Sociology* (1964) and Peter Berger and Thomas Luckmann's *The Social Construction of Reality* (1966). Both of these books borrowed and synthesised previously published work, and, in this sense, neither are startlingly original, but they did serve an important expository function at the time, and they succeeded in informing and infuriating sociologists for at least the next twenty years.

It is impossible to doubt the radically foundationalist intentions of Cicourel's monograph. Its first sentence could not be clearer: 'concern for the foundations of social science research should require the continual examination and re-examination of its first principles' (Cicourel, 1964, p. 1). Cicourel was largely concerned with questions of the relationship between sociological theory, method and data, where the last of these terms was conceived largely in terms of linguistic or para-linguistic utterances directly solicited or indirectly observed by empirical researchers. Unlike Luckmann, Cicourel had not benefited from direct contact with Schutz; instead, he had come to study Schutz through the influence of Harold Garfinkel. Perhaps for this reason, Cicourel's version of the problem of the foundations of sociology stressed the role of linguistically formulated phenomena more directly than the version of Berger and Luckmann. Cicourel treats meaning as constituted in a pre-scientific substrate, and it is at this substrate that his foundations are to be located. His particular version of a foundational programme required work on the generic interpretive rules used by actors and researchers for deciding the import or the meaning of events, actions and gestures in their relevant environments.

Preferring not to mount a direct attack on the possibility of a scientific sociology as such, Cicourel instead argued that there was an absence of adequate knowledge concerning the relationship between numerical properties predicated by particular measurement systems in sociology and the pre-predicative properties of the social world. He was quite prepared to distinguish between social facts that do not pose a serious measurement problem (for example, demographic facts) and 'facts in relation to social action' (p. 140). His new foundations were to be inserted underneath an already existing structure, and while some of this work might undermine some of what is already built, other parts of it may be retained, even if in need of repair, re-decoration, alteration or extension.

Berger and Luckmann's monograph was framed as a contribution to a sociology of knowledge considerably wider than that envisaged by Mannheim in his famous essay on the problems of the sociology of knowledge. Defining the sociology of knowledge as being concerned with 'everything that passes for "knowledge" in society' (p. 26), their programme called for the placement of such studies at the centre of sociological investigation. This heavily cognitivist emphasis arises from their reading of Schutz. Arguing that sociology is capable of inheriting what had previously been thought of as philosophical questions concerning the nature of the foundations of knowledge in everyday life, their programme promises a comprehensive theory of social action, an account of the relationship between individual experience and social structure, a sociology of language, a sociology of religion and a social psychology. Central to all these endeavours was to be the analysis of three basic social processes – 'objectification', 'institutionalisation', and 'legitimation'. There can be no doubting the scope and ambition of this particular undertaking.

4 PROGRAMMATIC PURITY

Long-term success in the human sciences requires more than critical
and programmatic promise; it also requires the demonstration of an
accumulating body of findings capable of attracting the intellectual and
practical interests of students, colleagues and sponsors. That the
interpretivist programmes were less than wholly successful in such a
demonstration was due to two main facts.

The first was that many of their proponents continued to prosecute
doctrinal disputes not only with positivism, but also with other anti-
positivist but non-interpretivist sociologists and philosophers of social
science (cf. Lassman, 1974; Keat and Urry, 1975). Useful as such
debates might prove in the clarification of the standing of programmatic proposals, they were often undertaken at the expense of
empirical inquiries. Indeed, internal differences between those
sharing a broadly interpretivist approach also played their part in the
continuation of programmatic disputes. A reading of the exchange
between Denzin and Zimmerman and Pollner on the relationship
between symbolic interactionism and ethnomethodology should con-
firm the difficulty that would be experienced in the production of any
single synthetic statement of theoretical commitment (see Douglas,
1973). On matters of method, the standard ethnographic practice of
symbolic interactionism was the object of direct critique despite the
general affiliation felt by some to the interactionist programme as
such. Schutz, for example, was critical of the capacity of ethnographic
participant observation to deliver the kinds of information relevant to
phenomenological interests:

> We should certainly be surprised if we found a cartographer in
> mapping a town restricting himself to collecting information from
> natives. Nevertheless, social scientists frequently choose this
> strange method. They forget that scientific work is done on a level of
> interpretation and understanding different from the naive attitudes
> of orientation and interpretation peculiar to people in social life.
> When these social scientists speak of different levels, they frequent-
> ly consider the difference between the two levels as entirely and
> simply one of the degree of concreteness or generality. (Schutz,
> 1962, p. 67)

Equally, the image of phenomenological work being carried out
wholly through the study of the investigator's own consciousness was

seen as an enterprise doomed to failure by more objectivist participants in such discussions. The danger courted by many convinced of
the potential power of the new programmes yet overwhelmingly
concerned with the exact provenance of their claims is well expressed
in Goffman's concern with methodological self-consciousness pushed
too far at the expense of empirical discoveries:

> Methodological self-consciousness that is full, immediate and per-
> sistent sets aside all study and analysis except that of the reflexive
> problem itself, thereby displacing fields of inquiry instead of
> contributing to them. (Goffman, 1974, p. 12)

The second fact was that there existed clear difficulties in following
through programmes strictly in accord with philosophical views that
had developed independent of the main substantive concerns and
methodological ambitions of sociology. In some ways it is puzzling that
it was thought possible to found sociology upon such resources in ways
that would both remain true to the intent of their originators, and at
the same time serve as adequate foundations for sociology considered
as a whole. Most commentators on Schutz's work, including those
from within an interpretivist tradition, have no difficulty in drawing
attention to a series of problems that arise in any attempt to found
sociological analyses on assumptions concerning the standpoint of a
solitary ego, and many have commented on the difficulty of rescuing
much of the furniture of the social (including that of language) from
such a project. Bleicher (1980, 1982), Coulter (1979) and others have
made such points with some force.

Equally there is real dispute as to whether the acceptance of Winch's
arguments permits any space for sociology at all, at least that sociology
which seeks to share with him a concern with the nature of human
agency (see, for example, Gellner, 1968, 1975; Louch, 1963, 1965).
Many of his own comments (for example, 'sociology is misbegotten
epistemology') have served only to make the case for a Winchian
sociology more difficult to sustain.

5 STYLE BECOMES SUBSTANCE

Despite the presence of these, and other, doctrinal disputes, however,
by the mid 1970s it became possible to discern much more clearly both
the developing research preferences and the substantive and theoreti-

cal achievements of what Baldamus had seen as a vaguely related set of projects and programmes. In his 'Hermeneutics, Ethnomethodology and the Problems of Interpretative Analysis', Anthony Giddens (1976a) outlined the recurrent themes in such analyses, and in this section of the chapter I will expand his treatment of some of these themes to bring out certain features of the achievement of interpretivist sociologists during the post-programmatic period.

Interpretivism has been conspicuously successful in generating knowledge about a series of connected matters previously defined as sources of difficulty when encountered in the practice of positivist sociology. For positivism, there were a series of stubborn and recalcitrant features of the social world that hindered the effort to formulate those stable descriptions of social events that could successfully replace lay descriptions and thereby play their proper part in the apparatus of theory construction and empirical testing essential for the accumulation of scientific knowledge. The achievement of interpretative sociology has been to turn these nuisances into researchable topics; the general process could be referred to as 'converting noise into information'.

5.1 Dimensions of Human Agency

The fragmentation of the individual actor characteristic of positivist work and the neglect of human agency in structuralist work have both been the subject of complaint by interpretivist sociologists. The provision of alternative 'constructivist' or 'performativist' frameworks for the description of social action and interaction results from efforts to overcome these shortcomings. Such frameworks permit the representation of action as 'achieved' or 'accomplished' through the use of acquired competences, rather than being determined by mechanisms located either at the level of social structure or at the level of the actor's brain, mind, or personality. It is possible to identify two differing approaches to this overall project. The first has been concerned with the provision of integrated and cumulative sets of general concepts for the analysis of social action and interaction. Two examples may serve to illustrate what has been achieved: 'conversation analysis', and the work of Erving Goffman.

The main goal of conversation analysis is the description and explication of the competences that ordinary speakers use and rely on in participating in intelligible, socially organised interaction. Workers in this field have been particularly successful at demonstrating the way in which aspects of social action and interaction can be shown to exhibit recurrent and remarkably complex organisational features arising from, and oriented to, individuals. Any and every interaction can be analysed so as to make these features visible, and participants' orientation to them can also be demonstrated. The literature in this field is both extensive and difficult to summarise or illustrate, but good examples and summaries may be found in Atkinson (1978), Atkinson and Drew (1979), Atkinson and Heritage (1984) and Heritage (1984a and b).

Another attempt to develop a systematic set of concepts for the analysis of social action and interaction can be seen in the work of Goffman. Between 1952 and his death in 1983, Goffman published a remarkable series of studies. The aim of his research was to isolate and record recurrent practices of face-to-face interaction. He was especially concerned with those social practices whose formation and analysis might help to build a systematic framework useful in studying interaction throughout our society. From the beginning, in his study of a Shetland island community carried out for his doctorate at the University of Chicago, he treated conversational interaction as one species of social order, and all his work was concerned to promote acceptance of this domain as an analytically viable one – a domain which he called, for want of any better title, the interaction order. What was important in Goffman's statements about this domain of study is the idea that it was to be studied *in its own right*. He argued that the treatments normally accorded to face-to-face interaction in sociology were markedly different from what he was proposing. There were two predominant ways of attending to such material: the first, social structural in its focus, involved studies in which accounts of what happened in the course of face-to-face interactions were used to illustrate claims concerning social institutions; the second, though focused on the individual actor, took a narrowly utilitarian view of action.

For Goffman, the key to the nature of the interaction order was that it was a *ritual order*. And he used this term in two ways: the first to refer to the 'moral' character of interaction, the second to refer to the 'standardised' character of interaction – the latter, then, perhaps better described as 'ritualisation'. These two senses clearly intermingle, but they can, I think, be teased out a little. In *The Presentation of Self in Everyday Life* (1959), for example, the moral character of intervention is given considerable but generalised treatment. The view taken in this text is that social life is organised on the principle that an individual who possesses certain social characteristics has a moral right to expect that others will treat him/her in an appropriate way. In return, any individual who claims to have certain characteristics, ought in fact to be what he or she claims to be. In consequence, then, when persons project definitions of the situation and thereby make claims to be persons of particular kinds within it, they exert moral demands upon the others, obliging them to value and treat him or her in the manner persons of those kinds have the right to expect. All encounters (roughly speaking, all instances of particular face-to-face engagements) necessarily involve the alignment of participants to one another, to the situation and to themselves.

Ritual has another, complementary, sense in Goffman's work: it is not simply that somehow individuals' appearance and manner provide evidence of their social character, status or relationships, but also that there are fixed forms in the way in which individuals may conduct themselves in face-to-face interaction. The utilisation of such fixed forms allows others to gather things about one another. Interactants are in a position to facilitate this process, or block it, or misdirect those who want to know something about them. All this is made possible through the standardisation or ritualisation of behaviour. It was this order that Goffman was at pains to describe by means of the large repertoire of concepts and observations that make up his corpus of work.

Not all interpretivist work on human agency has been concerned to develop such complex networks of concepts as those referred to above. An alternative approach has preferred to work with a small number of sensitising concepts comprising a loosely outlined framework for the description of social events. Often, as Garfinkel has observed, such a framework has adopted one or several 'natural metaphors'. For example, metaphors of negotiation and strategy have often played an important part in the production of work responsive to the demand for the portrayal of active human agency. The work of Strauss and his colleagues (1964) on 'negotiated order' demonstrates a sophisticated understanding of the ways in which participants in formal organisations are able to utilise organisational rules and resources in a flexible way, and a number of subsequent studies have confirmed the usefulness of this descriptive concept. Strauss himself (1978) has reviewed a large body of this material. Analyses of the strategic character of action have been supplied by many researchers. Glaser and Strauss's (1965) description of the strategic considerations necessary in different types of 'awareness contexts' are a conspicuous example of such efforts, and their work in the United States has been successfully extended to the British context in a subsequent study of communication and awareness in the cancer ward of a Scottish hospital (McIntosh, 1977).

Finally, it is noticeable that one of the most compelling ways in which studies concerned with the intentional nature of human action can demonstrate their success is by undertaking to portray action previously only represented as determined (or, in some cases, random) as in fact the product of quite finely tuned performances by participants. Peter Barham's (1984) account of schizophrenic patients and David Goode's (1979) work on the world of the congenitally deaf-blind both represent this kind of effort, but one of the most successful of such studies has been MacAndrew and Edgerton's work (1976) on drunkenness. In an extraordinary ethnographic review, they demonstrate the failure of both neurological and psychological theories of drunkenness to account for what is known of the comportment of drunken persons. Arguing instead that drunkenness is a learned behaviour, both produced and controlled much more carefully than these accounts allow, they provide both the conceptual and empirical resources for a reassessment of a significant, common and deeply problematic form of action.

5.2 The Nature and Use of Social Knowledge

A second theme of interpretivist work has been to give increased emphasis to the issue of cognitivity in social life, and there have been many investigations concerned with both the content of actors' knowledge, and the ways in which such knowledge is linked to actions. These may usefully be separated into three areas of study: general practices of sense-making, locally organised cognitive practices, and the formation of specific intentional objects.

In *Cognitive Sociology* (1974), Cicourel argued that orderly social action depended on at least two levels of cognitive operations. The first was the ability to operate a set of surface rules – the rules which link actions to their conventional meanings. The second was the ability to operate a set of 'interpretive procedures', which are invariant properties of everyday practical reasoning. His account of these invariant procedures is modelled closely on Schutz's formulations of the cognitive style of everyday life, and they are listed by Cicourel as: the 'reciprocity of perspectives', the 'etcetera assumption', 'talk as reflexive', the 'retrospective-prospective sense of occurrence', and finally, 'vocabularies as indexical expressions'. These procedures are understood by Cicourel to 'provide continuous instructions to participants in the mutual adjustment undertaken by those who are parties co-present in a social situation'. Not all interpretivists have accepted such claims, and Goffman has commented that Schutz's original formulations have 'hypnotised some students into treating them as definitive rather than suggestive' (1974, p. 6) Goffman's own effort to represent cognitive competences at this very abstract level was the subject of *Frame Analysis* (1974), a study which claimed to 'isolate some of the basic available frameworks of understanding in our society for making sense of events and to analyse the special vulnerabilities to which they are subject' (Goffman, 1974, p. 10).

The work of Zimmerman and Bittner can be used to illustrate research into locally organised cognitive practices. Zimmerman (1969a, 1969b, 1971) was primarily concerned with the ways in which documentary records achieve the status of official and authoritative accounts of the condition and treatment of individuals who are the clients of bureaucratic organisations, and his studies describe the detailed practices used by receptionists and caseworkers in an American public assistance agency to assemble case records by means of which the client's eligibility for financial assistance can be determined. Faced with potential discrepancies between what applicants may claim to be their identity, resources and needs on the one hand, and what can be shown to be their 'actual' identity, resources and needs on the other hand, caseworkers in the agency are forced to take an investigative stance towards the work of assessing client eligibility. Zimmerman's work then describes in detail the practices for which the term 'investigative stance' is a summary gloss.

Bittner (1967) has discussed practical skills utilised by 'skid-row' police officers that are partly constitutive of peace-keeping in such an environment. By practical skill, Bittner refers to 'those methods of doing certain things, and to the information that underlies the use of the methods that practitioners themselves view as proper and efficient' (Bittner, 1967, p. 701). Three elements of these skills are the subject of his detailed attention: the particularisation of knowledge of the area acquired by the police officers concerned, the rather restricted notions of criminal culpability that are applied to the residents of the area, and the exigency of decisions concerning the use of arrest and other coercive interventions in the life of skid-row. Bittner demonstrates the way in which the processes of arrest and detention that take place in such a setting are undertaken against a background of *ad hoc* decisions which include reference to situational and biographical facts as well as a consideration of the significance of the use of coercion in the lives of such individuals.

Work on the formation of specific intentional objects, the final area of cognitively oriented research, demonstrates the continuing influence of the phenomenological programme. Schutz made a number of attempts to describe the character of the cognitive world that would be the subject of his investigations; in one of them he described the commonsense world as consisting of:

> the most heterogeneous kinds of knowledge in a very incoherent and confused state. Clear and distinct experiences are intermingled with vague conjectures; suppositions and prejudices cross well-proven evidences; motives, means and ends, as well as causes and effects are strung together without clear understanding of their connections. There are everywhere gaps, intermissions, discontinuities . . . On the other hand, these experiences and rules are sufficient to us for mastering life. The ideal of everyday knowledge is not certainty, nor even probability in a mathematical sense, but just likelihood. The consistency of this system of knowledge is not that of natural laws, but that of typical sequences and relations. (Schutz, 1962, pp. 72–3)

Laurence Weider has commented that:

> it would be the task of a phenomenological sociology to describe and explicate such intending objects [i.e. objects intended through acts of consciousness] as . . . the experience ordinarily referred to by way of the concepts social role, norm, institution, cultural object, the other person, motive, language and the like. (Weider, 1973, p. 14)

Weider describes the developing sense of a code of behaviour and behavioural maxims held to be operative by inmates in a halfway house for ex-drug addicts. His observations and experiences of the operation of the code gradually uncovered its features as a self-elaborating scheme, so that he was able to show the way in which 'telling the code' was more than simply a matter of providing a commentary on events in the setting. Rather, it was productive of the social reality of the halfway house in question; it was, in his terms, 'persuasive and consequential'. Telling the code 'exhibits' the orderliness of the setting in question.

5.3 Context and Social Situation

A further concern of recent interpretivist sociology has been the attempt to adequately conceptualise and describe the contextual or situated character of social action. While many of the descriptions of conduct referred to in the previous sections give us some understanding of the ways in which individuals are able to link actions across different social settings, the nature of social settings themselves have also been the focus of inquiries.

Writing about the analysis of speech behaviour, Goffman (1964) commented critically on the neglect of the 'social situation' as a focus for analysis in sociology, arguing that a feature of such omnipresent relevance to the accomplishment and understanding of talk and action had been handled with regrettable imprecision by social analysts. It is undoubtedly true that the concept of context was not an easy one to express in the vocabulary of operational measurement. Interpretivist sociologists have not encountered such difficulties; the variety of terms used to refer to the situated character of action witnesses both a unity of interest in, and a diversity of resources brought to, the investigation of this topic. A partial listing includes: 'definition of the situation', 'social setting', 'situational specificity', 'occasionality', 'scene', 'setting', 'indexicality', 'frame', 'context' and 'episode'.

John Heritage (1984a) has written with considerable clarity about the sense of context that has informed the work of conversation analysis in particular and ethnomethodology in general. He uses the term 'double contextuality' to draw attention to two factual claims made by such researchers. The first is that actions are shaped by context – we cannot adequately understand an action except by reference to the context in which it is located. For conversation analysts, this has meant paying attention to context as the immediate local configuration of preceding actions, and they have made some efforts to demonstrate the way in which such a context is not simply a limp device of analysis, but is a phenomenon which speakers attend to in the detailed design of their utterances. The second sense in which actions are seen to be context-bound relates to the claim that conversational actions create or renew the current context in which they are located. Since every current action will form the immediate context for the next action in a sequence, it will inevitably contribute to the framework in terms of which the next action will be understood.

6 CONCLUSION

In the immediately preceding section, I have attempted to give some examples of the recent work of interpretivist sociologists which illustrate the contribution made by such work to certain central themes in the discipline of sociology. These contributions, taken together, amount to a very considerable achievement. However, I do not wish to claim that such studies constitute the fulfilment of the promise of those foundational programmes that arose from the enthusiastic participation of many interpretivists in the 'third stage' of the debate concerning the nature and scope of social knowledge. In conclusion, I offer some speculative ideas concerning the nature and influence of any such foundational programme in sociology.

I do not doubt that reference to such projects may serve useful rhetorical functions from time to time – it is difficult to conceive of the impetus underlying much of the research described in this paper without the influence of such an epistemological wager, but reputational difficulties soon arise if such foundationalist claims are taken too literally. Reference to 'foundation' presupposes the existence of some kind of epistemological certainty upon which the propositions of our discipline might rest. It is clear that some interpretivist work has conceived of such a possibility, and I have indicated some of the forms such conceptions have taken earlier in this chapter.

Two problems arise immediately we begin to examine the status of foundational claims for interpretivist sociology: one general to all such claims; another specific to the basis of this particular claim. The general problem consists of the embarrassing truth that recently the idea of the existence of epistemologically secure foundations for any discipline has been the subject of substantial and compelling doubt. Rorty (1980), Hacking (1982), and Foucault (1973) have all contributed to a critique of epistemology based on historical analyses of the development of this particular form of cognitive practice. Rorty at least believes that it can be shown that our concern to find 'foundations to which one might cling, frameworks beyond which one must not stray, objects which impose themselves, representations which cannot be gainsaid' (Rorty, 1980, p. 315) is an historical accident. Furthermore, he argues, it is an accident that has furnished a sterile project because of faults internal to it. Whether or not Rorty can establish that case is beyond my competence to judge, but his assertions concerning the principled impossibility of such a project would account for the failure of all previous attempts to establish such foundations in the human sciences. Interpretivist foundations, then, should expect to suffer the same fate as those that preceded them.

The second reason, specific to the particular foundational claims of an interpretivist kind, lies in the contradictory emphases of the various sources that came together to generate the cognitive style in question. Paradoxes abound here: the use of insights from analytic philosophy to support empirical social research; the utilisation of hermeneutics as part of a cumulative progressivist enterprise; the melding together of phenomenological and pragmatic impulses. Each paradox suggests contradictions that would disable a foundationalist programme from the very outset.

The move from cognitive style to substantive content has been achieved through the adoption of a particular attitude towards the connected issues of foundationalism, of programmatics, and of the doctrinal purity that accompanies such efforts. Zimmerman (1971), following Garfinkel, has pointed to the important distinction to be made between the pursuit of a problem within a tradition of thought (where the problems will have their own local complexion), and the use of a tradition to reflect upon, speculate about and imaginatively play with research issues that have an altogether different frame and countenance. The adoption of this latter approach has been crucial to the achievements of interpretivist sociology. It is this view of basic principles, sources and traditions that is most common among those that I have referenced in this chapter, and it has led to the rejection of doctrinal purity and of the overwhelming constraints characteristic of foundationalist conceits. Let me provide a short illustrative example. The theory of 'social typing' generated by Hargreaves, Hester and Mellor (1975) has certainly contributed to our knowledge of the ways in which deviant stereotypes of (in their case) children as 'trouble-makers' may be built up from the characterisation of small items of behaviour, become the subject of discussion with other participants and subsequently remain resistant to reformulation in the light of contrary evidence. However, a reading of their work, like a reading of many others earlier mentioned, will show the use of a variety of assumptions concerning both substance and method which draw on seemingly contradictory sources. While they admit that many of the interests that led them to undertake their work arose from a reading of phenomenological and symbolic interactionist texts, they felt no need to follow such models exactly.

Interpretivist sociology in general cannot hope to meet a Cartesian standard of 'seeing through the eyes of God', but such a standard was a

fantasy of cognitive potency anyway (Dunn, 1983). Neither epistemo-
logical nor ontological purity adds anything to the likely success of
sociological work. If we are concerned with reasons for the recent
failure of sociology to retain the interest and support of those outside
the discipline, we might do worse than consider the effects of the
cognitive pretensions that sociologists have so often been accused of
displaying; pretensions which have served to minimise the importance
of just those aspects of social life that interpretivist sociologists have
sought to examine. Such a sociology can record significant achievements in its provision of working solutions to problems in our
understanding of certain basic features of the social (especially those of
subjectivity, context, and reflexivity). These solutions became possible, at least in part, because of the blurring of boundaries between
sociology and philosophy at a particular historical moment. It would,
of course, be wholly mistaken to believe that other solutions are
impossible to attain, or that our sense of what the central problems of
sociology are will not itself change. The history of our discipline is such
that we can be confident that attempts to introduce and defend
inflexible interpretative schemata will succeed, if at all, only in the
short run. It is this fact that ensures the provisional character of even
the most basic achievements of sociology; it is this fact, too, that
guarantees the continuing relevance of this discipline to all attempts to
gain knowledge of the arrangements by which we organise our
individual and collective lives.

Notes

1. The major figure here is Habermas. Accounts of the relationship of
   Habermas's project to the work discussed in this chapter can be found in
   Apel (1972, 1979), Bernstein (1976, 1983), Bleicher (1980, 1982) and
   Giddens (1976a).
2. I mean this claim to resemble that made by Foucault (1973) in his
   discussion of the conditions of possibility of the human sciences.

References

Apel, K. O. (1972) 'The A-priori of Communication and the Foundation of
the Humanities', *Man and World*, vol. 5, pp. 3–12, 14–16, 22–37.
—— (1979) 'Types of Social Science in the Light of the Theory of Cognitive
Interests', in S. C. Brown (ed.), *Philosophical Disputes in the Social Sciences*
(Brighton: Harvester).
Atkinson, J. M. (1978) *Discovering Suicide* (London: Macmillan).
—— and Drew, P. (1979) *Order in Court* (London: Macmillan).

—— and Heritage, J. (eds) (1984) *Structures of Social Action* (Cambridge: CUP).

Baldamus, W. W. (1966) 'Some Recent Developments in Sociological Theory', *Working Papers in Sociology* (Birmingham: University of Birmingham).

Barham, Peter (1984) *Schizophrenia and Human Value* (Oxford: Blackwell).

Bauman, Z. (1973) 'On The Philosophical Status of Ethnomethodology', *Sociological Review*, vol. 21, pp. 5–23.

—— (1978) *Hermeneutics and Social Science* (London: Hutchinson).

Berger, P. and Luckmann, T. (1966) *The Social Construction of Reality* (Harmondsworth: Penguin).

*Bernstein, R. J. (1976) *The Restructuring of Social and Political Theory* (Oxford: Blackwell).

—— (1983) *Beyond Objectivism and Relativism* (Oxford: Blackwell).

Bittner, E. (1967) 'The Police On Skid Row', *American Sociological Review*, vol. 32, pp. 677–99.

Bleicher, J. (1980) *Contemporary Hermeneutics* (London: Routledge & Kegan Paul).

—— (1982) *The Hermeneutic Imagination* (London: Routledge & Kegan Paul).

Blumer, H. (1969) *Symbolic Interactionism: Perspective and Method* (Englewood Cliffs/NJ: Prentice-Hall).

Cicourel, A. (1964) *Method and Measurement in Sociology* (New York: Free Press).

—— (1974) *Cognitive Sociology* (Harmondsworth: Penguin).

Coulter, J. (1979) *The Social Construction of Mind* (London: Macmillan).

Cuzzort, D. (1969) *Humanity and Modern Social Thought* (New York: Holt, Rinehart & Winston).

Douglas, J. D. (ed.) (1973) *Understanding Everyday Life* (London: Routledge & Kegan Paul).

Dunn, J. (1983) 'Social Theory, Social Understanding and Political Action', in C. Lloyd (ed.) *Social Theory and Political Practice* (Oxford: OUP).

Foucault, M. (1973) *The Order of Things* (New York: Vintage Press).

Gellner, E. (1968) 'The New Idealism: Cause and Meaning in the Social Sciences', in I. Lakatos and A. Musgrave (eds), *Problems in the Philosophy of Science* (Dordrecht: Reidel).

—— (1975) 'A Wittgensteinian Philosophy of (or against) the Social Sciences', *Philosophy of the Social Sciences*, vol. 5, pp. 173–99.

Giddens, A. (1976a) 'Hermeneutics, Ethnomethodology and Problems of Interpretive Analysis', in L. A. Closer and O. Larsen (eds), *The Uses of Controversy in Sociology* (New York: Free Press).

—— (1976b) *New Rules of Sociological Method* (London: Heinemann).

Glaser, B. and Strauss, A. (1965) *Awareness of Dying* (London: Macmillan).

Goffman, E. (1959) *The Presentation of Self in Everyday Life* (Harmondsworth: Penguin).

—— (1964) 'The Neglected Situation', *American Anthropologist*, vol. 66, pp. 133–6.

—— (1974) *Frame Analysis* (Harmondsworth: Penguin).

Goode, D. (1979) 'The World of the Congenitally Deaf–Blind, in H. Schwartz and J. Jacobs, *Qualitative Sociology: A Method to the Madness* (New York: Free Press).

Hacking, I. (1982) *Representing and Intervening* (Cambridge: CUP).

Hargreaves, D., Hester, S. and Mellor, D. (1975) *Deviance in Classrooms* (London: Routledge & Kegan Paul).

Heritage, J. (1984a) *Garfinkel and Ethnomethodology* (Cambridge: Polity Press).

—— (1984b) 'Recent Developments in Conversation Analysis' *Working Papers in Sociology* (Coventry: Department of Sociology, University of Warwick).

Keat, R. and Urry, J. (1975) *Social Theory as Science* (London: Routledge & Kegan Paul).

Kuhn, T. (1962) *The Structure of Scientific Revolutions* (Chicago: University of Chicago Press).

Lassman, P. (1974) 'Phenomenological Sociology', in J. Rex (ed.), *Approaches to Sociology* (London: Routlege & Kegan Paul).

Louch, A. R. (1963) 'The Very Idea of a Social Science', *Inquiry*, vol. 6, pp. 273–86.

—— (1965) 'On Misunderstanding Mr Winch', *Inquiry*, vol. 8, pp. 212–16.

Lyman, S. M. and Scott, M. B. (1976) *A Sociology of the Absurd* (New York: Appleton-Century-Crofts).

MacAndrew, C. and Edgerton, R. (1976) *Drunken Comportment* (Chicago: Aldine).

McIntosh, J. (1977) *Communication and Awareness in a Cancer Ward* (London: Croom Helm).

Morris, M. (1977) *An Excursus into Creative Sociology* (New York: Columbia University Press).

Rock, P. (1979) *The Making of Symbolic Interactionism* (London: Routledge and Kegan Paul).

*Rorty, R. (1980) *Philosophy and the Mirror of Nature* (Oxford: Blackwell).

Schutz, A. (1962) *Collected Papers*, vol. 1 (The Hague: Martinus Nijhoff).

—— (1967) *The Phenomenology of the Social World* (London: Heinemann).

Strauss, A. (1978) *Negotiations* (San Francisco: Jossey-Bass).

—— *et al.* (1964) *Psychiatric Ideologies and Institutions* (New York: Free Press).

Tiryakian, E. (1965) 'Existential Philosophy and the Sociological Tradition', *American Sociological Review*, vol. 30, pp. 687–702.

Weider, L. (1973) *Language and Social Reality* (The Hague: Mouton).

Winch, P. (1958) *The Idea of a Social Science* (London: Routledge & Kegan Paul).

Zimmerman, D. H. (1969a) 'Tasks and Troubles', in D. Hansen (ed.), *Explorations in Counselling* (New York: Basic Books).

—— (1969b) 'Record Keeping and the Intake Process', in S. Wheeler (ed.), *On Record* (New York: Basic Books).

—— (1971) 'The Practicalities of Rule Use', in J. Douglas (ed.), *Understanding Everyday Life* (London: Routledge & Kegan Paul).

4 The Sociological Study of History: Institutions and Social Development

Stephen Mennell

Classical sociology arguably *is* historical sociology. We may debate the relationship in Western sociology since the Second World War between the empirical–analytical, the hermeneutic and the historical–institutional threads in sociology as a discipline. Yet in the preceding few generations, a concern with the development of human societies – particularly but not exclusively the institutions of 'industrial', 'capitalist' or 'Western' societies, call them what you will – was *central* to the work of those we recognise as the 'founding fathers' of sociology. This is obviously true of the Holy Trinity of the sociologists' pantheon, even if Durkheim expressed the concern in a slightly different way from Marx and Weber (see Bellah, 1959). It is also true of the dozen or so principal apostles who keep them company in the pantheon – such as Comte, de Tocqueville, Spencer, Toennies and Mannheim. These people framed most of the central problems of the discipline, and framed them originally in an historical or developmental way.

In the post-war period, however, the main bulk of sociological research has *not* been of an historical or developmental kind. These decades have been marked by what Wittfogel (1957) called 'developmental agnosticism' and Elias (1987b) 'the retreat of sociologists into the present'. This tendency may in part be the outcome of sociologists' wish to measure their 'achievement' against the utilitarian yardstick of usefulness in rectifying the ills of contemporary society. I think there are deeper reasons, and perhaps this is a question itself in need of sociological investigation. But several intellectual influences are worth mentioning, including those of anthropology, of cross-section data and variable analysis, and of philosophers of science – Sir Karl Popper notable among them.

Anthropology, especially in Britain, has always enjoyed higher prestige than its parvenu cousin, sociology, partly because of its intimate association with colonial administration. The rise within anthropology after the First World War of the functionalist approach associated especially with Malinowski and Radcliffe-Brown had a strong but markedly delayed impact in sociology. Functionalism was at its peak in sociology during the two decades after the Second World War when Talcott Parsons – who had spent a year at the London School of Economics under Malinowski in the 1920s – dominated American sociology, and American sociology dominated the world. In anthropology, functionalism had begun as a methodological rule-of-thumb in field work: it represented a reaction against the tendency of Victorian social evolutionary anthropologists to resort to 'conjectural history' in seeking to explain the customs of preliterate societies, when for the most part any firm evidence about the past of such societies was entirely lacking. Seeking synchronic relationships between patterns which could actually be observed in the field made better sense for anthropologists. Why the same ahistorical approach should have had such appeal to sociologists studying societies blessed with abundant records of their own past development gives more pause for thought.

A prevalent relativism helped compound the ahistorical bias of anthropology. Ethnographic relativism, which also began as a methodological precept essential to understanding the modes of life and thought of unfamiliar cultures, was transformed in the hands of such distinguished anthropologists as Evans-Pritchard (1937) into an epistemological relativism, any questioning of which was liable to bring charges as severe as 'racism' down on one's head. Rightly rejecting the evaluation of societies as 'superior' and 'inferior', most anthropologists also moved away from the more basic notion of sequential orders of development, even multilinear ones. Admittedly, it was never so unacceptable to despise one's own ancestors as to despise someone else's, yet something of this seems to have spilled over into sociology and hastened the retreat from the past. For their part, sociologists were haunted by the ghost of Herbert Spencer and other Victorians who, in attempting to put their own society and its recent transformation in the perspective of the history of humanity as a whole, actually succeeded in putting the whole history of humanity in the perspective of their own society. 'Who now reads Herbert Spencer?' was the rhetorical question with which Talcott Parsons (quoting Crane Brinton) opened his immensely influential *The Structure of Social Action* (1937).

The influence of atemporal functionalism might have been less had it not coincided with the rapid development of cross-section survey methods and techniques of variable analysis. As members of the

Frankfurt School often pointed out in the debates arising out of their collaboration with Paul Lazarsfeld, survey methods implicitly carried with them an assumption that social reality could be explained from the properties of constituent atoms – individual people whose opinions apparently welled up spontaneously from sources deep inside each separate one of them – as represented in a snapshot taken at one moment in time (Adorno, 1976; Pollock, 1976).

Functionalism, though not cross-section data and variable analysis, was in retreat in sociology across the world by the late 1960s. The developmental agnosticism which it had helped sustain was then, however, to receive strong reinforcement through the influence (among a minority of sociologists anyway) of French structuralism. Inspired by the shift in linguistics since Saussure from diachronic to synchronic investigations, Claude Lévi-Strauss sought the supposed eternal unchanging properties of the human mind underneath the surface flux and diversity. Something of this can be seen echoed in the radically ahistorical interests of groups like the ethnomethodologists. But, more important, in the hands of Lévi-Strauss and Roland Barthes, all history becomes myth. The prevailing relativism, or ultimately solipsism, is once again evident.[1]

Finally, what of Sir Karl Popper? Whether he had a powerful independent influence, or whether his views simply resonated with the currents already described, is an open question. At any rate, his books *The Open Society and Its Enemies* (1945) and *The Poverty of Historicism* (1957) had, in Britain at least, a great impact on sociologists. Whatever may have been Popper's actual intention, my own generation of undergraduates – the generation of the early mid–1960s – somehow picked up the idea that it was neither academically nor politically acceptable to explain the present characteristics of society by any reference to the past.

Historical sociology, of course, never disappeared entirely from the scene. One of the earliest signs of a forthcoming upsurge came indeed from the very power-centre of the functionalist hegemony. Three papers published in the *American Sociological Review* in 1964 by Talcott Parsons, Robert Bellah and S. N. Eisenstadt were the product of a seminar at Harvard on the subject of social evolution. That Parsons and his colleagues should have thought in terms of evolution is not surprising. Evolutionary assumptions were implicit in functionalism all along: how else to explain the selection for survival of only the best-integrated social systems? There were, however, few sociologists on whom the irony was lost. Question: 'Who now reads Herbert

Spencer?' Answer: 'Talcott Parsons does'. And indeed, Parsons's own
theorising about social evolution (1966, 1971) represented no advance
on Spencer. In fact, he mainly quarried history to fill in his AGIL
boxes.

More recently, since about the mid-1970s, there has been a very
marked revival in more scholarly historical work within sociology.
Indeed, during the Noordwijk conference, Ansgar Weymann remarked that it was now the retreat of sociologists into the past that
required explanation, and John Eldridge expressed his puzzlement at
many sociologists' fascination with (for example) the behaviour of
French peasants on Shrove Tuesday in one small town in the sixteenth
century (Ladurie, 1979). That could easily be explained away:
historians' ethnographic case-studies of the past can have the same
fascination and value as anthropologists' ethnographic case-studies of
exotic tribes in present or recent times. But sociologists' renewed
interest in the past seems more substantial than that.

It would be agreeable to believe that this was due entirely to a
spontaneous recognition of the intellectual necessity of developmental
theories in sociology. It may not, however, be wholly unconnected
with the fact that in an age when research funds are in short supply,
studying historical sources is much cheaper than gathering and
processing large quantities of survey data. Nor is it, I think, unrelated
to the fine flowering of Marxist or neo-Marxist scholarship in several
disciplines, for Marxists – defying Popper's attempted knock-out blow
against them – strove to keep alive developmental perspectives when
they were most in eclipse in sociology at large.

At any rate, the revival has occurred. But what has it achieved? How
can its achievement be assessed?

IS HISTORY BUNK?

The achievements of historical sociology seem to me to be peculiarly
vulnerable to underestimation against utilitarian yardsticks, more
vulnerable than either history or sociology in general. Few of the
politicians who (in an ironic echo of the student generation of 1968)
scream for 'relevance' would actually dare to declare that 'history is
bunk'. Henry Ford was a philistine – everyone knows that. History is
an old-established discipline in the academy, and historians have
always enjoyed high prestige, power and popularity. Some of their
books are quite widely read for enjoyment and entertainment. Many

politicians read history at university, and a few even continue to practise the craft in their spare time or in retirement. Besides, historians – or most of them – cultivate the mystique of the archival sources, of sticking close to the 'facts' and the documents. Historical sociologists – or the boldest of them, as we shall see in a moment – take more risks. They stand back, and build more ambitious models of longer-term processes, in which the leap of interpretation is, if not greater, at least more explicit and acknowledged than in the most conventional kind of historical work. Historical sociologists often refuse to be confined to a single specialised period, and show no shame in relying sometimes on secondary sources. To conventional historians they are not respectable.

On the other hand, historical sociology for the most part relinquishes the sociologist's standard defence of pretending to be practically useful. Sociology is a late entrant to the academy, and therefore stands low down in the academic pecking order. In general, however, sociologists do not have too much difficulty in convincing some of the people some of the time that their work is directly or not too indirectly useful in improving social conditions, refining policy, or whatever. But this defence rests heavily on the present-centredness of the research in question, and is therefore much less easy to deploy around the activities of historical sociologists. Like so many marginal people, the latter end up having the worst of both worlds.

The picture I have drawn must now be modified slightly, to take account of the fact that some of those who practise historical sociology, and draw upon themselves the scepticism of conventional historians, are themselves historians by disciplinary affiliation.

Any comprehensive survey of major contributions to historical sociology since the Second World War would have to discuss, at least, the works of Reinhard Bendix (1978), S. N. Eisenstadt (1963), Norbert Elias (1978b, 1982, 1983), Barrington Moore (1966), Charles Tilly (1976, 1984) and Immanuel Wallerstein (1974, 1980) from among sociologists. But it would also have to include the works of Perry Anderson (1974a, 1974b), Phillipe Ariès (1962), Fernand Braudel (1976, 1983), E. L. Jones (1981), William McNeill (1977, 1982), E. P. Thompson (1963), Eugen Weber (1976) and Karl Wittfogel (1957) from among historians. It would also have to mention groups of scholars of diverse disciplinary origins, like the Cambridge Group for Historical Demography (notably Peter Laslett, E. A. Wrigley and M. Schofield). The list is no doubt arbitrary, and probably should include many more works published during the last ten years.[2] There is, in any case, nowhere near sufficient space to survey them all here. They are, besides, very diverse in content, approach and scope. What they principally have in common, and what helps make them major contributions, is that they are more ambitious in the synthesis they attempt than is common among the works either of most historians or most sociologists. They have an ambitious concern with, in Tilly's phrase (1984), 'big structures, large processes, huge comparisons'. Most of them, one way or another, would attract the wrath of guardians of historiographical orthodoxy such as, for instance, Sir Geoffrey Elton. Why should that be so?

THE SOCIOLOGY OF THE PAST VERSUS STRUCTURED PROCESSES OF DEVELOPMENT

To clarify the matter, it is useful to draw a distinction between two types of historical sociology. The first may be called simply the 'sociology of the past'. In this kind of research, the historical sociologist – whether a sociologist or an historian by affiliation – uses sociological concepts and theories to investigate groups of people living in some specific society at a specific period in the past. This kind of research does not differ fundamentally from research into groups of people living at the present: it is merely that documents form a larger part of the evidence than they would generally do in research into the present, because the usual apparatus of questionnaires and interviews is, shall we say, confronted with practical obstacles. As against this 'sociology of the past', other sociologists seek to discern and explain longer-term *structured processes* of development.

The distinction is not hard and fast. For example, Norbert Elias's *The Court Society* (1983) – among his works the most widely admired by historians – deals with a relatively closely defined place and period (France and its royal court in the century before the Revolution), but his underlying concern is with more general processes of development. Still less is the distinction one of academic worth. Many of the finest examples of historical sociology are instances of the 'sociology of the past'. To put it perhaps over-simply, their impulse is comparative rather than developmental.

The scale on which comparison is pursued or invited varies enormously. At one end of the scale, two widely admired books may be mentioned: Kai T. Erikson's *Wayward Puritans* (1966) and Leonore Davidoff's *The Best Circles* (1973), studies respectively of

deviance in colonial New England and of behaviour in nineteenth-
century London high society, are excellent examples of the sociology
of the past. Their value, however, seems to me not at all dependent on
the fact that they are studies of the *past*: they are in effect contributions
to our understanding of deviant behaviour and of endogamous status-
groups irrespective of time. The arrow of time may also be reversed for
comparative purposes: a present-day study may prove stimulating
when studying the past. For instance, Stan Cohen's modern classic,
Folk Devils and Moral Panics (1972) – a study of the battles of Mods
and Rockers and of popular reaction to them – might usefully be read
by historians labouring at the large body of research on witch crazes in
the past.

Also instances of the sociology of the past, but on a more
macrosociological scale, are books like Barrington Moore's *Social
Origins of Dictatorship and Democracy* (1966) and Theda Skocpol's
States and Social Revolutions (1979). They explicitly set out to study
comparable episodes at different periods in different societies. Taking
a small number of episodes they attempt to generalise to similar
situations – past, present, and future. Yet they do not advance any
theory of social development over the longer term.

Most macroscopic of all is the case where the scholar seeks to re-
create a past society in the round. Braudel's *The Mediterranean and the
Mediterranean World in the Age of Philip II* (1976) is the classic
instance. Great events are set by Braudel in the largely changing
material context of the *longue durée*, like tiny figures of classical
antiquity in a Claude Lorraine landscape. The magnificent result is yet
distantly reminiscent of functionalist sociology.

The sociology of the past, then, takes many forms. In all the best
examples, studies of people in the past serve, in Harold Garfinkel's
phrase, as 'aids to a sluggish imagination' when studying present-day
people (and they do so, to my mind, far better than any of Garfinkel's
'demonstrations'). Their value is appreciated by non-historical sociologists and also by conventional historians who will admire their
professional use of sources; but they do not set out primarily to build
developmental models of structured processes of change. That
characteristic they share with the work of such social-scientifically –
and especially anthropologically – informed historians as Peter Burke
(1974, 1978, 1987) or Robert Darnton (1984).

We are left, then, with only a minority of authors whose sociological
interest in the past centres on the construction of models of long-term
developmental processes.

The minority includes Immanuel Wallerstein, two volumes of whose *The Modern World-System* have so far appeared (1974, 1980). The study may from one angle be seen as a massive attempt at an historical disproof of John Stuart Mill's timeless 'law of comparative advantage', showing how initially small inequalities in ties of interdependence between societies and economies have been magnified over time to produce the massive differences between today's First, Second and Third Worlds. On a similarly ambitious scale the economic historian E. L. Jones, in *The European Miracle* (1981) and especially in *Growth Recurring* (1988), undermines the sense of Europe's uniqueness by demonstrating that it was more the result of chance that it escaped the disasters which afflicted other major civilisations. Related themes on the scale of world history are tackled by the anthropologist Eric Wolf in *Europe and the People Without History* (1982) and by William McNeill in *The Rise of the West* (1963). McNeill's later books, *Plagues and Peoples* (1977), a history of disease and its impact on human society, and *The Pursuit of Power* (1982), on technology and armed force since AD 1000, are no less ambitious.

The minority also includes Norbert Elias. He is still best known for *The Civilising Process*, first published in 1939 but virtually unknown until the 1970s and 1980s. In this extraordinarily complex two-volume work, Elias advances a theory of state-formation based on a study of Western Europe during the last millennium, and links that to the changes in psychological makeup undergone by individuals as they become gradually more subject in the course of generations to the social constraint imposed by the monopolisation of the means of violence by the state apparatus. In his later writings, Elias has continued to extend the theory in scope to mankind as a whole (1984, 1987b).

Finally, the minority includes many Marxist scholars. I will cite only one instance here: Perry Anderson's massive comparative and developmental study, begun in *Passages from Antiquity to Feudalism* (1974a) and *Lineages of the Absolutist State* (1974b), and as yet incomplete.[3]

The notion of theories of long-term processes of social development remains suspect for different reasons, both to many sociologists and many historians.

Many sociologists remained wedded to the ideal of nomothetic-deductive explanation. If one's theory cannot be expressed in the form or propositions or axioms from which the observed course of events can be logically deduced, it is not 'scientific'. The condition is, of course, rarely attained in historical studies (nor, if truth be known, is it very common in present-centred sociological studies). Elias, for one, argues (1987a) that the nomothetic-deductive model of explanation is based on an outmoded image of classical physics, that the biological sciences (and now even modern cosmology) do not in practice employ nomothetic-deductive theories but rather 'process-theories' which are more adequate to the character of their subject-matter, and *a fortiori* to the social sciences. Nevertheless, the model of nomothetic-deductive explanation has enormous emotional appeal, and the hunting of the snark continues. Joseph Needham, indeed, suggested it was a cultural trait which could be traced back to the Greeks. 'Although historians of science are never tired of hymning the services of Euclidean deductive geometry to the Western world,' he wrote, it was arguable

> that Europe had had more geometry than was good for it. Of course, geometry was an essential basis for modern science, but it did have the bad effect of inducing too ready a belief in abstract timeless axiomatic propositions of all sorts self-evident, and too willing an acceptance of rigid logical and theological formulations . . . China, however, was algebraic and 'Babylonian', not geo-metrical and 'Greek', . . . [tending] to be practical and approximate rather than theoretical and absolute, and men did not feel obliged to formulate such timeless axiomatic propositions. (Needham, 1965, pp. 46–7n.)

Theories of long-term processes of social development remain suspect to most – not all – professional historians as a prime source of 'mere speculation'. But the table can be turned on the conventional historians. Elias, for instance, asks why the shelf-life of works of historical scholarship is typically so short (1983, p. 4ff). Why is it that history seems to have to be written anew in every generation? Can it be *only* the continuous discovery of new historical facts? Leopold von Ranke was aware of the problem a century and a half ago:

> History is always being rewritten . . . Each period takes it over and stamps it with its dominant slant of thought. Praise and blame are apportioned accordingly. All this drags on until the matter itself becomes unrecognisable. Then nothing can help except a return to the original evidence. But would we study it at all without the impulse of the present? . . . Is a completely true history possible? (Ranke, quoted by Elias, 1983, p. 4)

Ranke's own solution was to base history on the most meticulous and scholarly study of the documentary evidence. But while his work marked an enormous advance in historical scholarship, his solution was not enough in itself. For while the methods he pioneered lead to the accumulation of well-established discrete details, they do not in themselves yield any systematic or verifiable framework of reference against which the details can be set. The details may be well-established yet the *connections between them* are often left to arbitrary interpretation and speculation:

> The constraints of the tradition of historiography that allows the individual historian very great latitude for personal hermeneutics in the establishment of narrative connections between carefully re-searched sources finds expression, among other ways, in a conscious renunciation of theory . . . Yet the proud renunciation of theory in this form of history writing leaves the door wide open for the formation of historical myths of all kinds. (Elias, 1977, p. 137)

It is all too easy for narrative historians – and the case for narrative as the central activity of historians is still made (Stone, 1983; cf. Hobsbawm, 1980) – to represent history as a jumble of 'unique' events, an unstructured sequence of the actions of particular people. The importance of writers such as we have mentioned is that they help to show that long-term, unplanned but explainable processes form the infrastructure of any such apparently random and structureless juxtaposition of people and events. The claim that historians study unique, unrepeatable sequences of events implies that 'uniqueness' is an inherent property of the objects or events studied. It is not: it is a property conferred on them by the low level of abstraction of the frame of reference with which such historians operate.

The claim of 'uniqueness' is linked, too, to the writing of history in a highly voluntaristic manner – that is, in terms of the motives and actions of apparently 'free' actors. The introduction of concepts at a higher level of abstraction, and especially longer-term process theories, is often seen by historians as bringing with it a quite opposite image of 'determinism'. But such absolutes as 'free' and 'determined' are metaphysical notions: in the real world, all human beings have always been interdependent with other human beings in various degrees and patterns. Voluntaristic studies of people's motives are valuable and essential, but process-theories – used consciously or unconsciously by most of those interested in long-term processes – aim to show how historical processes unfold through sequences of inter-

64   *The Sociological Study of History*

locking levers of accident and design, the unintended consequences of intentional actions forming the unintended conditions of subsequent intentional actions.

This links with a persisting suspicion, both among academics and among (non-Marxist) politicians, that any theory of long-term developmental processes is necessarily bound up with a belief in inevitable 'progress' and with predictions of an 'inevitable' future society – the legacy of Popper as much as anyone. The work of Wallerstein and of McNeill (*The Pursuit of Power* more than *Plagues and Peoples*) ought to be enough to show that developmental theories certainly do not always depict history in diachronic Panglossian terms as an ineluctable movement towards greater welfare. Elias too is always careful to stress that greater civilisation, in his technical sense, does not necessarily mean greater happiness: there are progressions, in his view, but no progress.

As for the 'inevitability' of social development and predictions of the future, Philip Abrams (1982, pp. 145–6) rightly singles out for praise Elias's discussion of the problem (Elias, 1978a, pp. 158–74). It rests on the basic distinction between necessary and sufficient conditions of a social change, or, as Abrams puts it, 'between that which is inevitable in the sense that all conditions necessary for its existence have been met and that which is inevitable in the sense that all other possibilities have been ruled out'. The historian and sociologist may frequently be able to demonstrate the former, but rarely if ever can possess the knowledge necessary to prove the latter. In other words, historical sociology may well be able to establish a sequential order, to demonstrate that an earlier pattern of social organisation (feudalism, for example) was a necessary precursor of the emergence of a later pattern (capitalism, shall we say), if the former in every case contained all the conditions necessary for the latter to come into existence. But that is not at all the same thing as being able to prophesy that the earlier pattern must inevitably give rise to the later; from the viewpoint of an earlier pattern, several alternative outcomes are usually possible. Popper sought to discredit 'historical prophecy', but any reasonably ambitious historical retrodiction seems to have been unnecessarily damaged by his argument too.[4]

CONCLUSION: WHAT IS ACHIEVED?

So far, I have perhaps sidestepped the question of what is achieved by the sociological study of the past. What use is it? It is possible to cite instances where the sociological investigation of the past has proved useful in the present in the most utilitarian ways. One example is the work of Eric Dunning and his colleagues on football hooliganism (1988). The very achievement of demonstrating that hooligan violence was not something which appeared abruptly in the 1960s, but had long historical roots and had been socially structured and channelled over time, had direct implications for the kinds of policies which would and would not succeed in controlling it. I myself have also found that my own purely historical sociological study of the development of culinary taste and appetite in England and France (Mennell, 1985) proved useful in designing current research to assist doctors in giving dietary advice to their patients.

It would, however, be hazardous to seek to justify historical sociology on utilitarian grounds. Any utilitarian, practical value is almost always incidental. But it does often serve to improve the human means of orientation. Perhaps the most practically useful result of the investigation of long-term developmental processes is to lend scale and perspective to the present. In this, its significance may spread beyond narrowly academic interests into influencing how people at large and even policy-makers interpret events they see before them at the present day. Only two examples will have to suffice by way of conclusion. The work of Wallerstein and of Jones could, for instance, eventually seep through into popular and political perceptions of the countries of the Third World. As recently as the 1960s, sociological interpretations were dominated by the 'culture of backwardness' approach associated with authors like Hoselitz (1960), and Almond and Coleman (1960). Using conceptual schemes derived from Talcott Parsons and previously bowdlerized from Max Weber, they seriously discussed the 'value-orientations' of 'societies' in isolation, usually diagnosing the need for an intravenous transfusion of the Protestant Ethic (Eisenstadt, 1968). No one could now take that seriously who has read Wallerstein, Jones, and related writers' accounts of the long-term structured processes in the course of which economic, political and cultural gulfs gradually widened in the context of increasingly unequal power-balances. Nevertheless, it is probably true that people at large in the rich industrial countries, and probably most politicians also, still see the situation in terms closer to the earlier, static, sociological view.

A second instance is the widespread belief that contemporary society is more insecure and more violent perhaps than ever before. To have read Wittfogel, McNeill and Elias – among others – adds perspective and makes one sceptical of any such claim.[5] Yet again, the popular view is extraordinarily hard to dislodge, if only because people who live in inner cities and feel insecure find it hard to believe that things could ever have been worse than they are for them. Sociologists, however, should never allow themselves to be too sanguine about their chances of reforming the perceptions of people in society at large. Even our own social scientific colleagues sometimes find it hard to accept research findings: for instance, Sir Edmund Leach (1986) poured scorn on Eric Dunning's painstaking documentary investigation of football hooliganism in the past – it was easy, he claimed, when you already knew what you would find – and preferred to rely on his own personal recollection of rowdyism after the Boat Race in the 1930s. Historical sociologists *can* hope to influence the way people see the world, shaking them out of old perceptions and into new. But it is a slow business. It, too, in its own right, may be a long-term, structured process of social development.

Notes

1. Scepticism about the reliability of historical sources is of course perfectly healthy. During the Noordwijk conference, Robin Williams expressed just such a scepticism about one recent fashion in history and sociology: oral history. He gave us an example – Studs Terkel's book *The Good War* (1984), compiled from the recollections of American veterans. He pointed out that Americans did not speak of the Second World War as 'the good war' *until after the Vietnam War*, when hindsight revised their perceptions retrospectively.
2. A conspicuous absentee is the philosopher Michel Foucault, whose works have sometimes been read as historical sociology. They certainly contain many nuggets of striking fact and insight. As a *theorist*, however, he seems to me to be confused and incoherent; it is notable how fast Foucault shares fell on the intellectual stock market after his death.
3. Harvey J. Kaye, *The British Marxist Historians* (1984), provides an extremely useful discussion of the work of Maurice Dobb, Rodney Hilton, Christopher Hilton, Eric Hobsbawm and E. P. Thompson.
4. For a critique of Popper and defence of developmental sociology, see Dunning (1977).
5. For quantitative evidence on long-term trends in interpersonal violence, see Gurr (1981) and Stone (1983).

References

*Abrams, P. (1982) *Historical Sociology* (Shepton Mallett: Open Books).
Adorno, T. W. (1976) 'Sociology and Empirical Research', in P. Connerton ed.), *Critical Sociology* (Harmondsworth: Penguin) pp. 237–57.

Almond, G. and Coleman, J. S. (1960) *The Politics of Developing Areas* (Princeton: Princeton UP).

Anderson, P. (1974a) *Passages From Antiquity to Feudalism* (London: New Left Books).

—— (1974b) *Lineages of the Absolutist State* (London: New Left Books).

Ariès, P. (1962) *Centuries of Childhood* (London: Jonathan Cape).

Bellah, R. N. (1959) 'Durkheim and History', *American Sociological Review*, vol. 24, pp. 447–61.

—— (1964) 'Religious Evolution', *American Sociological Review*, vol. 29, pp. 358–74.

Bendix, R. (1978) *Kings or People: Power and the Mandate to Rule* (Berkeley: University of California Press).

Braudel, F. (1976) *The Mediterranean and the Mediterranean World in the Age of Philip II*, 2 vols (New York: Harper & Row).

—— (1983) *Capitalism and Material Life*, 3 vols (London: Fontana).

Burke, P. (1974) *Venice and Amsterdam* (London: Temple Smith).

—— (1978) *Popular Culture in Early Modern Europe* (London: Temple Smith).

—— (1987) *The Historical Anthropology of Early Modern Italy* (Cambridge, CUP).

Cohen, S. (1972) *Folk Devils and Moral Panics* (London: MacGibbon & Kee).

Darnton, R. (1984) *The Great Cat Massacre* (London: Allen Lane).

Davidoff, L. (1973) *The Best Circles* (London: Croom Helm).

Dunning, E. (1977) 'In Defence of Developmental Sociology: A Critique of Popper's Poverty of Historicism . . .', *Amsterdams Sociologisch Tijdschrift*, vol. 4, pp. 327–49.

—— , Murphy, P. and Williams, J. (1988) *The Roots of Football Hooliganism* (London: Routledge & Kegan Paul).

Eisenstadt, S. N. (1963) *The Political Systems of Empires* (New York: Free Press).

—— (1964) 'Social Change, Differentiation and Evolution', *American Sociological Review*, vol. 29, pp. 375–86.

—— (ed.) (1968) *The Protestant Ethic and Modernisation* (New York: Basic Books).

Elias, N. (1977) 'Zur Grundlegung einer Theorie soziale Prozesse', *Zeitschrift fuer Soziologie*, vol. 6, pp. 127–49.

—— (1978a) *What is Sociology?* (London: Hutchinson).

—— (1978b) *The Civilising Process*, vol 1, *The History of Manners* (Oxford: Blackwell).

—— (1982) *The Civilising Process*, vol 2, *State-Formation and Civilisation* (Oxford: Blackwell).

—— (1983) *The Court Society* (Oxford: Blackwell).

—— (1984) *Uber die Zeit* (Frankfurt: Suhrkamp).

—— (1987a) *Involvement and Detachment* (Oxford: Blackwell).

—— (1987b) 'The Retreat of Sociologists into the Present', *Theory, Culture and Society*, vol. 4, pp. 223–47.

Erikson, K. T. (1966) *Wayward Puritans* (New York: Wiley).

Evans-Pritchard, E. E. (1937) *Witchcraft, Oracles and Magic Among the Azande* (Oxford: Clarendon Press).

Gurr, T. R. (1981) 'Historical Trends in Violent Crime: A Critical Review of the Evidence', in M. Tonry and N. Morris (eds), *Crime and Justice: An*

Annual Review of Research (Chicago: University of Chicago Press) vol. 3, pp. 295–353.

Hobsbawm, E. (1980) 'The Revival of Narrative: Some Comments', *Past and Present*, no. 86, pp. 3–8.

Hoselitz, B. F. (1960) *Sociological Aspects of Economic Growth* (Glencoe: Free Press).

Jones, E. L. (1981) *The European Miracle* (Cambridge: Cambridge University Press).

—— (1988) *Growth Recurring* (Cambridge: Cambridge University Press).

Kaye, H. (1984) *The British Marxist Historians* (Oxford: Polity Press).

Ladurie, E. L. (1979) *Carnival at Romans* (New York: Braziller).

Leach, E. R. (1986) 'Violence', *London Review of Books*, 23 October 1960.

McNeill, W. H. (1963) *The Rise of the West* (Chicago: University of Chicago Press).

—— (1977) *Plagues and Peoples* (Garden City, NY: Doubleday).

—— (1982) *The Pursuit of Power* (Chicago: University of Chicago Press).

Mennell, S. (1985) *All Manners of Food* (Oxford: Blackwell).

Moore, B., Jnr (1966) *Social Origins of Dictatorship and Democracy* (Boston: Beacon Press).

Needham, J. (1965) *Time and Eastern Man* (London: Royal Anthropological Institute).

Parsons, T. (1937) *The Structure of Social Action* (New York: McGraw-Hill).

—— (1964) 'Evolutionary Universals in Society', *American Sociological Review*, vol. 29, pp. 339–57.

—— (1966) *Societies: Evolutionary and Comparative Perspectives* (Englewood Cliffs, N.J.: Prentice-Hall).

—— (1971) *The System of Modern Societies* (Englewood Cliffs, N.J.: Prentice-Hall).

Pollock, F. (1976) 'Empirical Research into Public Opinion', in P. Connerton (ed.), *Critical Sociology* (Harmondsworth: Penguin) pp. 225–36.

Popper, K. R. (1945) *The Open Society and Its Enemies* (London: Routledge & Kegan Paul).

—— (1957) *The Poverty of Historicism* (London: Routledge & Kegan Paul).

Skocpol, T. (1979) *States and Social Revolutions* (Cambridge: CUP).

Stone, L. (1983) 'Interpersonal Violence in English Society 1300–1980', *Past and Present*, no. 101, pp. 22–23.

Terkel, S. (1984) *The Good War* (New York: Pantheon).

Thompson, E. P. (1963) *The Making of the English Working Class* (London: Victor Gollancz).

Tilly, C. (1976) *The Vendée* (Cambridge, Mass: Harvard University Press).

*—— (1984) *Big Structures, Large Processes, Huge Comparisons* (New York: Russell Sage Foundation).

Wallerstein, I. (1974, 1980) *The Modern World-System*, 2 vols (New York: Academic Press).

Weber, E. (1976) *Peasants Into Frenchmen* (Standord: Stanford University Press).

Wittfogel, K. A. (1957) *Oriental Despotism* (New Haven: Yale University Press).

Wolf, E. R. (1982) *Europe and the People Without History* (Berkeley: University of California Press).

5 Tales of Innocence and Experience: Developments in Sociological Theory since 1950
Christopher G. A. Bryant

1 INTRODUCTION

Assessment of achievement in sociological theory since 1950 could fill a series of books. 'Theory' after all contains a multitude of possibilities. Merton (1957c) listed six – methodology, general orientations, analysis of concepts, *post factum* interpretations, empirical generalisations, and the formulation of scientific laws (statements of invariance derived from a theory) – and implied a seventh – the codification of scientific laws. Of these only the last two, deduction of propositions for empirical test and their cumulation, apparently constitute theory proper. Boudon refers to similar manoeuvres in his 'Theories, theory and Theory' (1970). By contrast I shall uphold a more catholic conception, partly so as not to overlap Henk Becker's chapter on the analytical tradition, and partly out of my own reluctance to disqualify as 'theory' work of quality commonly so called just because it is not dedicated to particular conceptions of scientific laws and theory building (cf. Section 4). Cutting my task down to the size allowed by a single chapter is therefore not easy. In order to make it manageable I have chosen to concentrate on the following three themes:

1. the volume and quality of work on the history of social thought and the writings of the great names from the past;
2. the presentation of developments in theory since 1950 in terms of first the orthodoxy of structural functionalism, then the challenges to it from various quarters (including Marxism and conflict theory and the different strands of the hermeneutic or interpretive tradition) which issued in the war of the schools, and finally the

circumspection which has followed the excesses of that war and the attempts at synthesis and integration;
3. reassessment of the differentiation of propositional theory by level, range and type in the light of post-empiricist philosophy of social science.

In each case I can do no more than advance the basic arguments and point to key publications or specific examples.

In each of the three themes one motif in particular recurs – loss of innocence and subjection to the hard lessons of experience. The real achievement in theory has been the winning of a kind of wisdom. Such a claim may sound impossibly pretentious but I shall return to it in my concluding section and try to make it stick.

2 THE HISTORY OF SOCIAL THOUGHT

When confronted with Whitehead's dictum that 'A science which hesitates to forget its founders is lost', those sociologists who continue to pour vast efforts into commentary on, and translation of, sociological figures long dead sometimes console themselves with the thought that a science which forgets its origins neither knows how far it has travelled nor in what direction. I have never found this rejoinder very convincing. Quite apart from its unthinking acceptance of a particular conception of science, it does not justify the sheer volume of labour devoted to the classics and their successors. After all, a quick glance back is often enough to establish origins and directions. There are, however, other ways in which one can, and should, justify these labours – although it is doubtful whether anyone could ever show that the particular configuration of scarce human and other resources invested in study of the history of social thought is, at any given time, exactly the right one.

2.1 Recovering the Classics

In many European countries the big breakthrough for sociology in higher education came in the 1960s. Even in America, where sociology had had its place in many institutions from their inception, the 1960s saw a major expansion. It is difficult now to grasp just how inadequate was the state of knowledge of sociological theory on the eve of these developments. Sociology was no new discipline, and sociological theory, however defined, no new activity. On the contrary, from Saint-Simon to Schutz an enormous amount of value and import had already been written. Unfortunately some of it had not been published, much was out of print and not readily accessible, more still was not in English translation. Let me illustrate this by referring to the three most illustrious figures of all – Marx, Durkheim and Weber. Basically most of those who knew their Marx – not many in America – did not know about the *Economic and Philosophical Manuscripts* and the *Grundrisse*. The former had first been published in full in German in 1932 but did not become widely known until Bottomore and Rubel published extracts in English in 1956 and Bottomore put out a full English translation in 1963. The latter had been published in German in 1939 but had not been much noticed. It was republished in German in 1951 but the first English edition did not appear until 1973. Those who knew their Durkheim only in English had translations of *The Elementary Forms of Religious Life* (1915), *The Division of Labor* (1933), *The Rules of Sociological Method* (1938) and *Suicide* (1951) but nothing on education, socialism and professional associations (except the preface to the second edition of *The Division of Labor*). They also lacked many key articles. Readers of Weber in English did not get a complete *Economy and Society* until 1968 or the last of the *Wissenschaftslehre* essays until 1981 and they still await translations of many of his political writings. Works on the world religions only came out in English between 1951 and 1958. Other key works, including many articles, came still later. The availability of numerous other figures, from Comte to G. H. Mead, was, if anything, even less satisfactory.

The authors of these writings had for the most part worked independently of one another. Typically their critical engagement extended from developments in philosophy, history and economics to the complex economic and political changes in the societies in which they lived. Their legacy to the brave new sociology teachers of the 1960s was vast, rich, fragmented and intellectually challenging in the extreme. Is it any wonder that it has taken several decades of commentary, editing and translation on the part of a host of scholars to come to grips with it? How could it possibly have been otherwise?

Some of this work has been of very high quality. Lest anyone doubt this, it is enough to consider the huge projects of the *Complete Works of Marx and Engels* in English and the *Max Weber Gesamtausgabe*; the superb readers on Marx by McLellan (1977) and Marx and Engels by Tucker (1972 and 1978); Roth and Wittich's invaluable complete edition of Weber's *Economy and Society* (1968); commentaries such as

Rubel and Manale's *Marx Without Myth* (1975), Lukes's *Emile Durkheim: His Life and Work* (1973), Bendix's *Max Weber: An Intellectual Portrait* (1960), Matthews's *Quest for an American Sociology: Robert E. Park and the Chicago School* (1977) and Jay's *The Dialectical Imagination: A History of the Frankfurt School and the Institute of Social Research 1923–50* (1973); or the English translations of Marianne Weber's *Max Weber: A Biography* (1975), Simmel's *The Philosophy of Money* (1978) or Schutz's *Der sinnhafte Aufbau der sozialen Welt* (translated as *The Phenomenology of the Social World*, 1967). Indeed the list of achievements, in articles as well as books, is almost endless.

It can be argued that as more and more of our inheritance is rendered accessible, diminishing returns must set in on further works of this kind – whether they be critical reappraisals, new editions, translations of more minor works or re-translations of major ones. Though plenty remains to be done, I have considerable sympathy with this argument. I also accept that over-absorption in the concepts, methods and perspectives of Marx and the mid-Victorians, or the 1890–1920 generation or any other past group sometimes desensitises us to the genuinely different realities of today (cf. Nisbet (1966) on sociology as a response to the French and Industial Revolutions and their consequences, or Ossowski (1963, pp. 2–3) on things of which Marx could have no conception including nuclear weapons). But there still seem to me good reasons why intense interest in past writers should continue. They have to do with the linguistic turn of the 1960s and 70s and the greater attention we now pay to the problems and opportunities of interpretation.

2.2 The Meaning of Texts from the Past

The conceptual vocabulary of sociology has never been standardised. The strong version of the thesis of the essential contestability of concepts says that it *cannot* ever be standardised because there is a *two*-way tie between sociological and natural language (Giddens's double-hermeneutic where Schutz had stressed only the rootedness of secondary in primary constructs), and natural language cannot be fixed once-and-for-all, or even for protracted periods, outside utopia (Giddens, 1984, p. 374; Schutz, 1953). (Sartori (1984) and other leading figures in the ISA and IPSA Committee on Conceptual and Terminological Analysis clearly think otherwise, but few take much notice of them.) It is therefore only to be expected that scholars will seek to render texts understandable by trying to recover their authors' meanings and by other exercises in contextualisation. If, however, texts are in some sense period-pieces, is the effort worth it? They may throw light on the past, but have they relevance for today? I shall suggest that they can have by building on an argument of Ricoeur's. Ricouer distinguishes between spoken discourse and the written text. Speech is an event. Writing fixes not the saying but the said. 'With written discourse, the author's intention and the meaning of the text cease to coincide' (Ricoeur, 1971, p. 534); the career of the text escapes the career of the author. The text also frees itself from the ostensive references of speech; instead, '[f]or us, the world is the ensemble of references opened up by the texts' (pp. 535–6). Finally, whereas speech is addressed to someone, the text has a universal range of addressees; '[a]n unknown, invisible reader has become the unprivileged addressee of the discourse' (p. 537).Ricoeur's object is to consider whether the model of the text also serves the analysis of human action. I want only to consider the understanding and interpretation of sociological texts.

Some work on the writings of figures long dead is a kind of hypercontextualisation, an attempt to understand by recovering the actuality, the situational references, of their production. This is the quest-for-the-historical Weber school of exegesis. It is hard to do but has for many an intrinsic fascination, and it does sometimes resolve puzzles or shed new light on old texts. An example would be McLellan's *Karl Marx: His Life and Thought* (1973). Other work goes for complete decontextualisation. Ricoeur discusses structuralists whose *epoché* of the situational world of the text renders it worldless and possessed only of an inside. He cites Lévi-Strauss (1958) on myth and adds that the latter's systematic oppositions and combinations would lack all significance for us were they not about birth and death, blindness and lucidity, sexuality and truth. Structuralists may some-times pretend a formalism as contentless as algebra, but their appeal lies in what they tell us about the human condition. There would seem, then, two ways of presenting the interpretation of decontextualised texts – one in terms of their internal order and the other in terms of a virtual order which is simultaneously out-of-time and out-of-place and of universal relevance. Althusser and Balibar's *Reading Capital* (French 1965) provides an example of the first; Coser's use of Simmel in *The Functions of Social Conflict* (1956), in which the *flâneur* disappears altogether, tends towards the second.

What I want to add is that there is a multitude of possibilities between the extremes of hypercontextualisation and both nowhere decontextualisaton and everywhere decontextualisation. One can attempt a critique, a specification of the conditions and the limitations, not only of individual texts, but also of oeuvres, genres, schools and traditions. One can also place all of these in many different contexts of production and consumption. Connecting production and consumption is difficult but it is not a new problem. Rickert and Weber encountered it when trying to connect practical and theoretical value-relations (cf. Bryant, 1985, pp. 64–98). Ricoeur concentrates on consumption:

> To understand a text is at the same time to light up our own situation, or, if you will, to interpolate among the predicates of our situation all the significations which make a [non-ostensive] *Welt* of our [ostensive] *Umwelt*. It is this enlarging of the *Umwelt* into the *World* which permits us to speak of the references *opened up* by the text – it would be better to say that the references *opened up* the world. (Ricoeur, 1971, p. 536)

I do not see how one can place any limit on the capacity of past texts in sociological theory to open up the world for us, partly because they address questions of the human condition and partly because they invite us to grasp the character of our own age by locating it in contexts which transcend it.

3 ORTHODOXY AND HETERODOXY

There is, I think, much to be said for the presentation of developments in theory since 1950, in terms of three stages: first the orthodoxy of structural functionalism, then the challenges to it and the war of the schools, and finally the circumspections of the present and the renewed interest in synthesis. Simplification it may be but it does reflect the changing temper of debates not just in theory but in sociology generally.

For the record, however, I had better say what the simplifications are. First, the 'orthodoxy' of structural functionalism contained its own variations. The four-function paradigm of Parsons and Smelser's *Economy and Society* (1956), for example, is significantly different from Parsons's theory of *The Social System* (1951); both in turn differ in some respects from the functional analysis endorsed by Merton in his classic 'Manifest and Latent Functions' (1949 and 1957); and so on. Second, even in the 1950s and early 1960s there existed the semi-submerged tradition of symbolic interactionism in America, a tradition of Marxist studies in Europe and a mass of empirical work, especially in America, singularly uninformed by any consciously articulated theory whatsoever. Third, the war of the schools sounds as if there were clearly demarcated battle lines. In practice the contest between functionalisms, conflict theories (some Marxist, others more Weberian), Marxisms, variants in the interpretive or hermeneutic traditions, structuralisms (again some Marxist and others not), etc., was never that tidy. Schools overlapped, alliances shifted, targets were redefined. For example, conflict theory, for which Dahrendorf's *Class and Class Conflict in an Industrial Society* (German, 1957, English 1959) remains the most impressive statement, shares certain assumptions with the functionalism it opposes; and no target has undergone more redefinition than that labelled positivist (cf. Bryant, 1985). Also the metaphor of a 'war' suggests that people were destroyed. In a few places – certain German universities come to mind – the disputes generated real personal fear and loathing, but much more often the 'war' was simply a time of intense intellectual debate in which a lot of sociologists learned a great deal. Certainly many in Britain look back on the war with affection. Fourth, circumspection is common today but by no means universal; and among the circumspect not everyone is interested in attempts to set forth structures of theory within which different modes of theorising can then be located, or in attempts at synthesis.

Where lies the achievement in all this? In formulating an answer, I want to cheat on the post-1950 brief and refer first to Parsons's *The Structure of Social Action* (1937). On the first page of that massive work, Parsons recalled that in Spencer there had once been a theorist who dominated social theory. His influence had, however, long given way to a multiplicity of approaches. On the penultimate page, he deplored the prevailing pessimism that 'there are as many systems of sociological theory as there are sociologists, that there is no common basis, that all is arbitrary and subjective' (p. 774). Fortunately deliverance was at hand; his own voluntaristic theory of action would put an end to this unhappy state! Over the decades which followed, Parsons's theoretical development went through a number of stages but at the heart of all of them there persisted a determination to establish the common basis, not just of all sociology, but of all social science. Now consider the breakdown of functionalist orthodoxy in the late 1960s and the subsequent war of the schools. Were there not then, too, as many systems of sociology as there were sociologists? And look at the contemporary quest for integration; is this not also an attempt to bring order where there was disorder? Could it not be said that the wheel has turned full circle? *Plus ça change, plus c'est la même chose?*

3.1 Responses to Anti-Foundationalism

Many disciplines oscillate between periods of convergence and periods of divergence. I think sociology may again be in a converging phase, but this turn of the wheel, like others before it, does not return the wheel to its point of departure but rather moves it on. Things are not as they always were. There seem to me three elements to this advance: widespread recognition of the problem of foundationalism, near-universal acknowledgement of the linguistic turn, and a growing interest in social science as moral inquiry. I will comment briefly on each.

The metaphor of a sure foundation for our knowledge originates in Descartes. Strictly speaking it belongs to epistemology but, like many notions in epistemology, it also shades into ontology in so far as ideas of what we can know are connected to ideas about how the world is. It refers to knowledge as a mirror of nature; alternatively, to knowledge as a faithful representation of how the world is. What marks contemporary social scientific discourse off from both structural functional orthodoxy and the alternative paradigms in the war of the schools is widespread doubt about the availability of any such sure foundation. The reasons for this include the patent impossibility of sealing off sociological from natural discourse and the consequent elusiveness of a universal categorial system for all sociology, the evident limitations of all known research methods, and real doubt as to what objectivity would consist of – let alone whether we could achieve it. Perhaps the most telling challenge to foundationalism is Rorty's *Philosophy and the Mirror of Nature* (1980); perhaps the most obvious evidence of doubt about it occurs in the debate on post-modernism. Once foundationalism is discarded, claims to both objectivism and realism become highly problematic. By 'objectivism' I mean the idea 'that there must be some permanent, ahistorical matrix or framework to which we can ultimately appeal in determining the nature of rationality, knowledge, truth, reality, goodness, or rightness' (Bernstein, 1983, p. 8); and by realism I mean Francis Bacon's thesis that science reveals the true and hidden nature of the world.

3.1.1 Scientific Realism

There seem to be four main responses to the assault on foundationalism. The first, that of the scientific realists, of whom Bhaskar (1975, 1979) is probably the most influential among sociologists, is much favoured in Britain. It depends on a distinction between the phenomena and events of the actual observable world and the realities which underlie them. In effect it reclaims the Baconian realist idea of a nature which is hidden and opposes it to what it deems to be the prevailing 'positivist' view that excludes all such non-observables as metaphysical and unscientific. Bhaskar attributes to real entities 'the capacity . . . to bring about changes in material things', i.e. in the world as distinct from our idea of it (1979, p. 16). To have this capacity, to cause, is, however, to govern but not to determine. It is in the essential nature of something that it has the power to generate certain effects, but whether it actually does or not depends on the other mechanisms which are operative in what are open systems of phenomena and events. It also depends on the extent to which agents reproduce or transform the relations of production in which they are implicated.

Scientific realists reject attempts to dispose of *ceteris paribus* problems in the specification of causes by using the elaboration techniques – partialling in and factoring out – associated with multivariate analysis (cf. Pawson, 1986). Realist explanatory closure is logical in that it connects actual phenomena and events with those underlying realities and generative mechanisms which, were they to exist, would have the power to cause them. As such it differs from actualist explanatory closure which is statistical in its connection of actualities with other actualities. The affinities of scientific realism with structuralism are obvious and it is no surprise that Marx, and sometimes Durkheim, are pleaded in aid. Given that underlying realities are said to govern but not to determine, empirical confirmation of their being and presence presents grave difficulties. Scientific realist truth can hardly be said to rest on sure foundations! But these difficulties are no different from those which accompany attempts to establish the utility of any ideal-type, logical construction or deductive system, such as those of classical economics, in the explanation of the actual social world or the real economy in the economist's sense of 'real'. All that scientific realism has done, it seems to me, is to make additional ontological assumptions for no additional explanatory benefit – contrary to the principle of Occam's razor. Nevertheless it does bring those who have turned aside from ideal-typification or classical economic models or other intellectual constructions because they object to the substantive content and political import of frequently cited exemplars, into greater *methodological* alignment with those who do heed them. Accordingly, its influence may yet prove convergent.

3.1.2 Habermas's Ideal Speech Situation

The second response is that of Habermas. Habermas acknowledges much of the anti-foundationalist case. In particular he rejects realism and adopts a consensus theory of truth whose two most important elements are the ideal speech situation and the theory of communicative action. Habermas treats truth as the product of rational consensus; as such it is universal and objective. Rational consensus is the outcome of an ideal speech situation: that is, a situation in which all parties have equal opportunities to speak, and equal competence in speaking, there are no asymmetries of power and influence between them, and where, freed from both internal and external forces, they are persuaded by the 'unforced force of the better argument' (quoted in McCarthy, 1978, p. 292). What is the status of this idealisation? Before answering it is helpful to quote a passage from Habermas's essay on universal pragmatics:

> anyone acting communicatively must, in performing any speech action, raise universal validity claims and suppose that they can be vindicated [or redeemed: *einlösen*] . . . The speaker must choose a comprehensible [*verständlich*] expression so that the speaker and hearer can understand one another. The speaker must have the intention of communicating a true [*wahr*] proposition (or a propositional content, the existential presuppositions of which are satisfied) so that the hearer can share the knowledge of the speaker. The speaker must want to express his intentions truthfully [*wahrhaftig*] so that the hearer can believe the utterance of the speaker (can trust him). Finally, the speaker must choose an utterance that is right [*richtig*] so that the hearer can accept the utterance with respect to a recognized normative background. Moreover, communicative action can continue undisturbed only as long as participants suppose that the validity claims they reciprocally raise are justified. (Habermas, 1976, pp. 2–3)

Undistorted communication requires redemption of all four validity claims – comprehensibility, truth, truthfulness and rightness. According to Habermas it is anticipated by all sincere participants in discourse. Undistorted communication in an ideal speech situation has, he claims, a transcendental status; 'on this unavoidable fiction rests the humanity of intercourse among men who are still men' (Habermas, quoted in McCarthy, 1978, p. 140). It grounds the critique of actual communication and institutions.

It is this transcendental character which gives Habermas's ideal speech situation a privileged status over other idealisations such as Weberian ideal-types. In a way there is here a surprising affinity with Popper. As Hesse has pointed out:

That an ideal speech situation occurs is falsifiable but not verifiable, like the occurrence of a true theory for Popper. Like Popper's true theory, it may never be realized in history, and indeed it seems as though we could not certainly recognize it if it were. Like Popper's true theory, it is a regulative ideal, presupposed in the decision to enter a certain form of life, that is, the scientific community of rational discourse . . . But Popper . . . also maintains that truth is to be understood as correspondence with reality . . . Habermas, on the other hand, rejects the correspondence account, and locates truth in the consensus which the scientific community would reach at a postulated limiting point of this process. (Hesse, 1980, p. 217)

In another respect the difference with Popper is stark because the ideal speech situation is a regulative idea not just for science but for all rational discourse and all claims to knowledge. How ironic, in the light of the *Positivismusstreit*, that where Popper sought to demarcate science from non-science without condemning non-science as non-sense, Habermas demands that all claims to knowledge, scientific and non-scientific, be redeemed in the same way.

The privileged status of Habermas's idealisation is, it seems to me, open to two objections above all others. First, it is assumed that undistorted communication in an ideal speech situation will always issue in rational consensus. By contrast I cannot see why it should not sometimes issue in rational dissensus. I cannot see why, even after emancipation from internal compulsion and external repression, reason should be able to dissolve all differences of language and value. Second, it is assumed that the limiting case of the ideal speech situation serves as a useful, indeed necessary, normative standard. But a device which ignores practical impediments of place and cost in communication between participants and practical limitations of time in reaching consensus is itself liable to be ignored.

3.1.3 Relativism

Habermas is a modernist in his belief that post-conventional cognitive domains, such as science and law, replace traditional codes of conduct with warranted principles. He thus stands opposed to the third response to the assault on foundationalism – relativism. Bernstein has defined relativism as:

> the basic conviction that when we turn to the examination of those concepts that philosophers have taken to be the most fundamental – whether it is the concept of rationality, truth, reality, right, the good, or norms – we are forced to recognize that in the final analysis all such concepts must be understood as relative to a specific conceptual scheme, theoretical framework, paradigm, form of life, society or culture. Since the relativist believes that there is (or can be) a nonreducible plurality of such conceptual schemes, he or she challenges the claim that these concepts can have a determinate and univocal significance. For the relativist, there is no substantive overarching framework or single metalanguage by which we can rationally adjudicate or univocally evaluate competing claims of alternative paradigms. (Bernstein, 1983, p. 8)

Relativists are, for example, ready to accept that 'our' and 'their' standards of rationality are 'radically incommensurable'. Put as strongly as this, it is not easy to name any relativists. Dévotés of the over-encapsulated conception of culture sometimes attributed to Winch (1958) might be one example, vulgar interpreters of Kuhn (1962) on the incommensurability of paradigms, or Feyerabend (1975) on 'anything goes', another. Subscribers to internal critique who eschew all extra-discursive references might also qualify. For the most part, however, relativism is more spectre than substance.

3.1.4 The New Pragmatism

The fourth response, and the one I favour myself, is the pragmatic one. It does not deny the non-availability of a single metalanguage but refuses to draw from this the conclusion of radical incommensurability. Instead it treats comparisons between paradigms and conceptual vocabularies, cultures and epochs, as exercises in translation in which there may be some direct equivalences but there will also have to be many discursive glosses. The object of these exercises is to construct a 'conversation' between one's own culture, age, position or whatever, and some other(s). For distinguished examples of this kind of work, one can turn to Geertz (1973); for more of its rationale, one can turn to Rorty (1980 and 1982) in philosophy and Bernstein (1971 and 1983) in sociology. It is a pragmatic approach in that it is guided by the notion that knowledge is better regarded not as a representation of reality but rather as a means of coping with it. The pragmatic response to the anti-foundationalist challenge is still being worked out, but it is already possible to discern something of its sources of inspiration and its uses. The former include Rickert and Weber on theoretical and practical value-relations, and the American pragmatists. The latter include proponents of the interactive and dialogical models of applied social research (such as Weiss, 1980; Bulmer, 1982; and Giddens, 1987) which capitalise on the two-way tie (Giddens's 'double-hermeneutic', Rorty's 'conversation') between ordinary members' and sociologists' language and knowledge.

3.2 The Linguistic Turn

The expression 'the linguistic turn' originated in Bergmann's *Logic and Reality* (1964):

> All linguistic philosophers talk about the world by means of talking about a suitable language. This is the linguistic turn, the funda-mental gambit as to method, on which ordinary and ideal language philosophers . . . agree. (Bergman, 1964, p. 177)

Rorty's use of it for the title of his 1967 volume on philosophical method made it generally known. In sociology it has prompted what has sometimes been called 'the hermeneutic turn' (cf. Phillips, 1986, p. 2). Execution of this turn requires acknowledgement of the language and understandings of the (types) of person whose action one seeks to explain and about whom one seeks to generalise. Schutz's insistence, in 1953, that social scientists' (secondary) constructs be relatable to lay (primary) constructs via the postulates of subjective interpretation and adequacy, is an example of negotiation of the linguistic turn before it had even been formulated as such. Schutz, however, was of little influence before the 1960s and a better idea of progress on this issue can be gained by comparing statements from Parsons and Merton in the 1950s with that of Giddens in the 1980s.

In 1951 Parsons and Shils presented their work on the general theory of action as a categorial system (an interdependent system of classes and definitions) for all the social sciences. This they saw as a necessary step on the way to first a theoretical system (a categorial system plus laws which relate elements of the system), and then an empirical-theoretical system (a theoretical system which affords predictions under real, as distinct from experimental, conditions) (1951, pp. 50–1). Their model was that of classical mechanics. They no more allowed that actors might vary their behaviour in the light of what social scientists say about them than they considered planets in the solar system would vary theirs. Whilst Parsons was the grandest grand theorist of that time, many sociologists had more sympathy with Merton's call for theories of the middle range. But Merton, too, made plain his desire for the 'systematics' and 'codification' of theory and for *'verifiable statements of relationships between specified variables'* (1957, p. 9, his italics). His footnote at this point to Lundberg's article on 'The Natural Science Trend in Sociological Theory' (1955) confirmed his pursuit of laws similar to those attributed to natural science.

Compare this with Giddens (1984) on generalisations and the knowledgeability of actors:

> Generalizations tend towards two poles, with a range and variety of possible shadings between them. Some hold because actors themselves know them – in some guise – and apply them in the enactment of what they do. The social scientific observer does not in fact have to 'discover' these generalizations, although that observer may give a new discursive form to them. Other generalizations refer to circumstances, or aspects of circumstances, of which agents are ignorant and which effectively 'act' on them, independently of whatever the agents may believe they are up to. Those I shall call 'structural sociologists' tend to be interested only in generalization in this second sense – indeed, this is what is meant when it is claimed that the 'theory' in social theory should comprise explanatory generalizations. But the first is just as fundamental to social science as the second, and each form of generalization is unstable in respect of the other. The circumstances in which generalizations about what 'happens' to agents hold are mutable in respect of what those agents can learn knowledgeably to 'make happen' (Giddens, 1984, p. xix)

Giddens not only makes the linguistic turn where Parsons and Merton do not, he also offers a formulation which is superior to Schutz's in so far as it acknowledges that social science may inform the knowledge-ability of actors.

3.3 Social Science as Moral Inquiry

The issue of social science as moral inquiry follows from that of the linguistic turn. (I have taken the expression 'social science as moral inquiry' from the title of a volume edited by Haan *et al.*, 1983). In the 1950s and 60s sociologists sought an objectivity and value-neutrality in which social science and moral inquiry are quite separate. Once the double-hermeneutic is recognised, however, this dissociation loses all plausibility. The language sociologists use in constituting their objects of inquiry can never be purged of all normative content, and what they say and write can, and often does, directly, or more likely as mediated by people of influence, the press, broadcasters, etc., enter extra-sociological discourse. The great advance of the last decade consists of increasing recognition of the problem, rather than any single agreed way of dealing with it (cf. Haan *et al.* (eds), 1983; Callahan and Jennings (eds), 1983; and Wardell and Turner (eds), 1986).

Work on the historical texts referred to in Section 2 of this chapter has helped generate awareness of the problem. Marx, Durkheim and Weber, in particular, adopted positions on it which are much subtler than the scientific socialism, scientific sociology and objective and ethically neutral social science attributed to them in the 1950s and early 60s (cf. Bryant, 1976). Gouldner's famous anti-minotaur article (1962), for example, should have been directed not at Weber but at the American travesty of Weber. Having said that, recovery of the classics has yielded two positions, neither of which is satisfactory. The first looks to some kind of scientific determination of moral and political choice in which choice is really a misnomer. There are versions in Marx and Durkheim but both are widely discredited. The second acknowledges the value content in science (social science is value-related and only in very restricted senses value-free), but disclaims any possibility of establishing that the values concerned in any particular sociological analysis or empirical research are indeed the right ones. The upshot is, as Habermas complained, an arbitrary decisionism. Either sociologists show no interest in how values can be rationally justified, or, worse still, they deny that any rational justification is possible (thereby calling to mind Weber's argument that ultimate values are the demons that hold the very threads of our lives).

What the recent debate has achieved is the reinstatement of the rational justification of values on the social science agenda. Three approaches to justification have generated particular interest. The first figures in Rawls's theory of justice (1971) and involves a distinctive restatement of social contract and rational choice theories:

> the guiding idea is that the principles of justice for the basic structure
> of society are the object of the original agreement. They are the
> principles that free and rational persons concerned to further their
> own interests would accept in an initial position of equality as
> defining the fundamental terms of their association. (p. 11)

In this 'original position' those who choose the principles of justice do
so behind a 'veil of ignorance' as to their own social position and their
corresponding interests. Devices such as these do make possible
rational discussion of things Weber treated as beyond the pale of
rational discourse, but they are also open, I suggest, to the kinds of
criticisms Marx levelled at Feuerbach. The second is Habermas's use
of the ideal speech situation in his legitimation theory. It bears some
resemblance, I submit, to Rawls, and is also open to the objections
already mentioned in Section 3.1.2. The third is suggested by the new
pragmatism. Again the object is not to resolve questions of value in
some timeless and placeless way but rather to help people in specific
situations find ways of coping with them.

3.4 Circumspection and Integration

I have claimed that anti-foundationalism, the linguistic turn and
recovery of the moral dimension to social science have moved very
many sociologists in the late 1980s to practise a kind of continuous
auto-critique. Where once they promoted their favoured modes of
analysis with a partisanship which brooked no alternatives, now they
have an awareness of the conditions and limitations of what they do
and the possibilities of proceeding differently. In addition to prudence
and circumspection, there is, however, a further characteristic of the
contemporary scene worthy of comment – the interest in synthesis and
integration. (With his writings on unities in sociological theory, one of
our symposiasts, Mennell (1974 and 1980) could be said to have
anticipated it.)

All synthesis and integration is difficult, but the simplest is the kind
attempted by Johnson, Dandeker and Ashworth (1984) in which one
seeks a kind of paradigm for theory in the Mertonian sense, i.e. a
structure, as distinct from a mere list, of issues and dilemmas. Perhaps
Alexander's four volumes (1982–4) on 'theoretical logic' can be
regarded in the same way. More difficult still is the kind of integration
attempted by Elias in his figurational sociology (German 1939, English

1978, 1982), Berger and Luckmann in their thesis of the social construction of reality (1966), Bhaskar in his reproduction/transformation model of society (1975, 1979) and Giddens in his structuration theory (1979, 1984). Crucially, all four set out to overcome the dualisms of structure and agency and structure and process; and two at least, Elias and Giddens, are now the focus of international discussion. Most difficult of all is the kind of (non-positivist) integration of social science, politics and ethics attempted by Habermas. Habermas does not so much reject the positivist and hermeneutic traditions as seek their dialectical transformation in a critical theory which serves our real human interests. In his refusal to reduce epistemology to the philosophy of science, and ethics to politics, he upholds a rationalism in which sociology plays but one part.

Theory in the late 1980s consists of more than peaceful co-existence in lieu of the war of the schools; it also offers prospects of advancement from fragmentation to integration. To have shifted sociology to such a position is an intellectual feat that few thought possible only a decade ago. There is real achievement here; do not let anyone deny it.

4 REASSESSMENT OF THE DIFFERENTIATION OF PROPOSITIONAL THEORY ACCORDING TO LEVEL, RANGE AND TYPE IN THE LIGHT OF POST-EMPIRICIST PHILOSOPHY OF SOCIAL SCIENCE

Merton argued that only the last two of his six or seven activities which had commonly gone by the name of theory consituted theory proper. In effect he equated theory with propositional theory, the specification and elaboration of generalisations or 'laws'. Now I agree that specification of general propositions is a regulative idea of sociology's, but I would also claim that sociologists have become much more sophisticated since the 1950s about the differentiation of propositional theory by level, range and type. In addition, post-empiricist philosophy of social science, without ever abandoning its propositional goals, is notable for the points of contact it affords with modes of theorising which disciples of Merton would not countenance as theory at all.

4.1 Differentiation of Theory

I have already referred to the four levels of theory which Parsons and Shils put forward in 1951. The categorial system for all the social sciences which they sought to establish represents only the second level of theorising. It is an improvement on the first, *ad hoc* classifications – which by definition are uncoordinated, but is inferior to the third, a theoretical system – which consists of a categorial system plus laws or empirical generalisations couched in its terms. This in turn is deemed inferior to the fourth level, a theoretical system which applies in real conditions and which affords precise empirical-theoretical predictions. Only economics among the social sciences had, they claimed, anything approaching even a theoretical system.

Parsons's failure to establish such a categorial system cannot leave us unmoved, in so far as routine, but systematic, comparison and cumulation of social research findings – what Kuhn (1962) later called normal science – is impossible in the absence of conceptual consistency and routine commensurability between researches. Either we must succeed where Parsons failed or we must reconsider our theoretical goals.

Merton, of course, had seen Parsons's failure coming:

> To concentrate entirely on the master conceptual scheme for deriving all subsidiary theories is to run the risk of producing twentieth-century equivalents of the large philosophical systems of the past, with all their varied suggestiveness, all their architectonic splendor and all their scientific sterility. (Merton, 1957, p. 10)

Instead he advocated theories of the middle range (on, though he does not say so explicitly, both the third and the fourth of Parsons's levels). These he defined as:

> theories intermediate to the minor working hypotheses evolved in abundance during the day-to-day routines of research, and the all-inclusive speculations comprising a master conceptual scheme from which it is hoped to derive a very large number of empirically observed uniformities of social behavior. (Merton, 1957, pp. 5–6)

Their range is more modest with respect to both the behaviours and the times and places to which they apply. It was in these terms that he presented his own work on reference groups and on social structure and anomie.

Most theory in American sociology has been of this character. (I have drawn attention elsewhere to the partial overlaps between Merton on middle-range theories, Mullins with Mullins (1973) on standard American sociology, Willer and Willer (1973) on empiricism, Warshay (1975) on small theories, and Wells and Picou (1981) on quantitative structuralism (cf. Bryant, 1985, pp. 168–73); see also Menzies (1982, ch. 7) on differences between theorists' and researchers' versions of middle-range theory.) It is also the theory of the theory building promoted by Lazarsfeld and Rosenberg (1955) or Stinchcombe (1968) or Dubin (1969) or Blalock (1969) and the kind of theory for which Wagner (1984) makes claims of growth.

By contrast some other propositional theorists (such as Peter Abell) point with dismay to the continued preoccupation of so many 'theorists' with activities which are not really theory at all, to the dearth of theories generated by sociologists, to the import of rational choice theory from economics and cognitive psychology, and to the concomitant danger that sociology could forfeit some of its traditional territory if it does not do more to generate propositional theory for itself. Some of the issues figure in the chapters on the analytical tradition and methodology. All I will say myself here is that formalised middle-range theorising justifies itself pragmatically if the explanations it affords are adequate for the purposes, academic and practical, for which they are sought; and that this is more likely where such theorising extends beyond actual co-variation to more abstract modelling, and is sensitive to the linguistic turn.

There are many ways in which theories can be differentiated according to type. I want to mention just one – the difference between theories which revolve around idealisations and those which attend to how things actually are. It raises issues associated with Parsons's movement from his third to his fourth levels and with arguments about the utililty of models. In so far as theories pertain to the actual, one may consider their validity in the light of empirical tests. In so far as they pertain to the ideal, one may consider their utility in the light of empirical applications. If, however, favoured models and idealisations fail to account for how things are, one need not necessarily abandon them. One can either make their assumptions more realistic in the sense of conforming more closely to actualities, or one can try to make actualities conform more closely to the model. Where there is a discrepancy between theory and world, one can change the theory or the world or both. Changing the theory is usually easier but ideologues and activists often have enough conviction to try to change the world, that is to change the language and action of their fellow men and women in the belief that certain consequences will follow. Of course the consequences of change are seldom exactly what their authors intend, but the linguistic turn and the double hermeneutic do provide for attempts to change social laws, the ways in which constituents of the social world are regularly connected.

4.2 Post-Empiricist Philosophy of Social Science

Arguing for a post-empiricist account of science, Hesse writes that:

1. In natural science data is not detachable from theory, for what count as data are determined in the light of some theoretical interpretation, and the facts themselves have to be reconstructed in the light of explanation.
2. In natural science theories are not models externally compared to nature in a hypothetico-deductive schema, they are the way the facts themselves are seen.
3. In natural science the lawlike relations asserted of experience are internal, because what count as facts are constituted by what the theory says about their interrelations with one another.
4. The language of natural science is irreducibly metaphorical and inexact, and formalizable only at the cost of distortion and the imaginative constructions in terms of which nature is interpreted by science.
5. Meanings in natural science are determined by theory; they are understood by theoretical coherence rather than by correspondence with facts. (Hesse, 1980, pp. 172–3)

As Alexander (1987) notes, post-empiricism blurs the distinction between the history of sociological thought and systematic theorising in so far as both involve interpretation. In its emphases on metaphor, models which may or may not be imaginary, networks of terms and statements, and theoretical coherence, plus its refusal to dichotomise either the pre-theoretical and the theoretical, or the theoretical and the empirical, it opens the way to connections between propositional and other modes of theorising.

Post-empiricist philosophy of science no longer allows a stark contrast between natural science and social science, let alone between the analytical and hermeneutic traditions within the social sciences. This is not to proclaim some new version of a unified science – the double hermeneutic, crucially, applies only to social science – but it is to suggest that the philosophical grounds for the mutual respect of

adherents to the analytical and hermeneutic traditions i.
stronger than the partisans of each once supposed. As
more widely acknowledged, the expedient truce which f\
war of the schools gives way to renewed respect for complen
and integration.

5 CONCLUSION

I said in the Introduction to this chapter that the real achievement in
theory over the last four decades has been the winning of a kind of
wisdom. Ours are, I submit, tales of initial innocence and subsequent
experience. (I had better add that the expression 'innocence and
experience' has long since escaped its author's intentions and my use of
it here is without allusion to William Blake's singular prophetic
vision.) What does this wisdom consist of? I think we are vastly more
sophisticated about the constitution of society, the identity of sociology as a *social* science distinct from both natural sciences and
humanities but sharing certain features of each, and the relationships
between sociological and natural discourses. These may not seem
much to those who look to sociology for solutions to the problems of
the modern world but they are integral to a sociology better able to tell
the difference between those demands made of it which are meetable
and those which are not.

References

Alexander, J. C. (1982–4) *Theoretical Logic in Sociology*, 4 vols (London:
    Routledge & Kegan Paul).
——(1987) 'The Centrality of the Classics' in Giddens and Turner (1987)
    pp. 11–57.
Althusser, L. and Balibar, E. (French 1965) *Reading Capital* (London: New
    Left Books 1970).
Barnes, B. (1974) *Scientific Knowledge and Sociological Theory* (London:
    Routledge & Kegan Paul).
Bendix, R. (1960) *Max Weber: An Intellectual Portrait* (New York:
    Doubleday).
Berger, P. L. and Luckmann, T. (1966) *The Social Construction of Reality*
    (New York: Doubleday).
Bergmann, G. (1964) *Logic and Reality* (Madison: University of Wisconsin
    Press).
Bernstein, R. (1971) *Praxis and Action* (Philadelphia: University of Pennsyl-
    vania Press).
——(1983) *Beyond Objectivism and Relativism* (Oxford: Blackwell).

Bhaskar, R. (1975) *A Realist Theory of Science*, 2nd edn (Brighton: Harvester, 1978).
——(1979) *The Possibility of Naturalism* (Brighton: Harvester).
Blalock, H. M. (1969) *Theory Construction* (Englewood Cliffs/NJ: Prentice Hall).
Bloor, D. (1976) *Knowledge and Social Imagery* (London: Routledge & Kegan Paul).
*Bottomore, T. B. and Nisbet, R. A. (eds) (1978) *A History of Sociological Analysis* (New York: Basic Books) (UK edn, London: Heinemann, 1979).
——and Rubel, M. (eds) (1956) *Karl Marx: Selected Writings in Sociology and Social Philosophy* (London: Watts).
Boudon, R. (French 1970) 'Theories, theory and Theory', in his *The Crisis in Sociology* (London: Macmillan, 1980).
Bryant, C. G. A. (1976) *Sociology in Action: A Critique of Selected Conceptions of Sociology in Action* (London: Allen & Unwin).
——(1985) *Positivism in Social Theory and Research* (London: Macmillan).
Bulmer, M. (1982) *The Uses of Social Research: Social Investigation in Public Policy-Making* (London: Allen & Unwin).
Callahan, D. and Jennings, B. (eds) (1983) *Ethics, the Social Sciences, and Policy Analysis* (New York: Plenum Press).
Coser, L. (1956) *The Functions of Social Conflict* (London: Routledge & Kegan Paul).
Dahrendorf, R. (German 1957) *Class and Class Conflict in an Industrial Society* (London: Routledge & Kegan Paul).
Dubin, R. (1969) *Theory Building: A Practical Guide to the Construction and Testing of Theoretical Models* (New York: Free Press).
Durkheim, E. (French 1893) *The Division of Labor in Society* (New York: Macmillan, 1933).
——(French 1895) *The Rules of Sociological Method* (Chicago: University of Chicago Press, 1938).
——(French 1897) *Suicide: A Study in Sociology* (Glencoe/Ill: Free Press).
——(French 1912) *The Elementary Forms of the Religious Life* (London: Allen & Unwin, 1915)
Elias, N. (German 1939) *The Civilizing Process:* vol. 1, *The History of Manners;* vol. 2, *State Formation and Civilization* (Oxford: Blackwell, 1978 and 1982).
Feyerabend, P. (1975) *Against Method: Outline of an Anarchistic Theory of Knowledge* (London: New Left Books).
Geertz, C. (1973) *The Interpretation of Cultures* (New York: Basic Books).
Giddens, A. (1979) *Central Problems in Social Theory: Action, Structure and Contradiction in Social Analysis* (London: Macmillan).
——(1984) *The Constitution of Society* (Cambridge: Polity Press).
——(1987) *Social Theory and Modern Sociology* (Cambridge: Polity Press) (see ch. 2, 'Nine Theses on the Future of Sociology'; and ch. 8, 'Social Theory and Macroeconomics').

*——and Turner, J. H. (eds) (1987) *Social Theory Today* (Cambridge: Polity Press).

Gouldner, A. (1962) 'Anti-Minotaur: The Myth of a Value-Free Sociology', *Social Problems*, vol. 9, pp. 199–213.

Haan, N., Bellah, R. N., Rabinow, P. and Sullivan, W. M. (eds) (1983) *Social Science as Moral Inquiry* (New York: Columbia University Press).

Habermas, J. (German 1976) 'What is Universal Pragmatics?', in his *Communication and the Evolution of Society* (London: Heinemann, 1979).

Hesse, M. (1980) *Revolutions and Reconstructions in the Philosophy of Science* (Brighton: Harvester) (see (a) ch. 7, 'In Defence of Objectivity'; and (b) ch. 9, 'Habermas's Consensus Theory of Truth').

Jay, M. (1973) *The Dialectical Imagination: A History of the Frankfurt School and the Institute of Social Research 1923–50* (London: Heinemann).

Johnson, T., Dandeker, C. and Ashworth, C. (1984) *The Structure of Social Theory* (London: Macmillan).

Kuhn, T. S. (1962) *The Structure of Scientific Revolutions*, published as *International Encyclopedia of Unified Science*, vol. 2, no. 2 (Chicago: University of Chicago Press).

Lazarsfeld, P. F. and Rosenberg, M. (eds) (1955) *The Language of Social Research: A Reader in the Methodology of Social Research* (Glencoe/Ill: Free Press).

Lévi-Strauss, C. (French 1958) *Structural Anthropology* (New York: Basic Books, 1963).

Lukes, S. (1973) *Emile Durkheim: His Life and Work* (London: Allen Lane/Penguin).

Lundberg, G. A. (1955) 'The Natural Science Trend in Sociology', *American Journal of Sociology*, vol. 51, 1955–6, pp. 191–202.

McCarthy, T. (1978) *The Critical Theory of Jürgen Habermas* (London: Hutchinson).

McLellan, D. (1973) *Karl Marx: His Life and Thought* (London: Macmillan).

——(ed.) (1977) *Karl Marx: Selected Writings* (Oxford: OUP).

Marx, K. (written 1844) *Economic and Philosophical Manuscripts*, in T. B. Bottomore (ed.), *Karl Marx: Early Writings* (London: Watts, 1963).

——(written 1857–8) *Grundrisse: Introduction to the Critique of Political Economy* (Harmondsworth: Penguin, 1973).

——and Engels, F. (1975 onwards) *Collected Works*, 50 vols (London: Lawrence & Wishart).

Matthews, F. H. (1977) *Quest for an American Sociology: Robert E. Park and the Chicago School* (Montreal: McGill-Queen's University Press).

Mennell, S. (1974 and 1980) *Sociological Theory: Uses and Unities* (Walton-on-Thames: Nelson, 1st and 2nd edns).

Menzies, K. (1982) *Sociological Theories in Use* (London: Routledge & Kegan Paul).

Merton, R. K. (1949 and 1957a) 'Manifest and Latent Functions', in his *Social Theory and Social Structure* (Glencoe/Ill: Free Press, 1957d).

——(1957b) 'Introduction', to his 1957d.

——(1957c) 'The Bearing of Sociological Theory on Empirical Research', in his 1957d.

Mullins, N. C. with Mullins, C. (1973) *Theories and Theory Groups in Contemporary American Sociology* (New York: Harper & Row).

Nisbet, R. A. (1966) *The Sociological Tradition* (New York: Basic Books).

Ossowski, S. (Polish 1963) *Class Structure in the Social Consciousness* (London: Routledge & Kegan Paul, 1967).

Parsons, T. (1937) *The Structure of Social Action* (Glencoe/Ill: Free Press, 1949).

——(1951) *The Social System* (Glencoe/Ill: Free Press).

——and Shils, Edward A. (eds) (1951) *Towards a General Theory of Action* (Cambridge/Mass: Harvard University Press).

——and Smelser, N. J. (1956) *Economy and Society* (London: Routledge & Kegan Paul).

Pawson, R. (1986) 'Open Systems and Closed Systems', paper given at XI World Congress of Sociology, New Delhi, August 1986.

Phillips, D. L. (1986) 'Preface', to Wardell and Turner (eds) (1986).

Rawls, J. (1971) *A Theory of Justice* (Cambridge/Mass: Harvard University Press).

*Ricoeur, P. (1971) 'The Model of the Text: Meaningful Action Considered as Text', *Social Research*, vol. 38, pp. 529–62.

Rorty, R. (ed.) (1967) *The Linguistic Turn: Recent Essays in Philosophical Method* (Chicago: University of Chicago Press).

——(1980) *Philosophy and the Mirror of Nature* (Princeton: Princeton University Press).

——(1982) *Consequences of Pragmatism* (Minneapolis: University of Minnesota Press).

Rubel, M and Manale, M. (1975) *Marx Without Myth* (Oxford: Blackwell).

Sartori, G. (ed.) (1984) *Social Science Concepts* (Beverly Hills and London: Sage).

Schutz, A. (German 1932) *The Phenomenology of the Social World* (Evanston/Ill: Northwestern University Press, 1967). (German title, *Der sinnhafte Aufbau der sozialen Welt.*)

——(written 1953) 'Concept and Theory Formation in the Social Sciences', in his *Collected Papers*, vol. 1 (The Hague: Nijhoff, 1962) pp. 48–66.

Simmel, G. (German 2nd rev. edn 1907) *The Philosophy of Money* (London: Routledge & Kegan Paul, 1978).

Stinchcombe, A. (1968) *Constructing Social Theories* (New York: Harcourt Brace Jovanovich).

Tucker, R. C. (ed.) (1972) *The Marx-Engels Reader* (New York: Norton). 2nd edn, 1978.

Wagner, D. G. (1984) *The Growth of Sociological Theories* (Beverly Hills and London: Sage).

Wardell, M. L. and Turner, S. P. (eds) (1986) *Sociological Theory in Transition* (Boston: Allen & Unwin).

Warshay, L. H. (1975) *The Current State of Sociological Theory: A Critical Interpretation* (New York: McKay).

Weber, Marianne (German 1926) *Max Weber: A Biography* (New York: Wiley, 1975).

Weber, Max (German 1922) *Economy and Society: An Outline of Interpretive Sociology*, 3 vols, eds G. Roth and C. Wittich (New York: Bedminster Press, 1968).

——(1922) *Gesammelte Aufsätze zur Wissenschaftslehre*, 4th edn, ed. J. Winckelmann (Tübingen: J. C. B. Mohr (Paul Siebeck), 1973).

——(1982 onwards) *Gesamtausgabe*, 33 vols (Tübingen: J. C. B. Mohr (Paul Siebeck)).

Weiss, C. H. with Bucuvalas, M. J. (1980) *Social Science Research and Decision-Making* (New York: Columbia University Press).

Wells, R. H. and Picou, J. S. (1981) *American Sociology: Theoretical and Methodological Structure* (Washington: University Press of America).

Willer, D. and Willer, J. (1973) *Systematic Empiricism: A Pseudo-science* (Englewood Cliffs/NJ: Prentice-Hall).

Winch, P. (1958) *The Idea of a Social Science and Its Relation to Philosophy* (London: Routledge & Kegan Paul).

6 Methodological Achievements in Sociology Over the Past Few Decades with Special Reference to the Interplay of Quantitative and Qualitative Methods

Peter Abell

INTRODUCTION

Sociologists have always sought to understand the remarkably complex phenomena they choose to study by adopting a variety of research methods, amongst which are: surveys, case studies, participant observation, field and ethnographic studies, the secondary analysis of published statistics, documentary and content analysis, comparative historical methods and even occasionally fully fledged experiments.

In this respect sociology is rather unlike the other social sciences where the range of methods used is characteristically much more limited. But each method can claim to have advanced our understanding in certain areas and not others, and each has probably made significant analytical progress in the past decades. This progress has, though, been at different rates; it is, I think, indisputably true that the more quantitatively based methods have advanced relatively rapidly when compared with those of a qualitative nature, though there are now welcome signs that this situation may well be changing. And, of course, the divide itself is by no means a clear one.

Indeed I shall find it useful not to draw a line in this way, i.e.

between quantitative and qualitative methodologies, but rather between what I will term *variable-centred methodologies* – where data are assembled as variables (at any level of measurement)[1] – and *account-centred methodologies* – where data are more likely to be assembled in a natural language format (ethnographic accounts, etc.) (Abell, 1987).[2] In setting up this distinction I do not want to be seen as drawing a sharp line; finding ways of combining the two methodologies and translating back and forth between them (for example, triangulation), in a convincing manner, is to my mind of the first importance (Fielding and Fielding, 1986; Fararo, 1986). Looking back at the achievements of sociology, it does appear to me that those studies which most of us admire, and which may be said to have significantly enhanced our understanding of society, usually attempt to combine materials in the variable-centred and account-centred modes.

One development has, however, had an overwhelming effect upon the conduct of sociological research (indeed, upon research in all the social sciences) – namely, the computer. Initially, the main-frame computer, with its vast data storage and manipulation capacity, and then, over the last decade or so, the smaller personal computers, have revolutionised the conduct of social research. Certainly, within the context of variable-centred methodology, there is scarcely a comparison between what could be accomplished, say, in 1950, and now. Collins (1981) documents this well when remarking upon the impact of the computer on the research style in the two leading American sociological journals:

> Even a cursory glance at the types of journal articles published in 1946 and 1976 provides a feeling for what has happened. In 1946, 54% of the substantive articles published in the *American Sociological Review* lacked any type of mathematical analysis at all. In the *American Journal of Sociology*, 46% of the substantive articles were completely without mathematical analysis. By 1976 only 12% of the *ASR* articles and 14% of *AJS* articles lacked mathematical analysis. (Collins, 1981, p. 438)

Recently, with the development of the appropriate computer languages, we are also witnessing the incorporation of intelligent knowledge-based expert systems and production systems into the account-centred methodologies (Heise, forthcoming).

I should like to make one final observation by way of introduction: although, as I mentioned above, it does appear that the variable-centred methods have experienced the most rapid and extensive advance, the technical research on which these advances are based has largely been carried out outside sociology. To a significant degree, though not exclusively, sociologists have adopted and adapted techniques developed elsewhere by econometricians and statisticians. This is not as true, however, of the account-centred methods, though the very recent developments I mentioned in the last paragraph do find their genesis outside sociology. We must admit, I think, that sociology is not, as yet, technically speaking a strongly based discipline. This is partly because of its recruitment pattern, but springs also from the very eclecticism which I mentioned in my opening paragraph – in a sense, sociologists are 'jacks of all trades' with the inevitable consequence that they are 'masters of none'. But neverthless, this can be interpreted as a strength, and with the progressive technical realisation of account-centred methods I, for one, am confident of the future.

THE MAJOR ACHIEVEMENTS

There are, no doubt, many ways in which the methodological achievements within the discipline of sociology could be instanced, but trying to limit them to a manageable number and keeping an eye on the interplay of variable- and account-centred analysis, the following seem to me to be the particularly important ones:

1. The development of causal modelling (path analysis etc.) within the variable-centred tradition.[3] Statistically speaking, this has arisen by the incorporation of, initially, *The General Linear Model* and, later, *The Generalised Linear Model*, into the mainstream of sociological analysis. I would include here also the increasingly sophisticated use of stochastic models – particularly in the study of social mobility.
2. The development of rigorous techniques for translating between micro (individual) level and macro (group, collective) level variables. That is to say, the use of contextual variables and a full understanding of the issues surrounding ecological correlation and inference.
3. The development of rigorous methods for the analysis of structural data. That is to say, the use of techniques derived from graph and di-graph theory and network analysis.

4. The development of production system models and the incorporation of finite automata and generative models into social theory and research. (The cross-fertilisation with linguistic modelling is particularly important here.)
5. The development of a more rigorous framework within which to conduct comparative research – particularly at the societal level. (The cross-fertilisation with historiography is particularly important here.)
6. The development of reliable methods of recording and analysing micro interactional data. (The use of video, film and audio techniques are particularly important here.)

I believe that on each of these six counts one can unquestionably detect major advances over recent decades. Others, I am sure, would include different developments; some obvious ones which I have not included, for the reasons given below, are as follows:[4]

First, the development of statistical measures for the covariation of nominal and ordinal variables (e.g. Kruskal, 1958; Goodman and Kruskal, 1959); although, over the years, many new measures have been suggested, their use has largely been superseded by development of the generalised linear model (Maxwell, 1961; Wilson, 1974).

Second, the development of metric and non-metric scaling techniques (Kruskal, 1964a and b; Lazarsfeld, 1950, 1968; Torgerson, 1958; Goodman, 1978). A useful summary is to be found in Hildebrand, Laing and Rosenthal (1977). The main developments have taken place outside sociology and they have not, in my judgement, as of yet had a major impact upon the conduct of sociological inquiry (but see Kruskal and Wish, 1978).[5]

Third, the development and use of various statistical techniques for aggregating covariation structures (factor analysis, principal component analysis, etc.) (Harman, 1960; Kendall and Stuart, 1961; Maxwell, 1961; Gorsuch, 1974). Though sociologists have made sporadic use of these sorts of analyses, they have not made a major impact upon sociological research (but see Kim and Mueller, 1978). They have been developed outside sociology, and, what is more, to many statistical purists they remain suspect – particularly when applied to ordinal and nominal variables where normality assumptions break down.

Having dismissed these as major (though not insignificant) areas of achievement, I will now turn to the six areas of development I mentioned above and in each case attempt to chart the progress made.

Inevitably, I can do this, in the space available, in only the most superficial detail.

THE DEVELOPMENT OF CAUSAL MODELLING

A casual perusal of any one of the leading sociological journals – say *The American Sociological Review* – would quickly reveal a remarkable change in intellectual style over the last three decades.[6] Broadly speaking, simple bivariate (sometimes trivariate) analysis has given way to multivariate analysis within the statistical framework of, usually, linear regression models. Furthermore, journals like *Sociological Methods and Research* (first published in 1972) and the annual publication of The American Sociological Association, *Sociological Methodology* (first appearing in 1969), have provided a vehicle for the promotion and incorporation of causal modelling techniques into the body of sociological research. I estimate that some 60–70 per cent of the space of these publications has been devoted to this purpose, and recall the remarks of Collins (1981) with which I opened.

In retrospect we can see Blalock's publication of *Causal Inferences in Non-Experimental Research* (1964) as particularly influential in widening the appeal of causal modelling, followed later by more technical presentations (e.g. Goldberger and Duncan, 1973).

There is perhaps no clearer way of appreciating the achievements sustained by the introduction of multivariate causal modelling into sociology, than by comparing some outstanding sociological studies of the 1950s with some published in each of the succeeding decades. Those sceptical about the progress of sociology should compare, say, *Social Mobility in Britain* (Glass, 1954) or *Work and Authority in Industry* (Bendix, 1956) with, in the 1960s, *The American Occupational Structure* (Blau and Duncan, 1967) or, a little later, *Inequality* (Jencks, 1972) with *Intergroup Processes* (Blalock and Wilken, 1979) and *Opportunity and Change* (Featherman and Hauser, 1978). Such comparisons could scarcely fail to convince the reader about the increasing sophistication of sociological analysis within what I have termed the variable-centred tradition.

Most of these studies inevitably rely rather heavily on the use of survey technique as a source of data. There have, however, been no dramatic developments here over the course of the decades we are looking at. Survey techniques were essentially understood and made available to the practising sociologist in Hyman's classic of 1955,

Survey Design and Analysis (significantly with an introduction by Lazarsfeld). Nevertheless, refinements in sampling (e.g. Lazerwitz, 1968), interviewing techniques and the design of questionnaires and so on, have taken place continually.

So what is the intellectual essence in the development of multi-variate causal modelling? In the 1950s the analysis of variable-centred data was almost always conducted within the framework of Lazarsfeld's seminal work on the elaboration of three variable covariation – usually with categorical, often dichotomous variables (Lazarsfeld and Rosenberg, 1955). This framework, along with Simon's early papers (1957), delivered techniques which enabled sociologists to begin to sort out the causal precedence amongst a few variables. At this stage, the statistical issues concerned both with parameter estimation and inference were treated in a rather cavalier fashion. Though Lazarsfeld's formulation of three variable covariation was couched in terms of categorical variables, Simon, drawing upon parallel developments in econometrics, effectively relocated the debate within sociology in terms of interval and ratio measured variables. Blalock, among others, then developed causal modelling usually with such variables in mind.[7] It was only later that the practical and statistical problems of using categorical variables within the framework of fully fledged causal models began to be worked out.

In the period from about 1960 to 1975, the incorporation of causal modelling into sociological research had the following consequences (Duncan's *Introduction to Structural Equation Models* or Heise's *Causal Analysis* both give a good impression of the state of the art in sociology as of 1975)[8]:

1. Techniques became available for studying (N permitting) the causal structure of any number of variables (assuming the proposed model is identifiable and standard assumptions apply). Initially, recursive models and, later, non-recursive models allowed complex patterns of causal interdependence, including feedback loops, to be systematically studied.
2. The problems of statistical inference (under standard assumptions) became fully understood and incorporated into standard sociological research.
3. Non-linear (variable) and interaction effects were introduced into models with relative ease.
4. A number of standard computer packages became widely available and used in social research.

5. Endemic problems like measurement error in predictor variables and multi-collinearity (Blalock, 1963) became well understood, if not always surmountable.
6. The causal model framework became the standard way of interpreting the validity of single or multiple indicators of an underlying non-observable (theoretical) concept/variable. Hauser and Goldberger (1971) give a good introduction to the progress made in this field during this period. The LISREL program (Joreskog, 1973 and 1978) is the natural extension of this approach and became influential in the decade following 1975.
7. The explicit recognition of the problem of identifiability brought some needed discipline into the formulation of sociological models.

These achievements, in my opinion, fundamentally changed the way in which good variable-centred research was carried out in sociology. Nobody could deny this as a major achievement – an achievement which has subsequently been consolidated. Bielby and Hauser (1977) offer a review of causal modelling in sociology as of the mid 1970s.

The achievement was not, however, entirely unblemished. The use of causal models became so easy (given standard computer packages) that they could be run off with little thought as to whether the assumptions necessary for estimation and inference held. In particular, little attention was often given, in the haste to adopt the new paradigm, to specification effort. Possible causes, not brought into the study, were quickly assumed not to correlate with those explicitly included, when a little thought would have revealed this to be unlikely. In some ways, the early cautions which Lazarsfeld enunciated about spurious correlation were cast aside and the strength of estimated parameters was often given an unwarranted validity.

The early users of the causal modelling framework usually assumed that the variables involved were unbounded and continously distributed (or at least that this was a good approximation). Sociological variables are, however, often categorical in nature and in many cases simple proportions are the most likely form in which data presents itself. The recent development of the generalised linear model is progressively enabling sociologists to analyse their data within a framework appropriate to these sorts of variables (Nelder and Wedderburn, 1972; Haberman, 1974; Bishop, Fienberg and Holland, 1975).[9]

Goodman, in a series of important articles, has largely been responsible for introducing log-linear models to sociologists (Goodman, 1969, 1970, 1972, 1978). Studies of social mobility seem to have been the major beneficiaries of this development (Goldthorpe *et al.* 1980). Though some reservations must be expressed about incorporating log-linear models into complex causal analysis, there is now some general optimism that well-founded statistical techniques are becoming available where the constituent variables are measured at a variety of levels (Goodman, 1973; Plackett, 1974).

Most survey data is, of course, cross-sectional in nature – observations being made at one point in time. The problems of conducting research based upon repeated observations of the same units of analysis (panels) are well known. Nevertheless, recent arguments (e.g. Pickles *et al.*, 1985) point very strongly in the direction of longitudinal data in the face of endemic specification bias. We are at the moment witnessing a resurgence of interest in longitudinal studies despite the logistical problems they inevitably involve.

THE DEVELOPMENT OF TECHNIQUES FOR RELATING THE MICRO TO THE MACRO

Again we remain very much within what I have termed the variable-centred framework. From at least Durkheim's time, a central sociological ambition has been to relate the behaviour/action/attitudes, etc. of individuals to their group or collective context. On the other side of the equation, social theorists have often invited us to find ways of aggregating individual level measures to the collective level and then to relate these collective (macro) variables to others at the same level. Indeed, for many, the ability to translate back and forth between various levels of aggregation is the very touchstone of the sociological enterprise. It is for this reason that I have chosen to include a special section on these problems, and not because any great technical virtuosity has been involved in their resolution.

The technical matters at stake are those surrounding the use of so-called 'contextual variables' and the closely associated problem of 'ecological correlation and inference'. A series of articles have significantly advanced our understanding of these matters with the result that the analyst is able both to model contextual variables and to understand when ecological inferences are sound. Hañan (1971) is perhaps the crucial landmark. (Green's *Aggregation in Economic Analysis* (1964) is a useful technical source.)

Blau (1960) concentrated upon models where not only the individual level scores, on a given predictor variable, enter the estimation equation but the mean value of the variable across a specified subgroup also. Przeworski (1974) worked with an alternative formulation where the mean value of the dependent variable entered the equation on the predictor side. Davis, Spaeth and Huson (1961), Boudon (1963) and Valkonen (1969) have also introduced models where the macro level variable (i.e. the mean of an individual level independent variable) is specified as interacting multiplicitively with the individual level variable. Przeworski (1974), in a significant contribution, has linked the estimation of contextual effects into the more general debate about ecological correlations. Davis *et al.* (1961) have also studied models where the difference between the mean value and the individual value of a variable enters the equation (so-called deviancy effects). Hauser (1974) has shown how specification error in the class of contextual models can easily lead to misleading interpretations. Blalock and Wilken (1979) in a useful review, along with attempts to extend the contextual model to multiple group contexts, note the often present empirical problems of specification error and collinearity. Their conclusion – one which I will endorse in my closing remarks – is that we need more theoretical guidance to enable us to distinguish between the plethora of possible models.

Nevertheless, a very real advance has been made which permits variable-centred methodologists to treat contextual effects within the framework of causal modelling and the general linear model. Furthermore, whereas a few decades ago the problems involved in ecological correlation were scarcely understood (Jahn, 1950), they now enter into the standard training of undergraduate sociologists (Langbein and Lichtman, 1978). Once again, the problems have proved tractable by their being placed within the framework of causal modelling and specification bias. Groupings often alter or introduce specification bias (i.e. correlations between independent variables and disturbance terms) at the ecological level, rendering the inference from ecological parameters to individual parameters hazardous. An early paper by Duncan and Davis (1953) introduced the 'method of bounds' which took the debate into the realm of categorical data, though, as far as I am aware, little subsequent use has been made of the method.

In the future we may anticipate the incorporation of contextual variables into the generalised linear model thus providing a bridge into qualitative variable-centred methodology. Moreover, since from a theoretical point of view, contextual effects may, causally speaking, be conceived of as impacting upon the individual through patterns of social relationships, the incorporation of structural ideas (see next section) into the conceptualisation of such effects may also be anticipated.

THE ANALYSIS OF STRUCTURAL DATA AND MODELS

Sociology is not infrequently described as a 'structural science' and one of the most remarkable advances we have witnessed over the last three decades is the emergence of structural analysis as, some would say, an analytical paradigm in its own right.[10] This advance, based upon graph and digraph representation of phenomena, builds upon early work in sociometry (Moreno, 1960).[11] Harary, Norman and Cartwright's *Structural Models: An Introduction to the Theory of Directed Graphs* (1965) and Kemeny and Snell's *Mathematical Models in the Social Sciences* (1962) may now be seen as major early influences. They give some impression of the achievements as of the early 1960s.

In a related vein, the study of biased nets (Fararo and Sunshine, 1964) brought some statistical techniques into the analysis of larger-scale structures; the early work of Rapaport (1951) was also seminal here.[12] Hand in hand with the descriptive and analytical techniques made available by graph and network depictions, the development of algebraic models of structure has also proved important. White's *An Anatomy of Kinship* (1963) and, a little later, Boyd's 'The Algebra of Group Kinship (1969) are perhaps the most important early influences.

Atkin, in *Mathematical Structure in Human Affairs* (1974), introduced a multidimensional analogue of graphs (simplicial complexes) to sociologists, in the form of Q-analysis (see also, Atkin, 1977).[13]

Before we look in more detail at these developments, it is worth noting that, in contrast to developments in causal modelling, many of the technical advances made have in fact been achieved by sociologists (see, for instance, Alba, 1982; Berkowitz, 1982; Burt and Minor, 1983).

In many respects, networks and graphs are qualitative in nature, though there is no reason why linkages should not be measured in various ways (e.g. strength, duration, frequency of activation and so on) or why the vertices should not be 'labelled' by measured characteristics (Doreian, 1970).[14] Furthermore, large structures invite statistical summary measures. One of the appealing features of structural analysis is that it straddles the qualitative/quantitative boundary in a flexible way. The structural depiction of 'account-centred' data is also becoming increasingly important. Structural analysis often provides an elegant way of handling the combinatorial complexity which is implied by many theoretical writings. For examples, see Fararo and Doreian (1984), Wilson (1982) and Breiger (1974). These authors develop a structural language for relating individuals to roles, roles to groups, and groups to wider cultures.

It is impracticable in a chapter like this adequately to review the full range and detail of the achievements in structural analysis, but some of the salient ones are as follows. (In each case I have given early and later references, enabling the interested reader to judge the progress for him/herself.)

1. The detection of cliques and patterns of connectivity (compare Doreian, 1969 with Arabie, Boorman and Levitt, 1978). Clique detection techniques are designed to reveal the extent of substructures which have a high concentration of possible linkages. In a substantive context, such structures depict highly interacting social groups. Connectivity patterns give analytically useful pictures of indirect links in social structures.
2. The development of computer programs for analysing structures (compare Coleman and MacRae (1960) with UCINET available from the University of California at Irvine, or STRUCTURE from Columbia, New York). There are now many packages available offering a variety of analyses of cliques, blocks, connectivity, centrality, structural equivalence and so on.
3. Models of structural equivalence (compare Lorrain and White, 1971 with Doreian, 1987). Structural equivalence enables the analyst to detect vertices in a structure that are identically placed in terms of their patterns of connectivity.
4. Algebraic treatment of structure (compare Boyd, 1969 with White and Reitz, 1983). By representing a structure algebraically, the issue of mapping from one strucure to another can be reduced to a search for homomorphisms between the algebras. White, in particular, has promoted the algebraic treatment of structural data, claiming for it a very wide role in sociological analysis.
5. The analysis of biased nets (compare Rapaport, 1951 with Fararo, 1986). Although the earlier work on biased nets, for example that by Fararo and Sunshine (1964), was not actively developed,

Fararo has recently reopened the possibility of integrating the approach into some mainline theoretical considerations.

6. The development of Q-Analysis (compare Atkin, 1974 with Freeman, 1980 and Doreian, 1981). Q-Analysis has attracted its critics, and the advantages it offers over other similar techniques like multidimensional scaling are subject to dispute. Furthermore, none of the deeper algebraic ideas in combinatorial algebraic topology have been incorporated into any analyses I am aware of. Nevertheless, as a generalisation of graph theory, it offers a powerful descriptive language.

These six comparisons would, I think convince even the most sceptical reader of very real achievement. Unfortunately, much of this is still foreign to mainline sociology, though there are now welcome signs that structural ideas are beginning to penetrate into serious social theory (Fararo, 1986; Fararo and Skvoretz, 1986).

THE DEVELOPMENT OF PRODUCTION AND EXPERT SYSTEMS MODELS

The seminal work of Newell and Simon (1972) is beginning to have a profound impact on sociology. A summary of this impact, as of 1984, may be found in Fararo and Skvoretz's 'Institutions as Production Systems' (1984). A more recent review, which places production system modelling in a wider 'generative framework', is also due to Fararo (1986). These developments parallel similar ones in psychology (Schank and Abelson, 1977) and continue to draw on the burgeoning discipline of artificial intelligence (Bundy, 1984).

This sort of modelling, which is both 'qualitative' and account-centred, seeks to describe the generative rules which act upon a knowledge base to produce the orderly sequencing of institutionalised actions. A related approach (though one less tied to institutionalised contexts) of comparative narratives is due to the present author (Abell, 1987). Skvoretz (1984) has successfully placed the generative problem within the framework of finite automata theory. Heise, in 'Modeling Event Structures' (forthcoming), has also adopted something along the lines of the production system approach in providing a suite of computer programs (Entho) which enable the analyst to chart the structure upon the events as a di-graph. As the title suggests, the techniques are formed by ethnomethodological considerations.

The advantages of this approach to model-building in sociology which is, in my opinion, very much in the ascendency, are as follows:

1. The modelling starts with natural language accounts of events and actions and then attempts to formalise these with a minimum of distortion (Axten and Fararo, 1977; Axten and Skvoretz, 1980). It is this aspect of the model-building which should prove attractive to those for whom variable-centred analysis is epistemologically unacceptable.
2. The modelling naturally links into a basic emphasis on social action, interaction and exchange, thus providing common ground with the major modern orientations in sociological theory.
3. Though qualitative in nature, the approach lends itself to systematic formalisation and to computer analysis.
4. The modelling begins to bring some formal rigour to the ambitions of generative structural theory. Such theory has, with its evident success in linguistics, inevitably proved attractive to those sociologists who are interested in strings of human actions. Structural theory has though, in my view, not produced anything of lasting intellectual worth outside linguistics, but we might now hope with these developments that the story will be different. Heise's work will I suspect prove seminal here.

Although the modelling of rule-governed action systems is still in its infancy, we can, nevertheless, discern a series of very real achievements during the last decade and a half. The integration of these models into the variable-centred framework is also an intriguing possibility (Abell, 1987).

THE DEVELOPMENT OF MACRO-COMPARATIVE METHODS

Ragin (1987a) has noted that if one were to plot the number of empirical studies in sociology against the number of units of analysis each involved ('sample' size), then one would obtain a U-shaped curve with a flat minimum in the range of 8–30 cases. There are many intensive studies in the range 1–8, and many less-intensive studies, usually based upon surveys and the variable-centred methodology, with more than 30 cases. This distribution, of course, reflects a fundamental divide in research philosophy. The tradition of intensive comparative case-studies, where small numbers preclude statistical treatment, is no less vibrant than the survey-cum-causal-modelling tradition. Early classic studies established modern standards (e.g. Moore, 1966; Smelser, 1959; Lipset, 1963) and recent studies continue to adorn the tradition (e.g. Skocpol, 1979; Tilly, 1975, 1978). In my view, the achievements in this sort of study are equally as evident as in the better signalled high N studies.

Ragin (1987b), in a closely argued book, has set out the virtues and logic of the comparative method, pointing out that in many situations it is not merely that intensive study precludes a larger N but that N is naturally small. So it would be wrong to interpret the 'comparative' method merely as a second-best strategy. It is intrinsic to situations where, using Tilly's (1984) title, *Big Structures, Large Processes, Huge Comparisons* are the order of the day.

There have been no dramatic changes in the way in which good comparative research is carried out. Barrington Moore still stands as an exemplar of the genre, but one can certainly detect two important developments. First, 'comparativists' have become much more skilled in interweaving qualitative and quantitative materials. Authors like Tilly have demonstrated increased ingenuity in generating internal variance within any one case-study, by reducing the level of abstraction of the unit of analysis (e.g. nation to country or region). Second, systematic methods are being elaborated which permit the combination of account-centred natural language materials with conclusions drawn from variable-centred materials.

RECORDING AND ANALYSING MICRO-INTERACTIONAL DATA

Perhaps the most significant methodological development within the so-called qualitative or account-centred methodology in the past twenty-five years has been the emergence of ethnomethodology and conversation analysis. Following the major contributions provided through the work of Garfinkel (1967) and, in a very different way, Goffman (1959), there has emerged a paradigm which can handle, both rigorously and formally, the details of social interaction and, in particular, the production and intelligibility of social actions and activities. The pioneering work of the late Sacks (1963), and his colleagues Jefferson and Schegloff (Sacks *et al.*, 1974), has unearthed a hitherto unexplored domain of social organisation and provided the methodological and analytic resources to exploit recordings of naturally occurring human behaviour for the purposes of sociological inquiry. Their contribution has given rise to an extensive body of empirical studies and a substantial corpus of findings concerned with the structures of social action. These studies and their findings, coupled with the methodological developments, have had an important influence on related work within linguistics, social psychology and social anthropology. The methodological developments include a strict set of principles for the identification and detailed empirical analysis of social actions and activities, a widely used transcription system for talk, and various solutions for warranting and validating findings (Jefferson, 1983; Atkinson and Heritage, 1984). They have also been coupled in recent years with the use of various statistical procedures. There has also been a growing interest in visual as well as vocal aspects of social actions and activities, and, correspondingly, we have witnessed the emergence of various methodological developments for use in the analysis of video recordings of naturally occurring social interaction (Heath, 1986).

It should be added that these techniques are not specially tied to language or non-verbal behaviour; rather, their central concern is with the social organisation which informs the production and intelligibility of social actions (Abell, 1987; Heise, forthcoming). It was recognised early on that audio and audio-visual recordings provide the social scientist with unprecedented access to the social world, almost akin to the microscope in biology, allowing researchers to capture fragments of social interaction as they occur in natural settings (Grimshaw, 1982; Corsaro, 1982). The integration of this sort of work into the production systems modelling, outlined in the previous section, is something we must now await.

The significance of these methodological developments over the last twenty-five years is attested to not only by the substantial corpus of studies, but also by the way in which the methods and findings increasingly pervade research in other areas of social science – for example, pragmatics, language use and communications theory.

Although perhaps a little out of place here, I might finally mention some of the computer-aided interviewing and survey techniques which have emerged since the early 1970s (Freeman and Shanks, 1983). Programmes have been developed by survey analysts which run on micros and greatly facilitate the flexibility of the analysis in either face-to-face situations (CAPI: computer-assisted personal interviewing) or over the telephone (CATI: computer-assisted telephone interviewing). Recently, also, user-friendly programs have been developed which enable the researcher to place a personal computer in the home or at the place of work of the respondent which then intelligently enables the respondent to generate overtime panel data (KAPAR: computer-assisted panel research).

CONCLUDING REMARKS

I hope that the aforegoing sections of this chapter have demonstrated that significant technical advances have been achieved by sociological methodologists over the last few decades. Others would have presented the case differently and would, no doubt, have instanced different achievements; but however we cut the cake, the conclusion must be the same.

The most dramatic achievements have taken place in the use of quantitative methods. The incorporation of the general linear model, in the guise of causal or path analysis, into the everyday procedures of variable-centred methodologists has changed the practice of sociology most decisively. Our ability to handle complex multivariate situations is now routine. With the extension to the generalised linear model, we are also now witnessing an improved ability to handle qualitative variables, and though this development has not yet worked its way through the discipline, the signs for the future are good. Whereas the previous generation of sociologists was faced with a plethora of techniques, we are now able to see these as special cases of a more general model where, in particular, assumptions about the structure of errors vary from situation to situation.

On the account-centred front, developments have also been significant, though, as yet, not as influential. A decade ago, the qualitative/ quantitative distinction created an unnecessary divide in sociology; the latter rapidly developing in technical sophistication, the former being technically rather static. Indeed, 'account-centred' sociologists often appeared to take an uneasy refuge from the increasing technical demands of variable-centred methodology, in overblown epistemological arguments asserting the exclusive validity of their chosen methods. Although we still suffer from the legacy of this opposition, I hope it is now intellectually dead. Indeed, as we have seen, the account-centred techniques are now experiencing an accelerating growth in technical sophistication, with the inevitable consequence that they can no longer provide a refuge.

There is, nevertheless, a lingering doubt in my mind. I have painted a distinctly rosy picture of methodological progress; does this mean that the often-voiced criticisms of sociology, which in fact motivated this symposium, have no foundation? Unfortunately, I think not, and though it falls beyond my brief, I will conclude on what I imagine is a controversial note.

Despite the improvements in methods available to sociologists, the achievements of sociology in the round, over the same period, is much less impressive. And, I think, the reason for this is that, as a discipline, we are ill-served by our theoreticians. Social theory (in practice usually metatheory) has failed to keep abreast of technical developments and 'theoreticians' still operate in a largely quasi-philosophical, non-propositional framework. Indeed, in my view, contemporary social theory is a rather frivolous activity but unfortunately nevertheless attracts the attention of many young sociologists. It has glamour but little substance – often merely rehearsing old arguments in new vocabularies. In fact, it does appear that the most significant 'social theory' is now often produced outside sociology by economists (e.g. Roemer, 1982; Olson, 1965) or sociologists strongly influenced by economic thinking (e.g. Coleman, 1986). Particularly in the variable-centred tradition, the number of models which can be initially entertained from 'a common sense' point of view is usually myriad, and until we have a stronger body of propositional theory providing constraints, ruling some out, then the technical sophistication I have spoken of is to a degree short-circuited. We need a fusion of methods and theory; social theory innocent of the emerging technical infrastructure of the discipline must become a thing of the past. This will call for a new generation of theorists. There is a crisis in sociology, and it is a crisis of theory – or rather the lack of it. If theoretical sociologists do not come to recognise this, others will begin to do our theory for us.

Notes

1. Ordinal and nominal variables would usually be regarded as qualitative.
2. The distinction is used in Abell (1987) and a similar one in Ragin (1987b).
3. Though very much an achievement of the variable-centred tradition, where variables can be strongly measured, the generalised linear model opens up these models to qualitative variables in a systematic way.
4. In the following paragraph, I have included references which would enable the reader to gauge the achievement over the period.
5. Metric multidimensional scaling has also been developed significantly (Coombs, 1964: Kruskal and Wish, 1978); Lazarsfeld's early papers (1950) on latent structure analysis have proved seminal.

6. This is less evident in the European journals.
7. There is a debate going back at least to Orcutt *et al.* (1961) about dummy and ordinal variables.
8. I include here the specific technique of path-analysis. In my view, the introduction of path analysis dating back to Sewall Wright (1921) caused unnecessary confusion in the early 1960s. The question arose about the relationship of path coefficients and regression-based coefficients (Wright, 1960; Duncan, 1970). Causal modelling has been best served when based on the standard techniques of regression and the general linear model (Hauser and Goldberger, 1971).
9. GLIM is an available computer package.
10. I use the term 'structural' here not in the sense of generative structuralism, but in terms of patterns of relations between objects.
11. A graph is a set of points (vertices) where some or all pairs are connected by a line (edge). A digraph is similar except the lines are directed.
12. A biased net is a structure in the sense of the previous footnote, where the lines are not randomly distributed between pairs of points.
13. Q-Analysis studies the dimensions of the pattern of connectivity between vertices.
14. Both the vertices and edges (see note 11) can be measured at any level of measurement.

References

Abell, P. (1987) *The Syntax of Social Life: The Theory and Method of Comparative Narratives* (Oxford: OUP).
Alba, R. D. (1982) 'Taking Stock of Network Analysis: A Decade's Results', *Research in the Sociology of Organisations*, vol. 1, pp. 39–74.
Anderson, E. B. (1980) *Discrete Statistical Models with Social Science Applications* (Amsterdam: North Holland).
Arabie, P., Boorman, S. A. and Levitt, P. R. (1978) 'Constructing Blockmodels: How and Why', *Journal of Mathematical Psychology*, vol. 17, pp. 21–63.
Atkin, R. H. (1974) *Mathematical Structure in Human Affairs* (New York: Crane Rusak).
——(1977) *Combinatorial Connectivities in Social Systems* (Basel: Birkhauser Verlag).
Atkinson, J. M. and Heritage, J. C. (eds) (1984) *The Structure of Social Action: Studies in Conversational Analysis* (Cambridge: CUP).
Axten, N. and Fararo, T. J. (1977) 'The Information Processing Representation of Institutionalised Social Action', in P. Krishnan (ed.) *Mathematical Models in Sociology* (Keele: University of Keele).
——and Skvoretz, J. (1980) 'Roles and Role Programs', *Quality and Quantity*, vol. 14, pp. 547–83.
Bendix, R. (1956) *Work and Authority in Industry* (New York: Wiley).
Berkowitz, S. D. (1982) *An Introduction to Structural Analysis: The Network Approach to Social Research* (Toronto: Butterworth).
Bielby, W. T. and Hauser, R. M. (1977) 'Structural Equation Models', *Annual Review of Sociology*, vol. 3, pp. 69–84.

Bishop, Y. M. M., Fienberg, S. E. and Holland, P. W. (1975) *Discrete Multivariate Analysis: Theory and Practise* (Cambridge/Mass; MIT Press).

Blalock, H. M., Jr (1963) 'Correlated Independent Variables: The Problem of Multi-Collinearity', *American Journal of Sociology*, vol. 42, pp. 233–7.

——(1964) *Causal Inferences in Non-Experimental Research* (Chapel Hill: University of North Carolina Press).

——and Wilken, P. H. (1979) *Intergroup Processes: A Micro/Macro Perspective* (New York: Free Press).

Blau, P. M. (1960) 'Structural Effects', *American Sociological Review*, vol. 25, pp. 178–93.

——and Duncan, O. D. (1967) *The American Occupational Structure* (New York: Wiley).

Boudon, R. (1963) 'Propriétés individuelles et propriétés collectives: un problème d'analyse ecologique', *Revue Française de Sociologie*, vol. 4, pp. 275–99.

Boyd, J. P. (1969) 'The Algebra of Group Kinship', *Journal of Mathematical Psychology*, vol. 65, pp. 139–67.

Breiger, R. L. (1974) 'The Duality of Persons and Groups', *Social Forces*, vol. 53, pp. 181–90.

Bundy, A. (ed.) (1984) *Catalogue of Artificial Intelligence Tools* (Berlin: Springer-Verlag).

Burgess, R. (1984) *In The Field* (London: George Allen & Unwin).

Burt, R. S. and Minor, M. J. (eds) (1983) *Applied Network Analysis* (Beverly Hills: Sage).

Coleman, J. S. (1986) *Individual Interests and Collective Action* (Cambridge: CUP).

——and MacRae, D., Jr (1960) 'Electronic Processing of Sociometric Data for Groups of up to 1,000 in Size', *American Sociological Review*, vol. 25, pp. 722–7.

Collins, T. W. (1981) 'Social Science Research and the Microcomputer', *Sociological Methods and Research*, vol. 9, pp. 438–60.

Conrad, P. and Reinharzs, S. (eds) (1984) *Computer and Qualitative Data* (New York: Human Success Press).

Coombs, C. H. (1964) *A Theory of Data* (New York: Wiley).

Corsaro, V. A. (1982) 'Something Old and Something New, The Importance of Prior Ethnography in the Collection and Analysis of Audio Visual Data', *Social Research Methods*, vol. 11, pp. 145–66.

Davis, J. A., Spaeth, J. L. and Huson, C. (1961) 'A Technique for Analysing the Effects of Group Composition', *American Sociological Review*, vol. 26, pp. 215–25.

Doreian, P. (1969) 'A Note on the Detection of Cliques in Valued Graphs', *Sociometry*, vol. 32, pp. 237–42.

——(1970) *Mathematics in the Study of Social Relations* (London: Wiedenfeld & Nicolson).

——(1981) 'Polyhedral Dynamics and Conflict Mobilisation in Social Networks', *Social Networks*, vol. 3, pp. 107–16.

——(1987) 'Measuring Regular Equivalence in Symmetric Structures', *Social Networks*, vol. 9, pp. 1–19.

Duncan, O. D. (1970) 'Partials, Partitions and Paths', in E. F. Borgatta and G. W. Bohrnstedt (eds), *Sociological Methodology* (San Francisco: Jossey-Bass).

——(1975) *Introduction to Structural Equation Models* (New York: Academic Press).

——and Davis, B. (1953) 'An Alternative To Ecological Correlation', *American Sociological Review*, vol. 18, pp. 333–63.

Fararo, T. J. (1986) 'Action and Institution, Network and Function: The Cybernetic Concept of Social Structure, *Social Forum*, vol. 1. pp. 219–50.

——and Doreian P. (1984) 'Tri-partite Structural Analysis: Generalising the Breiger-Wilson Formalism', *Social Networks*, vol. 6, pp. 141–75.

—— and Skvoretz, J. (1984) 'Institutions as Production Systems', *Journal of Mathematical Sociology*, vol. 10, pp. 117–82.

——(1986) 'E-State Structuralism: A Theoretical Method', *American Sociological Review*, vol. 51, pp. 591–602.

——and Sunshine, M. H. (1964) *A Study of a Biased Friendship Net* (Syracuse University: Youth Development Centre).

*Featherman, D. L. and Hauser, R. M. (1978) *Opportunity and Change* (New York: Academic Press).

Fielding, N. G. and Fielding, J. L. (1986) *Linking Data* (Beverly Hills: Sage).

Freeman, H. E. and Shanks, J. M. (1983) 'Forward: Special Issue on the Emergence of Computer-Assisted Survey Research', *Social Research Methods*, vol. 12, pp. 115–18.

Freeman, L. C. (1980) 'Q-Analysis and the Structure of Friendship Networks', *International Journal of Man Machine Studies*, vol. 12, pp. 25–47.

Garfinkel, H. (1967) *Studies in Ethnomethodology*, (Englewood Cliffs/NJ: Prentice-Hall).

Glass, D. V. (1954) *Social Mobility in Britain* (London: Routledge & Kegan Paul).

Goffman, E. (1959) *The Presentation of Self in Everyday Life* (New York: Doubleday).

Goldberger, A. S. and Duncan, O. D. (eds) (1973) *Structural Equation Models in the Social Sciences* (New York: Seminar Press).

Goldthorpe, J. H. *et al.* (1980) *Social Mobility and Class Structure in Modern Britain* (Oxford: OUP).

Goodman, L. A. (1969) 'How to Ransack Social Mobility Tables and Other Kinds of Cross Classification Tables', *American Journal of Sociology*, vol. 75, pp. 1–40.

——(1970) 'The Multivariate Analysis of Qualitative Data: Interactions Among Multiple Classifications', *Journal of the American Statistical Association*, vol. 65, pp. 116–56.

——(1972) 'Some Multiplicative Models for the Analysis of Cross Classified Data', *Proceedings of the Sixth Berkeley Symposium on Mathematics, Statistics and Probability*, pp. 649–96.

——(1973) 'The Analysis of Multidimensional Contingency Tables when some Variables are Posterior to Others', *Biometrika*, vol. 60, pp. 179–92.

——(1974) 'The Analysis of Systems of Qualitative Variables when some of the Variables are Unobservable, pt 1: A Modified Latent Structure Approach', *American Journal of Sociology*, vol. 79, pp. 1179–259.

——(1978) *Analysing Qualitative/Categorical Data: Log-Linear Models and Latent-Structure Analysis* (Cambridge/Mass: Abt Books).

——and Kruskal, W. H. (1959) 'Measures of Association for Cross Classifications II: Further Discussions and References', *Journal of the American Statistical Association*, vol. 54, pp. 732–64.

Gorsuch, R. L. (1974) *Factor Analysis* (Philadelphia: Saunders Co.).

Green, H. A. (1964) *Aggregation in Economic Analysis, an Introductory Survey* (Princeton: Princeton University Press).

Grimshaw, A. D. (1982) 'Sound Image Data Records for Research on Social Interaction', *Social Research Methods*, vol. 11, pp. 121–44.

Haberman, S. J. (1974) *The Analysis of Frequency Data* (Chicago: Chicago University Press).

Hanan, M. T. (1971) *Aggregation and Disaggregation in Sociology* (Lexington/Mass: Lexington).

Harary, F., Norman, R. Z. and Cartwright, D. (1965) *Structural Models: An Introduction to the Theory of Directed Graphs* (New York: Wiley).

Harman, H. H. (1960) *Modern Factor Analysis* (Chicago: Chicago University Press).

Hauser, R. M. (1974) 'Contextual Analysis Revisited', *Social Methods and Research*, vol. 2, pp. 365–75.

——and Goldberger, A. S. (1971) 'The Treatment of Unobservable Variables in Path Analysis', in H. L. Costner (ed.), *Sociological Methodology* (San Francisco: Jossey-Bass).

Heath, C. (1986) *Body Movement and Speech in Medical Interaction* (Cambridge: CUP).

Heise, D. R. (1975) *Causal Analysis* (New York: Wiley).

*——(forthcoming) 'Modeling Event Structures', *Journal of Mathematical Sociology*, forthcoming.

Hildebrand, D. K., Laing, J. D. and Rosenthal, H. (1977) *Analysis of Ordinal Data* (Beverly Hills: Sage).

Horton, R. L. (1978) *The General Linear Model* (New York: McGraw-Hill).

Hyman, H. H. (1955) *Survey Design and Analysis* (New York: Free Press).

Irwin, L. and Lichtman, A. J. (1976) 'Across the Great Divide: Inferring Individual Behaviour from Aggregate Data', *Political Methodology*, vol. 3, pp. 411–39.

Jahn, J. A. (1950) 'The Measurement of Ecological Segragation: Derivation of an Index Based on the Criterion of Reproductability', *American Sociological Review*, vol. 15, pp. 100–4.

Jefferson, G. (1983) 'Two Explorations in the Organization of Overlapping Talk in Conversation', *Tilburg Papers in Language and Literature*, no. 28 (Tilburg: University of Tilburg).

Jencks, C. (1972) *Inequality* (New York: Basic Books).

Joreskog, K. G. (1978) *Lisrel IV: A General Computer Program for Estimation of Linear Structural Equation Systems by Maximum Likelihood Methods* (Uppsala: University of Uppsala).

Kemeny, J. G. and Snell, J. L. (1962) *Mathematical Models in the Social Sciences* (Boston: Ginn & Co).

Kendall, M. G. and Stuart, A. (1961) *Advanced Theory of Statistics* (London: Griffin).

Kim, J. and Mueller, C. W. (1978) *Factor Analysis, Statistical Methods and Practical Issues* (Beverly Hills: Sage).

Kruskal, J. B. (1964a) 'Multidimensional Scaling by Optimising Goodness of Fit to a Non-Metric Hypothesis', *Psychometrika*, vol. 29, pp. 1–27.

——(1964b) 'Non-Metric Multidimensional Scaling, a Numerical Method', *Psychometrika*, vol. 29, pp. 115–29.

——and Wish, M. (1978) *Multidimensional Scaling* (Beverly Hills: Sage).

Kruskal, W. H. (1958) 'Ordinal Measures of Association', *Journal of the American Statistical Association*, vol. 58, pp. 514–61.

Langbein, L. I. and Lichtman, A. J. (1978) *Ecological Inference* (Beverly Hills: Sage).

Lazarsfeld, P. F. (1950) 'The Interpretation and Computation of Some Latent Structures', in S. A. Stouffer *et al.* (eds), *Measurement and Prediction Studies in Social Psychology in World War II*, vol. 4 (Princeton: Princeton University Press).

——and Henry, N. W. (1968) *Latent Structure Analysis* (Boston: Houghton Mifflin).

——and Rosenberg, M. (1955) *The Language of Social Research* (Glencoe/Ill: Free Press).

Lazerwitz, B. (1968) 'Sampling Theory and Procedures', in H. M. Blalock, Jr (ed.) *Methodology in Social Research* (New York: McGraw-Hill).

Lipset, S. M. (1963) *The First New Nation: The United States in Comparative and Historical Perspective* (New York: Basic Books).

Lorrain, F. and White, H. C. (1971) 'Structural Equivalence of Individuals in Social Networks', *Journal of Mathematical Sociology*, vol. 1, pp. 49–80.

Maxwell, A. E. (1961) *Analysing Qualitative Data* (New York: Wiley).

Moore, B. (1966) *Social Origins of Dictatorship and Democracy: Lord and Peasant in the Making of the Modern World* (Boston: Beacon).

Moreno, J. L. (ed.) (1960) *The Sociometry Reader* (New York: Free Press).

Nelder, J. A. and Wedderburn, R. W. W. (1972) 'Generalised Linear Models', *Journal of the Royal Statistical Association*, A135, pp. 370–84.

Newell, A. and Simon, H. A. (1972) *Human Problem-Solving* (Englewood Cliffs/NJ: Prentice-Hall).

Olson, M. (1965) *The Logic of Collective Action* (Cambridge/Mass: Harvard University Press).

Orcutt, G. H., Greenberger, M. and Korbel, J. (1961) *Microanalysis of Socioeconomic Systems: A Simulation Study* (New York: Harper & Row).

Pelz, D. C. and Andrews, F. M. (1964) 'Causal Priorities in Panel Study Data', *American Sociological Review*, vol. 29, pp. 836–48.

Pickles, A., Davies, R. and Crouchley, R. (1985) 'Understanding Life Histories and Recurrent Choice: A Framework for Analysis', in M. Proctor and P. Abell (eds), *Sequence Analysis* (Aldershot: Gower).

Plackett, R. L. (1974) *The Analysis of Categorical Data* (London: Griffin).

Przeworski, A. (1974) 'Contextual Models of Political Behaviour', *Political Methodology*, vol. 1, pp. 27–60.

Ragin, C. (1987a) 'Comparative Social Science in the 21st Century', mimeo (Cleveland: North Western University).

——(1987b) *The Comparative Method: Moving Beyond Qualitative and Quantitative Strategies* (Berkeley: University of California Press).

Rapaport, A. (1951) 'Nets With Distance Bias', *Bulletin of Mathematical Biophysics*, vol. 13, pp. 85–91.

Reynolds, H. R. (1977) *Analysis of Nominal Data* (Beverly Hills: Sage).

Roemer, J. E. (1982) *A General Theory of Exploitation and Class* (Cambridge/ Mass: Harvard University Press).

Sacks, H. (1963). 'Sociological Description', *Berkeley Journal of Sociology*, vol. 8, pp. 1–11.

——, Schegloff, E. A. and Jefferson, G. (1974) 'A Simplest Systematics for the Organisation of Turn Taking in Conversation', *Language*, vol. 50, pp. 696–735

Schank, R. and Abelson, R. (1977) *Scripts, Plans, Goals and Understanding* (New York: Wiley).

Shanks, J. M. (1985) 'The Current State of Computer Assisted Telephone Interviewing', *Social Research and Methodology*, vol. 12, pp. 119–42.

Simon, H. (1957) *Models of Man* (New York: Wiley).

Skocpol, T. (1979) *States and Social Revolutions: A Comparative Analysis of France, Russia and China* (Cambridge: CUP).

Skvoretz, J. (1984) 'Languages and Grammars of Action and Interaction: Some Further Results', *Behavioural Science*, vol. 29, pp. 81–97.

Smelser, N. J. (1959) *Social Change in the Industrial Revolution: An Application of Theory to the British Cotton Industry* (Chicago: University of Chicago Press).

Tilly, C. (1975) *The Formation of National States in Western Europe* (Princeton: Princeton University Press).

——(1978) *From Mobilisation to Revolution* (Reading/Mass: Addison-Wesley).

——(1984) *Big Structures, Large Processes, Huge Comparisons* (New York: Russell Sage Foundation).

Torgerson, W. S. (1958) *Theory and Methods of Scaling* (London: Wiley).

Valkonen, T. (1969) 'Individual and Structural Effects in Ecological Research', in M. Dogan and S. Rokkan (eds), *Quantitative Ecological Analysis in the Social Sciences* (Cambridge/Mass: MIT Press).

Maanen, J. van (ed.) (1982) *Varieties of Qualitative Research* (Beverly Hills: Sage).

White, D. R. and Reitz, K. P. (1983) 'Graph and Semigroup Homomorphisms on Networks of Relations', *Social Networks*, vol. 5, pp. 193–234.

White, H. C. (1963) *An Anatomy of Kinship* (Englewood Cliffs/NJ: Prentice-Hall).

Wiley, D. E. (1973) 'The Identification Problem for Structural Equation Models with Unmeasured Variables', in Goldberger and Duncan (1973).

Wilson, T. P. (1974) 'Measures of Association for Bivariate Ordinal Hypothesis', in H. M. Blalock (ed.), *Measurement in the Social Sciences* (Chicago: Aldine-Atherton).

——(1982) 'Relational Networks: An Extension of Sociometric Concepts', *Social Networks*, vol. 4, pp. 105–16.

Wright, S. (1921) 'Correlation and Causation', *Journal of Agricultural Research*, vol. 20, pp. 557–85.

——(1960) 'Path Coefficients and Path Regressions: Alternative or Complementary Concepts', *Biometrics*, vol. 16, pp. 189–202.

7 Successful Applications of Sociology
Martin Bulmer

1 INTRODUCTION

Too many sociologists in the last quarter of a century have, like
Molière's famous character Monsieur Jourdain, been speaking prose
without realising it. Their work has had considerable impact on the
practical world, but for much of the time they have been steadfastly
denying its usefulness, even in one case going to the lengths of writing a
book entitled *Why Sociology Does Not Apply* (Scott and Shore, 1979).
Starting from the view that a dominant theme of American sociology
has been the argument that knowledge can transform society in
obvious, self-evident and desirable ways, Robert Scott and Arnold
Shore hold that many sociologists have a mistaken conception of the
influence of research on policy. They see a schism opening up between
social scientists doing routine disciplinary research and policy researchers doing work on policy questions.

Such self-doubt also accords with critical assessments of the
intellectual achievements of the social sciences as scientific disciplines.
Sociology is held not to have made advances in its application
comparable to those in subjects like medicine, physics or agriculture.
It is said that it cannot point to technological innovations such as
nuclear weapons, or nuclear electricity, new forms of therapy, or new
improvements in food production. Nor are its cognitive accomplishments seen to be on a par with many other sciences. Moreover, applied
research in sociology is held not to be comparable to applied research
in the natural sciences and medicine, in that it does not involve the
application of scientifically tested general principles to the explanation
and management of specific social problems; for such general principles do not exist as yet.

The argument of this chapter is that much of the self-doubt on the
part of sociologists about the practical usefulness of their subject is
misplaced, while the apparently powerful arguments against a credible
applied sociology rest upon a mistaken model of the process of
knowledge application in the social sciences. The early part of the
chapter considers some of the self-imposed blinkers on the part of

sociologists themselves, the middle part the adequacy of the analogy with applied natural science or medicine. This leads on to a discussion in the later part of the chapter of cases of successful application which point to more positive conclusions about the usefulness of the subject. Drawing primarily on the author's British experience, some brief reference is made also to developments in other West European countries and in North America.

2 BASIC DISTINCTIONS

Several distinctions need to be made which pertain to the terms of the discussion. The discussion of the applications of sociology has been handicapped over the years by an enduring distinction between 'basic' and 'applied' work, which are somehow seen to be fundamentally different. A glance at the practical effectiveness of economics might suggest that this distinction is inadequate. Classics of sociological analysis such as Gunnar Myrdal's *An American Dilemma* or Erving Goffman's *Asylums* cannot readily be classified as either 'pure' or 'applied', for they are both at the same time. Scott and Shore's polemic draws too sharp a distinction between the disciplinary proclivities of social scientists and the very specific applied focus required of the policy researcher. They draw too sharp a line between basic and applied research and imply that there are no bridges to be built across the gap between the two. As the influential Dainton Report (1971, p. 5) argued, such a distinction is unsatisfactory. The objectives 'pure' and 'applied' imply a division where none should exist and their use can be harmful:

> One can scarcely begin to solve societal problems until one understands them; conversely, one only understands a societal problem when potentially effective solutions to it can be imagined . . . basic and applied social research share the science and craftlore of the social science disciplines, but differ in their artful aspects; the theories, methods and procedures of basic and applied research are quite similar but the style of work encountered in each camp is not. (Rossi *et al.*, 1978, p. 173)

This view of the nature of applied research has had many adherents in the history of the social sciences, particularly sociology. Florian Znaniecki (1940) in *The Social Role of the Man of Knowledge* discussed the fusion of the roles of sage and technological leader, insisting that technical specialists alone cannot effectively apply social science knowledge. William F. Ogburn, himself something of a technical specialist in statistical studies of social change, insisted that basic and practical research tended to merge. Basic research sometimes produced results of great benefit to mankind; research on practical social problems (such as race relations) not infrequently yielded knowledge that is fundamental (Ogburn, 1964, p. 332).

Sociologists of widely differing standpoints have shared a conception of sociology as contributing to the better understanding of contemporary society. In different ways Max Weber and Emile Durkheim exemplified such a practical orientation, Weber through his participation in the 'Verein fuer Socialpolitik' and Durkheim through his reflections on the division of labour and corporate organisation. An influential re-statement of the task of sociology has been made by Edward Shils, pointing out the limitations of a technicist conception of social science in aid of the policy-maker:

The proper calling today of sociology is the illumination of opinion. Having its point of departure in the opinion of the human beings who make up the society, it is its task to return to opinion, clarified and deepened by dispassionate study and systematic reflection . . . Some sociologists might feel that this definition of the calling of sociology is one that undoes the progress of the subject. On the contrary, it shows the right direction for a subject that is at once a science, a moral discipline and a body of opinion. (Shils, 1961, p. 1441)

Rather than a dichotomy between pure and applied research, a threefold distinction is more useful, between basic discipline-bound research, strategic research, and tactical research. Basic research is oriented to theoretical problems of a disciplinary kind, tactical research to discrete technical problems of a severely practical kind. What the Dainton report called 'strategic research' falls between the two, being neither pure discipline-bound – addressed to problems of an internal, theoretical kind – nor purely instrumental – in the sense of being addressed directly to the solution of practical problems. The fields of inquiry considered draw upon general theories – for example, in positing a link between class position and voting – but analyse their subject to draw conclusions with practical implications – in the case of the sociology of education, about the organisation of secondary education. They develop middle-range theories – for example, of the workings of the labour market – but also provide usable knowledge about the working of social processes – for instance, identifying the contribution of amplifying factors to the onset of depression. All three types of research are pursued by sociologists working in a variety of settings, who retain a basic identity as a sociological researcher. But there is a further dimension to sociological application: the utilisation of knowledge by practitioners in political, policy, administrative, journalistic and field settings, and by citizens *qua* citizens, who make use of sociological knowledge but are not themselves sociologists. Practising sociology may be confined to the three types of sociological researchers, but those utilising sociology are a much larger and more diverse group. There are thus both producers and consumers of sociological work with practical import.

3 SELF-DOUBT AMONG SOCIOLOGISTS

One of the greatest obstacles to the adequate recognition of the usefulness of sociology is the self-doubt which permeates discussions of applying sociology among sociologists themselves. Sociology as an academic pursuit struggles under a number of burdens, some of which are self-imposed. The internal obstacles stem from the way in which the purposes of sociology as an intellectual endeavour are construed, and in particular the way in which three elements – theorising, empirical inquiry, and practical application – are seen as relating to each other. Consider Figure 7.1. The representation of the relationship between the three elements in this diagram is intended to highlight the strong links which have traditionally bound theory and empirical inquiry, on the one hand, and empirical inquiry and practical application on the other, together. Following the model of natural science, the most fruitful scholarly pursuit has been thought to be work which combined the development of theoretical propositions of considerable scope with empirical studies to test those propositions. Max Weber's *The Protestant Ethic* and Emile Durkheim's *Suicide* stand as exemplars. The inter-relationships between theory and inquiry were anatomised in two classic essays by Robert Merton (1957, pp. 85–117). This development, however, has not led to the application of sociological theory to the solution of public policy problems in the way that, for example, economic theory was applied to the management of the national economy during and after the Second

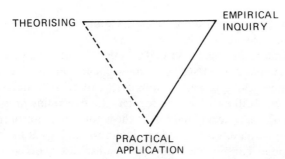

Figure 7.1 The relationship between theorising empirical inquiry and practical application

World War (cf. Winch, 1972). Nor at a more specific level has sociological theory informed the construction of social indicators in the way that economic theory has influenced the development of economic indicators (cf. Carley, 1986).

At the same time, though somewhat apart from the mainstream of the discipline, applied work of a markedly empirical character has gone on. Indeed, such contemporary research is a direct descendant of the tradition of 'political arithmetic' and the investigation of social conditions which has bound closely together empirical social inquiry with potential practical applications (cf. Bulmer, 1985). Such inquiries have not been notable for their theoretical orientation or sophistication, hence the dotted line in Figure 7.1.

On top of these two tendencies have been a number of recent trends in the subject which have pushed practical application further into the background. A strong strain, in European sociology in general and British sociology in particular, has been the cultivation of theoretical sociology as an end in itself untrammelled by empirical concerns, as if sociology were a brand of social philosophy rather than an empirical social science. Even those who have moved away from such solipsism to acknowledge the role of research regularly disparage applied research. Anthony Giddens, for example, has recently claimed that:

> the point of doing social research from a practical angle is simply to allow policy-makers better to understand the social world, and thereby to influence it in a more reliable fashion than would otherwise be the case. From this standpoint research does not play a significant part in shaping the ends of policy-making, but serves to provide efficient means of pursuing already formulated objectives. (Giddens, 1987, pp. 45–6)

Such a handmaiden function is, by implication, very much of a second order of importance.

Other tendencies which have had a dampening effect on recognising sociology's applied role have been the vogue for phenomenology and hermeneutic sociology, and various forms of critical sociology and neo-Marxism. In the case of the former, the overriding emphasis on the actor's perspective and the role of the actor in the interpretation of social phenomena tends to produce a micro-sociological focus and as an unintended consequence militate against direct practical application. There are striking examples of micro-studies with major impact – Goffman's *Asylums* comes to mind – but for the most part such studies have remained within a severely academic frame. General justifications also tend to play down the contribution which sociology may make. Giddens's appeal to the 'double hermeneutic' leads him to maintain that 'the most far-reaching practical consequences of social science do not involve the creation of sets of generalizations that can be used to generate instrumental control over the social world' (1987, p. 48). Instead, he argues, the role is to provide reflexively for the constitution and reconstitution of social knowledge through the concepts and theories which sociology produces.

In the case of critical sociology and neo-Marxism, the opposition to applied sociology has been more direct. On the one hand, the tradition of social arithmetic has been excoriated as being linked to a simple-minded reformism (cf. Rex, 1961), while, on the other, applied research has been seen as tainted by contact with the power structure of the state, and on that account to be repudiated. In doing so, a picture is painted of what applied research actually involves, and of the relationship between knowledge and social action. In essence, applied sociology is represented as highly instrumental, serving particular interests in a direct and manipulative way. It will be argued below that such a view is unrealistic, but its consequence has been to further diminish in the eyes of some of its practitioners the practical applicability of the subject.

These disparate tendencies have also had a further deleterious effect, in fragmenting the discipline and rendering a unified approach on which applications may be developed more difficult. As Basil Bernstein observed a decade ago in relation to the sociology of education:

In a subject where theories and methods are weak, intellectual shifts are likely to arise out of conflict between *approaches* rather than conflict between explanations, for by definition, most explanations will be weak and often non-comparable, because they are approach-specific. The weakness of the explanation is likely to be attributed to the approach, which is analysed in terms of its ideological stance. Once the ideological stance is exposed, then all the work may be written off. Every new approach becomes a social movement or sect which immediately defines the nature of the subject by redefining what is to be admitted, and what is beyond the pale, so that with every new approach the subject almost starts from scratch. (1974, p. 154)

Such intellectual fissiparousness is not conducive to the development of effective application, not only because it reinforces the tendencies already mentioned to dismiss such work as ideologically tainted, but also because it reduces the persuasiveness of the sociological product offered to non-sociologists.

Coupled with the dense and opaque prose which has found favour among some practitioners of some sociological approaches, the introspective character of the discipline has been reinforced. As a result, the predominant paths of communication have been between fellow specialists (often with quite narrowly defined interests) rather than between specialists and non-specialists. This has severely circum-scribed the potential applicability of sociological findings. To be sure, magazines such as *Society/Transaction* and *New Society* have served an important function in transmitting the results of sociological research to a wider audience, but by comparison with other fields in the social sciences sociologists have been hesitant to offer their wares to outsiders.

A further feature of sociology as an institutional activity has been, in Britain at least, the lack of a professional orientation characteristic of, for example, psychology or economics and their applied branches. Some years ago the British Sociological Association specifically rejected proposals to strengthen the element of professional certification. Sociology in Britain has remained an occupation rather than a profession, tending to be on the margin as a provider of social criticism rather than in the mainline of professional activity. There are exceptions to this – medical sociology, for example, is a widely practised and flourishing specialism – but the situation is markedly different from that pertaining in the Netherlands, where applied sociologists practising sociology have become well established in a number of fields, originally in spatial planning and the settlement of the Polders, more recently in industrial and public sector organisations.

The explanation of the perceived lack of relevance of sociology to practical concerns does not lie only in its internal characteristics. The milieu in which sociology becomes established may be more or less receptive to its product. There are undoubtedly good grounds for arguing, for example, that for various reasons the United States has been more receptive to the social sciences in both basic and applied forms than has Britain (cf. Soffer, 1982; Bulmer, 1987). Yet to a considerable extent sociology's recent lack of esteem in Britain has been self-inflicted. When one considers the promise which the field held out in the 1960s, the rapid expansion which took place with the creation *de novo* of sociology departments in more than fifty universities and polytechnics, perhaps one may be excused for wondering why sociology has not made more impact. At least part of the explanation lies in the employment of inappropriate models of knowledge use.

4 THE ANALOGY WITH NATURAL SCIENCE OR MEDICINE

Lay critics of sociology and many practising sociologists alike share a misapprehension about the idea of applying sociological knowledge, to the effect that sociology provides the evidence and conclusions to help 'solve' a policy problem. The sociologist is a technician who commands the knowledge to make the necessary investigation and interpret the results. Lay critics charge that sociology is generally ineffective in providing such knowledge, while many sociologists (such as Anthony Giddens, quoted earlier) consider such an 'instrumental' orientation to be intellectually shallow or serving interests other than scholarly ones. They share a common view of research as a mode of engineering.

The model is a linear one. A problem exists; information or understanding is lacking either to generate a solution to the problem or to select among alternative solutions; research provides the missing knowledge; and a solution is reached. Typically a single study will be involved. This – with its data, analysis and conclusions – will affect the choices that decision-makers face. Implicit in such an approach is agreement upon ends. It is assumed that policy-makers and researchers agree upon what the desired end-state should be. The role of research is to help in the identification and selection of appropriate

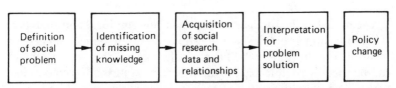

Figure 7.2 The 'engineering' model of research utilisation

means to reach that goal (Weiss, 1977, pp. 11–12). Such a view of the influence of research upon policy can be represented as in Figure 7.2.

The engineer (or the doctor) provides the role model for this kind of applied research. It involves the making of a sharp distinction between basic and applied research. The task of basic researchers is to develop and test a logico-deductive system of hypotheses and propositions. Theoretical knowledge is very general. Theoretical contributions are intended to systematise knowledge and stimulate empirical research. Applied social researchers, on the other hand, are concerned with the research applications of existing theoretical knowledge. Their task is to collect empirical data to solve specific problems. They are skilled in empirical research, and have the interpersonal skills to communicate their findings directly to policy-makers. 'They are, so to speak, social engineers' (Janowitz, 1972, p. 3). Hans Zetterberg (1962) argued that the applied social researcher, like a doctor, should be able to offer prescriptive recommendations on the basis of the special knowledge which he possesses. Unfortunately the examples adduced, such as advising public libraries, were not particularly impressive. The model of the social scientist as social engineer is nevertheless clear (see also, Dror, 1971; MacRae, 1976).

In Britain the engineering model received a powerful impetus from the influential Rothschild report of 1971 on government R & D which distinguished sharply between basic and applied research. Applied research for government, Rothschild argued, should be done on a customer/contractor basis. A customer (perhaps a government department) would commission research from a separate contractor (perhaps a research institute or university department). The customer, although he could be advised by the contractor, would set the objectives and the limits within which the contractor would work. The customer pays the contractor for his services (Rothschild, 1971). The model for such a role for research was taken from technology. Though Rothschild did not refer specifically to social research in his recommendations, he has nevertheless been read as endorsing the appropriateness of the engineering model for social science.

The model of the sociologist employing his empirical and analytical skills to answer problems and questions posed by policy-makers is a plausible one for those who favour it. It suggests that the sociologist can be socially useful, making an important contribution to national issues. The scientific status of social science is recognised both in its methods and explanatory theories. The professional status of research is much enhanced, while the social scientist is accorded a position of power as a technical expert comparable to that of the engineer or doctor. So what is wrong with it?

One powerful line of criticism suggests that the engineering model misstates and misunderstands the nature of the policy-making process:

> Information and analysis provide only one route among several to social problem-solving – because . . . a great deal of the world's problem-solving is and ought to be accomplished through various forms of social interaction that substitute action for thought, understanding or analysis . . . In addition . . . other forms of information and analysis – ordinary knowledge and causal analysis foremost among them – are often sufficient or better for social problem-solving. (Lindblom and Cohen, 1979, p. 10)

Policy research in the engineering model fails to take account of the complex processes by which decisions are reached, exaggerates the role of the 'decision-maker' for whom research is carried out, and gives unwarranted authority to the research input which the policy re-searcher provides. The results of policy research lack the degree of conclusiveness which their practitioners claim, either as scientific knowledge or as confirmation of ordinary knowledge.

Two strands in this criticism are particularly important. One concerns the nature of the policy-making process. If the policy-making process is confused, messy, inconclusive, involving mutual bargaining, the unintended consequences of actions, disjointed incrementalism and uncertain outcome, then the neat rationality of either David Glass's postwar optimism (cf. 1950) or modern 'policy science' may be beside the point. If the world does not work in a wholly rational way, the impact of a sociology designed specifically to serve policy will be correspondingly reduced. To posit the social sciences as enabling the policy-maker to make informed choices between competing alternative means to a given end on the basis of the fullest information available, does not fit with the available accounts of how policy emerges. (For an elaboration, see Bulmer, 1986, pp. 3–59.)

The second strand concerns the scientific status of the results of policy research in the engineering model. Perhaps Rothschild exempted social science from the customer/contractor principle because he recognised that many social sciences are unable to satisfy the customer by providing hard-and-fast answers to discrete 'technical' questions. Subjects like sociology are not well placed to provide definitive answers to questions like : How can (certain types of) vandalism be reduced? How can employee absenteeism be reduced? How can educational performance (of certain pupils) be improved? How can the health (of certain groups) be made better? Certainly some of the factors involved may be identified, and a distinction made between situation variables and policy variables, the latter being amenable to manipulation by the policy-maker. The findings of such research, however, are not only rarely absolutely conclusive, but also they frequently only explain a small proportion of the variance observed in the dependent variable. The scientific claims made for policy reseach in the engineering models are frequently much too strong, both on the part of lay outsiders and detractors among sociologists.

A more realistic view of the relationship between knowledge and application must therefore be found. The most persuasive recent adherent of an alternative to the 'engineering' model has been University of Chicago sociologist Morris Janowitz (1972), who has termed this approach the 'enlightenment' model. Janowitz argues that the sociologist is part of the process which he or she is studying, not outside it. For example, in studying the 'causes' of social problems as well as the technical means for analysing the issues, the sociologist has to make explicit criteria and standards of performance that are being applied. Minimum income levels and the procedures for welfare administration need to be considered, with a view not only to what is, but to what is possible:

> It is not the sociologist's task to *recommend* alternative policies and to insist that some administrative options are 'better' than others. But if he is not a proper catalyst of social change, neither ought a sociologist to serve as a justifier of received patterns, legitimating them with *post factum* omniscience as a product of 'inevitability'. If the sociologist may not expatiate upon what 'ought to be', he is still privileged to deal with another realm, 'the realm of what can be'. (Gouldner, 1954, p. 18)

The sociologist has to recognise that he is interacting with subject and audience, whom the findings may influence directly or indirectly. The findings and ideas which are put forward come in time to be part of the general culture, and specific social science theories and findings may become part of the defensive ideology of particular groups, as in the influence of social research on the self-perceptions of criminals and delinquents. (For one example, see McVicar, 1979.) 'The consequences of effective sociological inquiry . . . is to contribute to political freedom and social voluntarism by weakening myths, refuting distortions, and preventing an imbalanced view of social reality from dominating collective decisions' (Janowitz, 1971, p.6).

Empirical evidence in support of such a view of the role of applied social science is found in recent studies of policy- and decision-makers in government by Caplan (1976), Knorr (1977) and Weiss (1980). The neat model of the social engineer does not seem to accord with how government officials actually make use of social research. They seem to employ it more to orient themselves to problems than to find solutions to discrete policy problems. Research provides the intellectual background of concepts, orientations and empirical generalisations that inform policy. It is used to orient decision-makers to problems, to think about and specify the problematic elements in a situation, to get new ideas. Policy-makers use research to *formulate* problems and to set the agenda for future policy actions. Much of this use is not direct, but a result of long-term infiltration of social science concepts, theories and findings with the general intellectual culture of a society.

This is not to say that the engineering model is wholly inappropriate. Where the problem being tackled is a tightly delimited one, the theoretical model is precisely specified, and there are good data available on the independent and dependent variables, then a useful contribution can be made by focusing on variables susceptible to manipulation by the policy-maker (cf. van de Vall, 1986). There are examples from studies of borstal and parole prediction in criminology, changes in the school-leaving age in education, and labour market policies to deal with the consequences of redundancy, which exemplify this approach. Despite the problems of foreseeing the unintended consequences of planned social intervention (cf. Sieber, 1981), there are exceptional circumstances in which the sociologist is able to act as a social engineer.

As a general account, however, the enlightenment model is a more accurate portrayal, consistent with the range of roles played by the applied sociologist identified at the end of this chapter. Moreover, there need not be complete acceptance by the researcher of the fundamental goals, priorities and political constraints of the decision-maker. Decision-makers (at least in the United States) believe it is a good thing to have controversial research, challenging research, research that makes them rethink comfortable assumptions. Value consensus is not a prerequisite for useful policy research. There is a role for research as social criticism. There is a place for research based on variant theoretical premises. As new concepts and data emerge, their gradual cumulative effect can be to change the conventions policy-makers abide by and to reorder the goals and priorities of policy-makers (Weiss, 1977). 'Much of the more important empirical work of the postwar period has arisen out of applied concerns and the growth of sociology as a discipline has been profoundly affected by the knowledge about our society developed by empirical applied social research' (Rossi, 1981, p. 284). This American generalisation also holds for the European scene, although, there, theoretical interests have been pursued more actively alongside applied work.

5 CASES OF SUCCESSFUL APPLICATION OF SOCIOLOGY

The case-studies which follow suggest that in a number of fields in British sociology, the results of research have been applied in a not unsuccessful way. None of the fields discussed – in political sociology, the sociology of education, the sociology of labour markets, or the sociology of medicine – has been integrated into grand theory. They exemplify what T. H. Marshall once called an approach based on 'stepping stones into the middle distance'. Given the failings and disappointments to which grand theory has given rise, this has probably been the most fruitful level at which to combine a theoretical orientation with empirical inquiry. The cases examined look back some years, and this is a deliberate choice. It enables one to gain some perspective upon the effects of sociology, and distance from a present in which the identification of immediate effects is methodologically problematical. It also serves as a reminder that some of the effects of sociological understanding operate over a very long time-period, for example in influencing social beliefs and practices about the position of racial minorities or women.

5.1 Political Sociology

Political sociology exemplifies the successful application of sociology in an unusual way, by feeding into discussions of the contemporary political scene and the fortunes of parties in elections. This is taken so much for granted nowadays that it is worth pointing out that forty years ago it was not the case. The pioneer psephological studies date from the early 1950s, while Robert McKenzie's study of *British Political Parties*, applying Michels's theory in a study of the organisation of the Labour and Conservative parties, appeared in 1955. McKenzie himself, until his death in the mid-1980s, had a dual career as LSE sociologist and political broadcaster, taking a most active role as a television commentator on contemporary political developments. Subsequent to the 1950s, political scientists and polling organisations became more salient in election studies, but sociologists took the lead at the outset. Mark Benney's study of Greenwich, for example, was the first survey of British electoral behaviour (Benney *et al.*, 1956).

The 1959 election led to questions about the Labour Party's future chances, and a book by Mark Abrams and Richard Rose entitled *Must Labour Lose?* (1960) was an important stimulus to the study *The Affluent Worker* carried out at Cambridge in the early 1960s (Goldthorpe *et al.*, 1968a, 1968b, 1969). In turn, *The Affluent Worker* became a widely quoted sociological monograph on the part of political columnists and newspaper commentators discussing the behaviour of the electorate. More recently, the extent to which social class still constitutes a basis for political allegiance has been further examined, and sociologists were involved in the two major studies of the 1983 General Election (Heath *et al.*, 1985; Dunleavy and Husbands, 1985).

The point of this example is not that sociologists have dominated public discussion of electoral behaviour – they have not – but that in the until recently class-bound British political system sociological research provided significant insights into the ways in which the system worked, so that lay discourse was insensibly influenced and directed by the results of sociological research. The political world – particularly the behaviour of the electorate – was seen in a different way as a result of the work of sociologists (and political scientists). The involvement of academics such as Robert McKenzie in broadcasting brought this influence to bear directly, but it also influenced indirectly the orientation of political journalists and politicians, some of the latter (particularly for a period in the senior echelons of the Labour Party) themselves having a social science background. The influence which sociology has exercised in this area has been very diffuse, but it is nevertheless an identifiable one.

5.2 Sociology of Education

When one turns to the sociology of education, the traces of influence of particular types of research are more direct. The sociology of education in Europe is largely a post Second World War product, at least so far as a substantial sociological input was concerned (Szreter, 1980). But the focus of research connected both with interests in applied research and a political orientation:

> socialist influence on a choice of problems [in the sociology of education] was strong before the war, and continued after it, in the long tradition of empirical inquiry by royal commissions and private investigators of public issues. A Fabian social democratic use of data from such inquiries was concentrated characteristically on the analysis of social inequalities of educational opportunity. (Karabel and Halsey, 1977, p. 3)

The political source of this research interest later led Raymond Aron to exclaim: 'The trouble is that British sociology is essentially an attempt to make intellectual sense of the political problems of the Labour Party' (quoted in Halsey, 1982, p. 150).

In fact it would be a mistake to overemphasise this political source of the research on the social determinants of educational achievement. This focus stemmed from interests among LSE sociologists in social stratification, social mobility and the process of industrialisation (cf. Glass, 1959). It was oriented to social policy and social planning in the context of a society in which *in*equality of educational opportunity was a manifest feature of the social structure. Throughout, the emphasis was not just on diagnosis but on change:

> Once the facts of [educational] selection are established inquiry is directed towards the obstacles to 'perfect' representation of the population at large within selective schools and universities; and it is at this point that studies of the class conditioning of educational chances are supplemented by research into the influence of class on educational performance and vocational aspiration. Study of selection *for* education is supplemented by selection *through* education. (Floud and Halsey, 1958, p. 179)

The research done included a major study by Floud, Halsey and

Martin (1956) and an important longitudinal study under the direction of J. W. B. Douglas which produced (*inter alia*) an analysis of educational selection from 5 to 11 (Douglas, 1964). These academic studies exercised considerable influence in their own right and also upon the official advisory committees set up by government to examine aspects of educational provision. Over a period of thirteen years, four committees in turn drew attention to the wastage of talent occurring within the British system and the need to take measures to stem this flow. The Central Advisory Council's (CAC) Report on *Early Learning* of 1954 identified the variability in school drop-out by social class and recommended various ways of trying to overcome this. The Crowther Report of 1959 on education from 15 to 18 marshalled similar evidence of marked inequality of opportunity, showing, for example, that educational attainment correlated more closely with home background than with ability. It recommended raising the school-leaving age from 15 to 16. In 1963 the Newsom Report of 1963, *Half Our Future*, made use of research findings like its predecessor. Most extensive use of research was made by the last of the series, the CAC's report on primary education chaired by Lady Plowden, which reported in 1967.

At this period, interest was moving from the material factors affecting educational achievement – income, housing, child health – to the 'softer' cultural and attitudinal differences determining educational outcome. The considerable research which the Plowden Committee commissioned therefore focused on the attitudinal determinants of pupils' school performance. One student of the work of the committee has concluded that 'as much as anything else, the currents of academic research shaped the work of the committee' (Acland, 1980, p. 39). In organising its work, the committee created a working party chaired by Professor David Donnison, to investigate at the community level the influence of parental attitudes on schools and on educational performance. One particularly valuable presentation that they heard was from J. W. B. Douglas on the results of his longitudinal study. The working party later described his book as 'the most useful single document' that they had seen (Acland, 1980, p. 55).

Work in the sociology of education thus had a considerable impact on official bodies set up to make recommendations about educational change, all of which contributed to the political climate in the 1960s in which the minimum school-leaving age was raised from 15 to 16, and a system of comprehensive schools at secondary level, replacing the selective system, were instituted. There were other reasons for these changes, in the case of comprehensive education not least the perceived inequities of the 11+ system of selection, but sociological research made an important contribution nonetheless. Yet the influence again, as in the case of political sociology, was fairly indirect rather than direct. The Plowden Report itself, for example, although it sparked off the Educational Priority Area programme, did not lead to substantive changes in policy. 'As an immediate planning and social engineering exercise, Plowden scored no great success. Its success lies in other and less easy to define fields . . . [I]t undoubtedly reinforced and strengthened the liberating effects of progressive education in a large number of schools' (Kogan, 1973, p. 100). Within four years the Report had sold 150 000 copies, and had a very wide readership among professional educators and interested parents.

A brief analysis of this period also shows that a political interpretation of the influence of the sociology of education is not adequate. Aron's aphorism was only a partial truism. The egalitarian focus of the sociology of education existed alongside such ideas in the wider educational constituency. The research was in any case grounded in a broader sociological analysis of the effects of the stratification system. This found a reflection in the observations of more radical practitioners dissatisfied with the effects of selectivity in secondary education and the inequities resulting from the 11+ examination. Yet sociology did help to shift official opinion quite markedly. As the secretary of the Plowden Committee later observed, 'how would educational sociology have found its way into official acceptance if CAC's had not applied it in four successive Reports? The Councils, including Plowden, turned the radical sociology of nearly ten years into conventional wisdom' (Kogan, 1973, p. 102). At a later period one tends to take this change for granted, but it is important to observe how sociology exercised its subtle influence at the time this change was taking place.

5.3 Sociology of Labour Markets

The sociology of labour markets provides a contrasting case of sociological influence, since it was not a particularly contentious area politically, yet was one in which state intervention potentially could make a good deal of difference. This discussion abstracts from a larger body of work in the sociology of economic life to pinpoint several studies which focused upon plant closure, planned redeployment, redundancy, and movement between jobs in local labour markets.

Over a fifteen-year period a number of sociological studies appeared, including work on the motor industry by Hilda Kahn (1964), on the railway and electrical industries by Dorothy Wedderburn (1964, 1965), on the steel industry by John Eldridge (1968), on the mining industry by Rex Taylor (1969) and Martin Bulmer (1971), on the relocation of a Midlands food factory by Michael Mann (1973), on plant closure in a north Lancashire town (Martin and Fryer, 1973) and on the workings of the labour market in Peterborough by Bob Blackburn and Michael Mann (1979).

Cumulatively these studies identified a number of important features both of job recruitment and job loss. Among manual workers, means of recruitment were predominantly informal via personal networks, rather than through official channels such as the service provided by the Department of Employment. Formal job placement schemes were relatively ineffective. In situations of plant closure, there were strong tendencies for manual workers to resist moving house, and only a minority could be tempted to move even with well-planned relocation schemes. Job-finding after redundancy again made extensive use of informal networks, particularly approaches to employers via kin and friends. Local labour markets are complex entities in which, particularly among semi- and unskilled workers, there is a good deal of mobility. The creation of new jobs to replace those lost in declining industries does not necessarily open opportunities for the unemployed or newly redundant, but may rather result in a general shuffling around of positions within the system of occupational positions.

These substantive findings were linked to a number of theoretical developments. The whole trend of the research served to undermine an analysis of labour market behaviour in terms of economic rationality or rational choice. Affective and particularistic ties were shown to be important both in job-finding and in resistance to relocation. Several studies adopted a social action perspective, which came into industrial sociology at this period, emphasising the importance of the actor's definition of his or her situation and analysis of that situation (Eldridge, 1980, pp. 7–9). One or two studies more ambitiously sought to locate the plant or enterprise studied within the broader capitalist system and to relate the life-chances of individual employees to the wider changes taking place in the economy.

Unlike the sociology of education, there are no dramatic shifts in public policy one can point to as being directly influenced by the research. Several of the more significant pieces of legislation were introduced before the studies were carried out, as much as a result of trade-union pressure and links between the unions and the Labour government as to research findings. Nevertheless, as a whole this series of studies considerably enlarged knowledge about the workings of labour markets, and influenced officials, managers and trade unionists in their understanding of the workings of the system.

5.4 Sociology of Mental Illness

The fourth example will be dealt with more briefly but provides an interesting contrast because it shows sociological work impinging directly upon professional practice. The sociology of medicine in Britain is now a well-established sub-field, with its own directory of members and annual conference within the British Sociological Association. The study highlighted here is that carried out by George Brown of London University into the social origins of depression among working-class women (Brown *et al.*, 1975; Brown and Harris, 1978). As an attack on a practical problem, it exemplifies *par excellence* the proposition that social science is not primarily concerned with the collection of facts (empiricism) nor with constructing and testing causal laws (one form of grand theory) but with providing many different means of posing and answering questions by means of a process of inquiry.

Brown's work has been concerned with the problem of how social circumstances connect with particular health outcomes. The aim has been to specify some of the intermediate social processes at work connecting social class position on the one hand and the onset of depressive episodes on the other. Figure 7.3 shows one version of the resulting theoretical model, which identifies both primary aetiological factors and amplifying social factors leading to depression. This goes well beyond the sort of correlations between background social factors and the dependent variable (depression) produced by previous epidemiological work (cf. Brown, 1986). Moreover, the study goes some way to providing an account of the meaning of action to the actors concerned, since it involves interpretation of the subjective experience of three of the amplifying factors in relation to the onset or lack of onset of depression (Marsh, 1982, pp. 111–23). It demonstrates that while aetiological conditions grounded in circumstances of a severe loss or major difficulty are of causal importance, so too are social circumstances of the person affected.

This demonstration, albeit in relation to one condition only (depres-

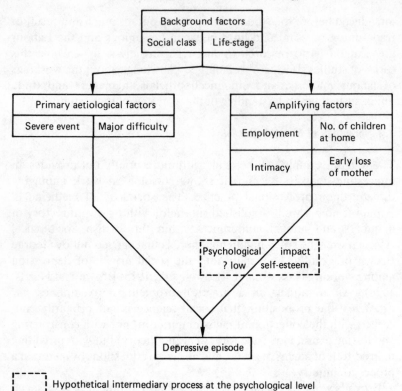

Figure 7.3   A simplified causal model of the relationship between social class
and depression
Source: Brown *et al.*, 1975, p. 246.

sion) for one population (working-class women), has had a considerable effect upon ways in which psychiatrists think about the social
causes of depression. The impact has perhaps been greatest among
academic psychiatrists in medical schools, but has permeated into
clinical practice to some extent. Medical sociology is perhaps unusual
in the closeness of its relationship to practitioners, but this association
provides for the possibility of the findings of sociological research
being taken up and applied in ways that are uncommon in other fields.

6 ANALYSIS AND APPLICATION

Such sociological research as the cases discussed here, poised between
academic theoretical concerns on the one hand and practical policy

problems on the other, goes some way to link the three corners of the triangle introduced in Figure 7.1 together. An awareness of this role also makes clear that there is more to the application of social science knowledge than simply the generation of factually useful, instrumental knowledge, which will be of immediate benefit to policy-makers. The difficulties with this engineering view of social science have already been adumbrated. The usefulness of social science consists much more in the gradual diffusion of understanding about how society works, its integration, strains and conflicts. But this analysis need not remain at the very general level to be found in, for example, discussions of 'the crisis of advanced capitalism'. It may be more fruitful if pursued within a delimited area of scope such as that of the four cases examined. Such studies establish links between the academic and practical worlds which can have important effects.

These bridges may be built in different ways. Sociology may contribute to the general cultural stock of ideas of the society, as in the example of political sociology influencing how electoral behaviour is understood through the media. In a different way, sociological research may inject new perspectives into politically contentious issues, as in the case of equality of educational opportunity. Another British example is provided by the study of poverty (cf. Banting, 1979). Sociology can also illuminate the workings of processes or institutions in a more detached and less partisan manner. The sociology of labour markets is one example, but one thinks also of studies in the sociology of the mass media and the sociology of total institutions. One interesting question for research, for instance, would be the impact of sociological studies such as Goffman's *Asylums* upon the moves gathering pace in Britain and the United States for the closure of large mental hospitals and the deinstitutionalisation of their inmates. And sociological research can feed into professional practice, as the example from the sociology of medicine demonstrated. Professions are variably receptive to social science input. An interesting contrast is provided by the place of socio-legal research in the United States and Britain.

There are thus different routes by which successful application may be achieved. The sociologist may also choose to play different roles. The public image of sociology in Britain – and the self-image fostered by critical sociologists in particular – is that of what Philip Abrams called 'advocacy', in which sociologists show their determination 'to insist on the proper continuity of sociological work beyond the printed page; recognising sociological knowledge as argumentative knowledge they follow their arguments through to the point of action' (1985, p. 197). This has affinities to what Patricia Thomas (1985) has identified as the 'gadfly' role of the applied social scientist as social critic.

There are, however, three alternative roles which the sociologist can play. The sociologist as adviser or consultant plays an intermediary role interpreting the findings of social science in a practical setting. In public policy this may take the form of acting as adviser to a minister (for example, A. H. Halsey to Tony Crosland when he was Secretary of State for Education), advising officials on an official committee, advising a committee of Parliament, or advising a non-governmental organisation. But there is also an important role in the private sector. Lisl Klein's role as an adviser at Esso (Klein, 1976) and more generally the Tavistock Institute of Human Relations' involvement in industrial sociology shows that there is a part to be played in industrial organisations, communicating the relevance of sociology.

Another role is the sociologist as illuminator, throwing light on the operation of society without acting in an official capacity or seeking to participate actively in political or pressure-group processes to bring about social change. This may be a matter of personal predilection, but is more often a reflection of the nature of the problem being investigated. Many subjects – the working of labour markets or the onset of disease, for instance – do not lend themselves to direct intervention. What Abrams termed 'enlightenment-clarification' has been a major applied emphasis in British sociology, 'contributing piecemeal through publication to the slow and erratic formation of a more sociological collective consciousness' (1985, p. 194).

The fourth role may be called the sociologist as communicator. It is represented in extreme form by political sociologists such as Robert McKenzie leading double lives as broadcasters, but the term refers to any sociologist who sets out to address a broader audience than that of their professional colleagues. It is a role which has been played by quite diverse British sociologists, in areas such as the sociology of deviance, medicine and education, addressing different types of audience. It is one that needs to be further developed, for the successful application of sociology depends not only on the quality of the sociological product but on the acceptibility of what is offered and on the effectiveness of the means by which it is communicated. More of what the French term *haute vulgarisation* is needed if the social effectiveness of sociology is to be enhanced.

The usefulness of sociology, then, is more diffuse, unspecific and longer-term than specific, targeted and instrumentally effective in the short term. Sociologists are unlikely, for instance, to provide panaceas for the treatment of particular social ills. This failure to demonstrate immediate utility has put sociology on the defensive, particularly in the British political climate of the 1980s. Sociologists need to be clear that the attempt to offer such short-term solutions is fruitless. This does *not* mean, however, that sociology cannot therefore be usefully applied. It can, but it is important to be clear as to the ways in which this can be done and the channels of its influence when such knowledge is brought to bear. And such fruitful applications of sociology are far more frequent than is commonly supposed.

References

Abrams, M. and Rose, R. (1960) *Must Labour Lose?* (Harmondsworth: Penguin).

Abrams, P. (1985) 'The Uses of British Sociology, 1831–1982', in Bulmer (ed.) (1985) pp. 181–205.

Acland, H. (1980) 'Research as Stage Management: The Case of the Plowden Committee', in M. Bulmer (ed.), *Social Research and Royal Commissions* (London: Allen & Unwin) pp. 34–57.

Banting, K. (1979) *Poverty, Politics and Policy* (London: Macmillan).

Benney, M., Gray, A. P. and Pear, R. H. (1956) *How People Vote: A Study of Electoral Behaviour* (London: Routledge & Kegan Paul).

Bernstein, B. (1974) 'Sociology and the Sociology of Education: A Brief Account', in J. Rex (ed.), *Approaches to Sociology: An Introduction to Major Trends in British Sociology* (London: Routledge & Kegan Paul) pp. 145–59.

Blackburn, R. and Mann, M. (1979) *The Working Class in the Labour Market* (Cambridge: Cambridge University Press).

Brown, G. W. (1986) 'Mental Illness', in L. H. Aiken and D. Mechanic (eds), *Applications of Social Science to Clinical Medicine* (New Brunswick/NJ: Rutgers University Press) pp. 175–203.

——, Bhrolcháin, M. N. and Harris, T. (1975) 'Social Class and Psychiatric Disturbance Among Women in an Urban Population', *Sociology*, vol. 9, pp. 225–54.

—— and Harris, T. (1978) *The Social Origins of Depression* (London: Tavistock).

Bulmer, M. (1971) 'Mining Redundancy', *Industrial Relations Journal*, vol. 2, no. 4, pp. 3–21.

—— (ed.) (1985) *Essays on the History of British Sociological Research* (Cambridge: CUP).

*—— (1986) *Social Science and Social Policy* (London: Allen & Unwin).

—— (ed.) (1987) *Social Science Research and Government: Comparative Essays on Britain and the United States* (Cambridge: CUP).

Caplan, N. (1976) 'Social Research and National Policy: Who Gets Used, By Whom, For What Purpose and With What Effects?', *International Social Science Journal*, vol. 28, pp. 187–94.

Carley, M. (1986) 'Tools for Policy-Making: Indicators and Impact-Assessment', in Bulmer (1986) pp. 126–54.

Dainton Report (1971) 'The Future of the Research Council System', in *A Framework for Government Research and Development*, Cmnd 4184 (London: HMSO).

Douglas, J. W. B. (1964) *The Home and the School* (London: MacGibbon & Kee).

Dror, Y. (1971) *Design for Policy Sciences* (New York: Elsevier).

Dunleavy, P. and Husbands, C. T. (1985) *British Democracy at the Crossroads: Voting and Party Competition in the 1980s* (London: Allen & Unwin).

Eldridge, J. E. T. (1968) *Industrial Disputes* (London: Routledge & Kegan Paul).

—— (1980) *Recent British Sociology* (London: Macmillan).

Floud, J. and Halsey, A. H. (1958) 'The Sociology of Education: A Trend Report and Bibliography', *Current Sociology*, vol. 3, pp. 165–233.

—— and Martin, F. M. (1956) *Social Class and Educational Opportunity* (London: Heinemann).

Giddens, A. (1987) 'Nine Theses on the Future of Sociology', in A. Giddens, *Social Theory and Modern Sociology* (Cambridge: Polity).

Glass, D. V. (1950) 'The Application of Social Research', *British Journal of Sociology*, vol. 1, pp. 17–30.

—— (1959) 'Education and Social Change in Modern England', in M. Ginsberg (ed.), *Law and Opinion in the Twentieth Century* (London: Stevens & Sons).

Goldthorpe, J., Lockwood, D., Bechhofer, F. and Platt, J. (1968a, 1968b, 1969) *The Affluent Worker; Industrial Attitudes and Behaviour; The Affluent Worker: Political Attitudes and Behaviour; The Affluent Worker in the Class Structure* (Cambridge: CUP) 3 volumes.

Gouldner, A. W. (1954) *Patterns of Industrial Bureaucracy* (New York: The Free Press).

Halsey, A. H. (1982) 'Provincials and Professionals: The Post-War British Sociologists', *Archives Européenes de Sociologie*, vol. 23, pp. 150–75.

Heath, A., Jowell, R. and Curtice, J. (1985) *How Britain Votes* (Oxford: Pergamon).

*Janowitz, M. (1971) *Sociological Models and Social Policy* (Morristown/NJ: General Learning Systems).

Kahn, H. (1964) *Repercussions of Redundancy* (London: Allen & Unwin).

Karabel, J. and Halsey, A. H. (1977) 'Educational Research: A Review and Interpretation', in their (eds), *Power and Ideology in Education* (New York: Oxford University Press). pp. 1–85.

*Klein, L. (1976) *A Social Scientist in Industry* (Aldershot/Hants: Gower).

Knorr, K. D. (1977) 'Policy-Makers' Use of Social Science Knowledge: Symbolic or Instrumental?', in C. H. Weiss (ed.), *Using Social Science Research in Public Policy-Making* (Farnborough/Hants: D. C. Heath) pp. 165–82.

Kogan, M. (1973) 'The Plowden Committee on Primary Education', in R. Chapman (ed.), *The Role of Commissions in Policy Making* (London: Allen & Unwin) pp. 81–104.

Lindblom, C. E. and Cohen, D. K. (1979) *Usable Knowledge: Social Science and Social Problem Solving* (New Haven/Conn: Yale University Press).

McKenzie, R. T. (1955) *British Political Parties* (London: Heinemann).

MacRae, D. (1976) *The Social Functions of Social Science* (New Haven/Conn: Yale University Press).

McVicar, J. (1979) *McVicar, by Himself* (London: Arrow Books).

Mann, M. (1973) *Workers on the Move* (Cambridge: CUP).

Marsh, C. M. (1982) *The Survey Method: The Contribution of Surveys to Sociological Explanation* (London: Allen & Unwin).

Martin, R. and Fryer, R. (1973) *Redundancy and Paternalist Capitalism* (London: Allen & Unwin).

Merton, R. K. (1957) *Social Theory and Social Structure* (New York: The Free Press).

Ogburn, W. F. (1964) *W. F. Ogburn on Culture and Social Change*, edited by O. D. Duncan, Jr (Chicago: University of Chicago Press).

Rex, J. (1961) *Key Problems in Sociological Theory* (London: Routledge & Kegan Paul).

Rossi, P. (1981) 'Applied Sociology', in J. F. Short, Jr (ed.), *The State of Sociology: Problems and Prospects* (Beverly Hills: Sage).

—— et al. (1978) 'The Theory and Practice of Applied Social Research', *Evaluation Quarterly*, vol. 2, pp. 171–91.

Rothschild, Lord (1971) 'The Organisation and Management of Government R & D', in *A Framework for Government Research and Development* Cmnd 4184 (London: HMSO).

Scott, R. A. and Shore, A. K. (1979) *Why Sociology Does Not Apply: A Study of the Use of Sociology in Public Policy* (New York: Elsevier).

Shils, E. (1961) 'The Calling of Sociology', in T. Parsons, E. Shils, K. D. Naegele and J. R. Pitts (eds), *Theories of Society* (New York: The Free Press) pp. 1405–48.

Sieber, S. D. (1981) *Fatal Remedies: The Ironies of Social Intervention* (New York: Plenum).

Soffer, R. N. (1982) 'Why do Disciplines Fail? The Strange Case of British Sociology', *English Historical Review*, vol. 97, pp. 762–802.

Szreter, R. (1980) 'Landmarks in the Institutionalisation of Sociology of Education in Britain', *Educational Review*, vol. 32, no. 3, pp. 293–300.

Taylor, R. (1969) 'Migration and Motivation', in J. A. Jackson (ed.), *Migration* (Cambridge: CUP) pp. 99–132.

Thomas, P. (1985) *The Aims and Outcomes of Social Policy Research* (London: Croom Helm).

Vall, M. van de (1986) 'Policy Research: An Analysis of function and Structure', in F. Heller (ed.), *The Use and Abuse of Social Science* (London: Sage) pp. 199–21.

Wedderburn, D. (1964) *White Collar Redundancy* (Cambridge: CUP).

—— (1965) *Redundancy and the Railwaymen* (Cambridge: CUP).

Weiss, C. H. (1977) 'Introduction', in C. H. Weiss (ed.), *Using Social Science Research in Public Policy-Making* (Farnborough/Hants: D. C. Heath) pp. 1–22.

*—— with Bucuvalas, M. J. (1980) *Social Science Research and Decision-Making* (New York: Columbia University Press).

Winch, D. (1972) *Economics and Policy* (London: Fontana).

Zetterberg, H. (1962) *Social Theory and Social Practice* (Totowa/NJ: Bedminster Press).

Znaniecki, F. (1940) *The Social Role of the Man of Knowledge* (New York: Columbia University Press).

8 Sociology in America
Nicholas C. Mullins*

INTRODUCTION

Sociology as an intellectual enterprise burgeoned in Western capitalistic societies beginning in the late nineteenth century. Its origins lie in a particular set of circumstances including the development of the research university as a source of legitimate knowledge and the establishment of welfare capitalism with its persistent demands for certified knowledge of the conditions of the general population. In current sociology, although the university still dominates the picture, government bureaus, business enterprises, and non-profit organisations, in America at least, utilise numerous sociologists, providing a varied social organisational base for the discipline.

[Despite the persistent demand and the varied base], sociology as a discipline in the late 1970s and 1980s is looking at a series of crises. These crises vary from changes in national policy brought about by a general swing to the political right, which has no love for most social science and denies it any legitimate place in the intellectual world, to local budget crises precipitated by declines in class enrolments at particular institutions. Attacks occur on the discipline at all organisational levels, from the national budget to particular universities.

The crisis of Western sociology seems to have caught us, its victims, by surprise, even though we have been warned of a crisis in our theory.[1] The current crisis shows itself in the destruction of the

*Illness prevented Nicholas Mullins from travelling to Noordwijk in November 1987 to present his paper in person. Instead he sent an uncompleted draft for the meeting to discuss in his absence. Subsequently he agreed to our request that he revise and expand it for publication. He died in July 1988 before completing a final draft. In particular, it was clear to us that he had not finished moving text around on his word processor, and we have had to exercise our own judgement as to the final location of some (part) paragraphs. We have also corrected obvious stylistic errors and supplied linking words of our own, always within square brackets, where necessary. We would add that Nicholas Mullins asked us, in a telephone call in May 1988, to do whatever we thought appropriate to prepare the text for publication.

C.G.A.B. and H.A.B.

institutional basis for sociology by targeted budget cuts and the abolition of programmes in a number of countries and universities, rather than in a theoretical reorganisation. Outside the range of this chapter, great cuts in social sciences and sociology particularly have occurred in Britain and the Netherlands. In the United States, an overall assault on social science research funding at the national level has been turned away, but particular catastrophes (for example, the closing of the sociology department at the University of Rochester, the abolition of the anthropology programme at Virginia Polytechnic and State University) have happened.

Comparative national studies of the sciences are not generally done, perhaps because science is believed to be universal, or because it is the operations of the components of scientific activity which have attracted the attention of scholars (Fuhrman and Snizek, 1987a). However, we can and do recognise different types of sociology. For example, Deutsch (1986), in recounting the origins of his article on the advances in the social sciences, recognised the great differences between American and European sociologies.

One explicit comparative study found that a particular European national (and linguistic) sociology was more realist whereas a comparable sample of American sociology was more individualist and nominalist. The study also found that theoretical commitment led to similar research methods choices in both countries. Fuhrman and Snizek present three reasons for the greater realism of Finnish studies: (i) a tradition of social statistics and the idea of a beneficent state; (ii) a homogeneous population and proportional representation of minority groups; and (iii) intellectual and educational traditions (Fuhrman and Snizek, 1987b, p. 215). These differences are mostly national, but the possibility of linguistic group sociology also exists. In his study of English-speaking Canadian, British and US sociologies, Menzies reports a 'strong similarity of sociological concerns in all three countries' (Menzies, 1982, p. 183). These general points would require further study of other countries and their sociologies.[2]

[Williams has indicated four of the factors any such studies would have to take into account. He writes that the theories of current sociology] 'represent a continuously emerging product of a complex interplay among (i) received ideas, (ii) social values and concerns, (iii) structural opportunities and constraints, and (iv) organizations and institutional factors' (Williams, 1976, pp. 81–2). All of these four factors are variable by country within the general pattern of Western capitalism and subject to change over time. Received ideas within each national system, for example, are derived from the formation of sociological theory in each country (France, Germany, the United States, etc.); their incorporation of different conceptual patterns and arguments leads to quite different sets of ideas developed within different institutional arrangements (Shils, 1970; Oberschall, 1972; Clark, 1973). For example, American sociology borrowed many theoretical ideas from various European sociologies and this was reinforced by the heavy influx of European émigrés in the 1930s and 1940s. [By contrast] current groups and ideas are heavily American and largely unchanged since the late 1960s (Mullins, 1983).

THE ORGANISATION OF TEACHING AND RESEARCH IN AMERICAN SOCIOLOGY

What has sociology achieved in America in the second half of the twentieth century? When one considers sociology from the perspective of European theory it is difficult to take the United States seriously. Obviously a great deal of work is done, but somehow it does not speak to the great sociological issues. Even the few quasi-European centres at Chicago, Harvard, and perhaps a few others, produce only some decent critiques but hardly major contributions to the mainstream of interpretative, structuralist, or other primarily European theoretical enterprises.[3] In these tough economic and political times for social science in many European countries, the United States begins to take on some aspects of a utopia, being a bit rural and rough like most utopias (compare Bloomington, Indiana, or Blacksburg, Virgina, as modern representatives of bucolic bliss). Foucault (1973) warns us that classifications based in utopias are sometimes so strange as to present us with difficulties in seeing how anyone could think like that. For the social scientist, the United States constitutes such a utopian place. In speaking of [sociology in America, and what it contains], we have a problem both with the specificity of our well-imagined utopia and with [coming to terms with its classifications].[4]

Many intellectual summaries of the received ideas of American sociology would provide the raw material for an analysis. It would not be adding to the sum of knowledge to try to recount them, with their cross-cutting and disputatious summaries of intellectual traditions, 'paradigms', and schools within sociology, or to extract the 'advances' that each school might assert that it makes (Eisenstadt and Curelaru, 1976; Martindale, 1960; Ritzer, 1975; Sorokin, 1928). Besides, typologies of differences in theories are non-Aristotelian and fuzzy-edged. I am at least reasonably certain that the particular mix of ideas in American sociology, although possibly a weakly contributing cause to this crisis, did not contribute significantly to the forces that came to dominate American sociology in the late 1970s and 1980s.[5]

The analysis of general American social values and concern is also a large and interesting possible exploration, but a small study will not add much to it (cf. Bellah *et al.*, 1985; Riesman, 1950; de Tocqueville, 1837). The question of the 'rightward shift', 'assertion of traditional values' and 'development of neocapitalistic individualism' is important. I just do not have much to say about it here.

I propose to concentrate on structural opportunities and constraints, and institutional opportunities, as shapers and sources of sociological theory and its achievements. The examination of the social resources of the discipline within one country continues the theme of my earlier book, which argued that (i) the increase in the number and size of graduate training and research institutions, (ii) the lack of centralised control, and (iii) the pressure on each scholar to produce some distinctive contribution, guaranteed a more diverse sociology in the 1960s than had existed before (Mullins, 1973). Pressures toward uniformity were identified as (i) common graduate training, (ii) available intellectual resources, and (iii) the social networks of peers whose evaluation tended to limit the range of alternatives.

This model makes assumptions about the social organisation of education and research in America. I would like to expand on that social organisation and select some important details. [In particular, I would emphasise that] *the educational and research system in the United States is complex and decentralised.*

First, note that *the system of post secondary education is large.* There are 3273 (2-year and 4-year) colleges, of which 456 universities offer the doctorate, and between 50 and 100 major research universities each with 10 000-plus students, 1000-plus faculty, and 100-plus acres of land (*1984–85 Fact Book*, table 106). The large number of universities provides many opportunities for teaching and research jobs for scientists of all sorts. Most of the jobs outside of the large research universities are primarily teaching, but small-scale research and writing opportunities abound.

The actual number of positions at any particular institution is dependent on the turnover of tenured faculty and the number of students taking courses in that discipline. The system of majors, required and optional courses, and distribution requirements is a complex and not-well-understood one. Each college and university has its own requirements, although the traditions of 'liberal arts', 'training for the market' and 'core curriculum' are influential in continuous small-scale, and less frequent large-scale, curriculum revisions. The number of majors in social science disciplines has been down since a high point in the early 1970s. This has restricted opportunities for new PhDs in the social sciences in general.

Second, note that *the control of the system of post secondary education is decentralised and lacks co-ordination.* The United States national government directly controls only about ten colleges and universities. Individual state systems are very large and include some major research universities (for example, the University of California, Berkeley, or the University of Michigan). Privately owned and operated colleges include Harvard University and Stanford University. Some of the private schools are owned by religious denominations, including Boston College and Notre Dame. One conclusion is that most social trends and value-changes will affect only part of the system at a time, with significant pockets resisting. For example, the trend to federal support of research is still not universally accepted. (Some religious fundamentalist schools have rejected any federal funding.)

Control of research funding is also decentralised. Although dominated by federal government resources, control of any science is shared among many different government agencies with only loose co-ordination. At least thirteen departments (with perhaps 83 different programmes), plus industry, states, and foundations, fund programmes in sociology.[6]

Not only universities and the research funding but also local departments of sociology are decentralised. American departments of sociology tend to be led by elected department chairs. The rotating chair system keeps individuals from long-term dominance of departments. There are often divisions within departments over recruitment, programmes, and personnel. These fights can be based on specialisations or on larger political issues. The American analytic research style supports a more apolitical sociology. Analytic style sociology also attracts research funding. Funding for research develops positions for students and other research team members. Not every professor has a research institute, and those without external funding have little support for their research activities. Both hermeneutic and ideological schools have less support. Other sources of external backing are local self help, social welfare, and the religious activist tradition.

THE INSTITUTIONAL CRISIS IN AMERICAN SOCIOLOGY

The crisis felt and discussed in American sociology is due to the reduced opportunities for, and increased structural constraints on, sociology. Its first manifestation was in the decline in enrolments for sociology courses and the concomitant reduction in teaching positions at a time when an increasing number of sociology PhDs were searching for such positions. At least 110 universities in the USA offer the PhD in sociology (ASA *Guide to Graduate Departments of Sociology*, 1985). Similar crises by slow attrition hit many other fields of graduate study, due to declining numbers in the universities.

[By contrast, the second manifestation of the crisis], the crisis in research funding, was specific to the social sciences. When the United States, like some European countries, had a right-wing government with a strong antisocial science bias, the outcome for sociology was buffered by the social structure of social science research. [Two factors were important here: the diverse sources of public funding for social science research which made their tight co-ordination difficult, and the new-found capacity which social scientists displayed for fighting back.]

In 1981, President Reagan's first budget proposed that all social science funding in the National Science Foundation be cut, first in half for fiscal year 1982, and then to zero for subsequent years. The social and behavioural sciences are supported by thirteen cabinet-level departments and eighteen independent agencies, according to data collected by the National Science Foundation. [There were many in these departments and agencies who were happy to see the 1982 budget proposal defeated or softened.] In response, social scientists and their social science associations founded the Consortium of Social Sciences Associations. COSSA is now funded by social science associations but was orginally a movement funded by individual contributions. The peculiarities of American tax law prevent the associations themselves from engaging in political lobbying. Dr Roberta B. Miller was the first executive director of COSSA and was a very effective lobbyist.[7] Her lobbying activities were initially supported by individual social scientists.

A support coalition, including congressmen and natural scientists, was developed between February and May, and beat back efforts to cut social science. This story has not been told in detail and I do not have the historical resources to do it. It appears from the outside that traditional lobbying of congressional staff and congressmen was very important. Each congressman was informed what social science research contributes to each locality which has a university. All congressmen were told what social science information contributes to the governability of the country in areas such as the census, housing, social welfare, economic policy, etc.

Supporters included middle-level bureaucrats in government as well as Congressional staff who use social science information. I believe that this is an important possible difference between American and other sociologies. The United States has developed social science experts from within the university system, who were also instrumental in the establishment of the social sciences outside the university. The social sciences have common origins 'in the transformation of political economy into economics, political science, and sociology in an America undergoing rapid industrialization . . . extra-university service by leading practitioners decisively shaped the intellectual limits of these disciplines and those of the professorate-at-large' (Silva and Slaughter, 1984, p. 4). In the US case, leading academics, working through their professional and scientific associations, and using the developing private foundations as sources of resources, demonstrated the uses of social knowledge. In these activities the social science expert had an important hand in shaping the modern American university. I would expect developments in other countries to vary according to differences in the development of the social science expert as well as historical factors.

In spite of these efforts, funding for the Division of Social and Economic Sciences of the National Science Foundation declined from $25.1 million to $17.56 million between fiscal years 1981 and 1982. The number of awards went from 489 to 432 and the average grant size was smaller (National Science Foundation, *Annual Report 1982*, 1983, p. 27). Social science programmes within the National Institute of Mental Health were also targeted to be reduced to zero and were cut severely.

[By mid-decade, the public funding of social science research had stabilised. Thus] there were few surprises in the President's budget proposals for 1986. Most programmes were in steady-state, receiving limited increases, while a few research areas continued to face annual proposals for reductions. Fewer still were targeted for substantial budget increases. Highlights of the funding situation were an increase in mental health research and the flat funding of education research. In addition, National Science Foundation social science programmes were in good shape, but the sociology programme had shifted towards the funding of data collection, particularly for large data bases, rather than analysis (Holt, Whitney and Garduque, 1985).

Neither of these two largest federal fund sources for academic social science has returned to 1981 funding levels. [Nor have some other programmes cut at that time. Even so, the situation today is far removed from the zero funding proposed in 1981.] The social sciences [have proved to be] much more embedded in the federal government structure than those who sought to eliminate them believed. Although damage has been done, social science funding continues, thanks to the good fight it has put up and to unexpected support.

ACHIEVEMENTS AND THE MARKET

[Differences in the social organisation of sociology yield variations in what counts as achievement.] Across all sciences and nations [Bryant and Becker suggest in their Introduction to the present volume], achievements are works of quality that are important in the emergence or development of a particular mode of inquiry, methodology or specialty including exemplary empirical researches. Achievements have a presence which cannot be ignored and they help others to orient their work. But we need to be careful when speaking of achievements in American sociology because we are talking of a strange land with strange ideas of what 'quality' or 'presence' are.

Alex Inkeles (1983) accidentally captured a great deal of American thinking on the subject of advances in his critique of an earlier and more general effort to summarise advances in the social sciences (Deutsch, Platt and Senghaas, 1971 – hereafter DPS). Inkeles first finds some things in the DPS list that he does not want to consider. He wishes to exclude developments that are primarily political and organisational innovations. Second, and most important, he claims that (i) a great deal that has been done in American sociology does not fit under the classification of achievements used by DPS; (ii) the DPS list of innovations is primarily conceptual; and (iii) much of what goes on in American sociology is cumulative progress. Inkeles wishes to consider gradual, nonconceptual, and methodological advances in sociology. He finds the DPS list too conceptual, and oriented to first statements of ideas rather than to their working-out. Interestingly, almost all the gradual, conceptual advances he finds in sociology are American.[8] The style of American sociology would seem to lend itself to the production of these gradual advances rather than to the large conceptual advances which dominate the DPS list.

Sociology in the United States has a market atmosphere. In the market of American academic life, sociology is a legitimate participant not only within the university but in interaction with other aspects of society. The large and high-quality institutions which have major sociology departments, including Columbia, Michigan, Wisconsin, Berkely, and Chicago, have large survey research organisations which do significant quantities of contract research for organisations in private industry, non-profit organisations and governments (both state and national). These survey centres are the training grounds for many students and provide the economic support for the activity of all parts of the departments of sociology. The development of such a market is an achievement of American sociology. The use of sociology in the media, albeit sometimes with ludicrous effects, is another success. *USA Today*, a national newspaper, uses sociology regularly for its 'facts for today' section. The latest discussions of national competitiveness find that an overdependence on market research, a sociology by-product, inhibits American corporations. Finally, within academia, the development of organisational behaviour, urban studies, family and child development, and social studies of science, all contain aspects of sociology in their intellectual background. The ability to legitimate intellectual offspring would seem to speak to the legitimation of the parent.

The achievements of American sociology include the establishment of a series of data bases which permit the gradual working-out of ideas through empirical methods. For example, the availability of rich census data has permitted demography to develop into almost a separate discipline. Crime statistics have led to criminology. Continuing status attainment and education data from several sources have not established a separate area, but their analysis has generated a major industry.

Project-oriented support rather than programme or institutional support encourages short-term reportable results which, when published, can be added to by others as well as by the original group. This type of support is most commonly available in America, and is much less available, although not totally unknown, in applied settings elsewhere.

[It is also of significance that] the American Court system, with its dependence on case law, has slowly acquired a number of areas, including school integration cases, where social science findings are becoming important parts of the law. Cases in other areas of the law refer to sociological findings, although the introduction of suitable information seems to depend on well-read lawyers and judges, rather than any formal connection.

Is American sociology shaped by the demands of the census and the criminal justice system for certain types of data analysis? The answer is that some academic programmes have a primary function to turn out people and reports for one or another of these services. Thus many research careers are shaped by the changes in those demands over time. However, the variety of potential sources and their lack of co-ordination appear to the formal eye of the economist as a market rather than as a hierarchy. There are many providers of funds (buyers), and many providers of information (sellers). The analysis of the market situation needs much elaboration (Williamson, 1975). Oligopolies may effect significant sections of research work. I see few true monopoly situations of only one buyer or one seller. If one existed I would expect a hierarchy of power around it. A particularly pernicious system would be a monopoly buyer in a short-term project-based system. One line for further research would be to see if the market and project systems go together in other areas.

As is always the case with social discoveries, they have unanticipated consequences. The relative weakness of the American academic department versus its senior and externally funded professors has been noted. The rise and fall of research institutions at a very high rate is another. Research support on institutional or programme features would have very different dynamics. A short-term project market shares some dynamics with a day labour market (Liebow, 1967). Institutional or programme-based systems would be very different as markets. The international comparison of these systems needs to be done with more concern for the type of research work being conducted in each of the types of system.

As in most market systems, not every taste is served. It is easier to get quantitative policy-based research funded than a long-term theoretic project. Theorists have learned to do without project funding by becoming primarily teachers. Theory textbooks required at both graduate and undergraduate levels provide a dazzling reward system. Theorists do critiques of other theorists too. What is lost is originality. It would be interesting to see what would result from a request for a couple of theory proposals. The alternative to the theory withdrawal is the current methodology emphasis in the journals and among younger scholars.

How does American sociology succeed? On average, most research projects fail. The despair that Inkeles points to – that all we will do is little pieces of work with no connection to one another – is real. Some areas are particularly desperate; [yet American sociology has succeeded well enough to withstand the worst of recent assaults upon it].

CONCLUSION

Achievements in sociology occur in national contexts. There is even some problem about the type of sociology one selects to investigate. If, as Bryant and Becker suggest, we connect the character and content of sociology to the external environment in which sociology operates – government, business, media, popular support; teaching; public and private funding of research – the meaning of achievement includes the development of opportunities for sociology to survive under extreme conditions. This is a test which American sociology has recently passed.

Some things about American sociology succeed. And some things do not. It produces large quantities of reports, which, when they embed theory, are so multivariate that the majority of the discipline sees them as simply descriptive or magical.[9] We continue to borrow many significant conceptual ideas from a system based on a different set of opportunities and commitments – the European. The social system of sociology seems to be sufficient to account for these differences. Between two such different systems, it would be hard to account for achievements in the same way. We have many experimental approaches, each with a high degree of risk, but some of them work (cf. Rosenberg and Birdzell, 1986).

This large, sloppy, system has been modified by the crises of the 1980s, but its very diversity and size will enable it to continue. The comparative study of national sociologies under comparable pressures would be an important and most interesting future study.

Notes

1. Gouldner (1970) saw the loss of the programmatic focus of Western sociology. He also ascribed the loss to changes in values and organisational structures. He was overly optimistic about those changes and did not see the direct challenge to the existence of the discipline.
2. Van de Vall and Leeuw (1987) do an interesting but not comparable study on the Netherlands.
3. Even the recovery of Parsons seems curiously to be a European enterprise.

4. When I first read Foucault's *The Order of Things* I laughed at his description of the Chinese encyclopaedia which, according to Borges, divided all animals into strange categories. Borges's classifications included such things as '(a) belonging to the Emperor, (b) embalmed, (c) tame, (d) sucking pigs, (e) sirens, (f) fabulous, (g) stray dogs, (h) included in the present classification, (i) frenzied, (j) innumerable, (k) drawn with a very fine camel hair brush, (l) et cetera, (m) having just broken the water bottle, (n) that from a long way off look like flies'. Foucault draws the inspiration for his book from the 'stark impossibility of thinking *that*' (Foucault, 1973, p. xix).

5. This argument needs to be developed in more detail. I will note only that 'sociology' was not specially targeted in this crisis. There was a general problem with the social sciences. This would suggest that any feedback from the subject-matter was very general indeed.

6. Quarles (1986, pp. 71–9) lists this number of different programmes. For each programme, COSSA lists: a contact person, a programme description, a budget, an application and review process description, a description of the funding mechanism, and a short list of examples of titles of previously funded projects.

7. See Miller (1987). Dr Miller has since gone on to be Director of the Division of Social and Economic Sciences for the National Science Foundation.

8. A large number of the discoveries in the classic mode he finds are the product of his own Columbia and Chicago group of Inkeles, Rossi, Goode, Lipset and Bendix. These are intended as examples, but they are telling, in that work like his own looms large in his view of the field, as it does for all of us.

9. On the Clark's law assumption that any sufficiently advanced technology is indistinguishable from magic.

References

Bellah, R. N., Madsen, R., Sullivan, W. M. Swindler, A. and Tipton, S. M. (1975) *Habits of the Heart: Individualism and Commitment in American Life* (New York: Harper & Row).

Clark, T. (1973) *Prophets and Patrons: The French University and the Emergence of the Social Sciences* (Cambridge: Harvard University Press).

Deutsch, K. W. (1986) 'What Do We Mean by Advances in the Social Sciences?', in Deutsch, Markowits and Platt (eds) (1986).

*—— , Markowits, A. S. and Platt, J. R. (1986) *Advances in the Social Sciences 1900–1980: What, Who, Where, How?* (Cambridge/Mass: Abt Books).

—— , Platt J. and Senghaas, D. (1971) 'Major Advances in the Social Sciences Since 1900: An Analysis of Conditions and Creativity', *Science*, no. 171, pp. 450–59; reprinted as Appendix to Deutsch *et al.* (1986).

Eisenstadt, S. N. and Curelaru, M. (1976) *The Form of Sociology: Paradigms and Crises* (New York: Wiley).

Foucault, M. (1973) *The Order of Things: An Archeology of the Human Sciences* (New York: Vantage Books).

Fuhrman, E. and Snizek, W. (1987a) 'Introduction: Comparative/ Historical Sociology of Science', *Sociological Inquiry*, vol. 57, pp. 117–19.

—— (1987b) 'Finnish and American Sociology: A Cross-Cultural Comparison', *Sociological Inquiry*, vol. 57, pp. 204–21.

Gouldner, A. W. (1970) *The Coming Crisis of Western Sociology* (New York: Equinox).

Holt, V. Whitney, D. D. and Garduque, L. (1985) 'Social and Behavioural Research in the FY1986 Budget', in Intersociety Working Group, *AAAS Report X: Research and Development, FY 1986* (Washington: American Association for the Advancement of Science).

*Inkeles, A. (1983) 'The Sociological Contribution to Advance in the Social Sciences', *Social Science Journal*, vol. 20, pp. 27–44; reprinted in Deutsch *et al.* (eds) (1986) pp. 13–31.

Liebow, E. (1967) *Tally's Corner* (Boston: Little, Brown).

Martindale, D. (1960) *The Nature and Types of Sociological Theory* (Boston: Houghton Mifflin).

Menzies, K. (1982) *Sociological Theories in Use* (London: Routledge & Kegan Paul).

Miller, R. M. (1987) Social Science Under Siege: The Political Response 1981–84', in M. Bulmer (ed.), *Social Science Research and Government: Comparative Essays on Britain and the United States* (Cambridge: CUP).

*Mullins, N. C. (1973) *Theories and Theory Groups in Contemporary American Sociology* (New York: Harper & Row).

—— (1983) 'Theory and Theory Groups Revisited', *Sociological Theory*, vol. 1, pp. 319–37.

National Science Foundation (1983) *Annual Report 1982* (Washington: NSF 83–1).

Oberschall, A. (ed.) (1972) *The Establishment of Empirical Sociology* (New York: Harper & Row).

Quarles, S. D. (ed.) (1986) *Guide to Federal Funding for Social Scientists* (New York: Russell Sage Foundation); prepared for COSSA.

Riesman, D. (1950) *The Lonely Crowd: A Study of the Changing American Character* (New Haven: Yale University Press).

Ritzer, G. (1975) *Sociology: A Multiple Paradigm Science* (Boston: Allyn & Bacon).

Rosenberg, N. and Birdzell, Jr. L. E. (1986) *How the West Grew Rich: The Economic Transformation of the Industrial World* (New York: Basic Books).

Shils, E. (1970) 'Tradition, Ecology, and Institution in the History of Sociology', *Daedalus*, vol. 99, pp. 760–825.

Silva, E. T. and Slaughter, S. A. (1984) *Serving Power: The Making of the Academic Social Science Expert* (Westport/Conn: Greenwood).

Sorokin, P. (1928) *Contemporary Sociological Theories* (New York: Harper & Row).

Tocqueville, A. de (1837) *Democracy in America* (New York: Anchor, 1969).

Vall, M. van de and Leeuw, F. L. (1987) 'Unity and Diversity: Sociology in the Netherlands', *Sociological Inquiry*, vol. 57, pp. 183–203.

Williams, Jr., R. M. (1976) 'Sociology in America: The Experience of Two

Centuries', in C. M. Bonjean, L. Schneider and R. Lineberry *Social Science in America: The First Two Hundred Years* (Austin: University of Texas Press).

Williamson, O. (1975) *Markets and Hierarchies* (New York: Free Press).

9 Sociology in Britain: A Going Concern
John Eldridge

There is no question mark in the title of this chapter, though some might think there should be. I want to reflect on some of the issues, problems and accomplishments that sociology in Britain manifests. What follows is not from the standpoint of a spectator but of a participant.

In his thoughtful and affectionate recollection of his time at LSE in the early 1950s, 'Provincials and Professionals: The Post-War Sociologists', A. H. Halsey mentions, in addition to himself, twelve people who in their various ways went on to play a significant part in post-war British sociology, several of them becoming professors of sociology in English universities and one a Director of the LSE. They were: J. A. Banks, Olive Banks, Michael Banton, Basil Bernstein, Percy Cohen, Norman Dennis, Ralf Dahrendorf, David Lockwood, Cyril Smith, J. H. Smith, Asher Tropp and John Westergaard (Halsey, 1985). By any account that is a significant cohort and in due season gave rise to a range of work in class and stratification, education, socio-linquistics, industry, youth and community studies, ethnic relations and social theory. It is important to remember this, not least when we sometimes are invited to believe that it is only in the 1980s that empirical, policy-relevant research in sociology has started to be taken seriously.

This generation was subject to a variety of immediate influences at LSE including T. H. Marshall, R. H. Tawney, David Glass, Karl Popper, Edward Shils and (in Halsey's view to a lesser extent) Morris Ginsberg. One would not expect them to be theoretically un-sophisticated or methodologically unskilled in such a climate and Halsey is surely right to claim that their work has provided a significant addition to knowledge of the changing social structure of Britain. It was certainly more than a simple response to the Fabian socialism which inspired the founders of LSE. 'In its most fundamental sense,' writes Halsey, 'it was the assimilation of international sociology and its application to the understanding of British society' (pp. 161–2). At the end of his essay Halsey refers to the break-up of this activity at LSE as people moved into other academic positions and the sociology department there became somewhat fragmented and lost its impetus. But in the provinces – Leeds, Leicester, Birmingham, Manchester and Liverpool – there was another story to tell. From the Liverpool Department, for example, came a series of empirical monographs mainly in the fields of industrial and urban sociology. They explored such questions as the impact of technical change on industrial relations, crime in the city, and the effect of new housing developments on social and community relations, and were associated with names such as J. A. Banks, Olive Banks, J. B. Mays, W. H. Scott, Enid Mumford, Joan Woodward and Tom Lupton in a department headed by T. S. Simey (Later Lord Simey).

John Rex, who worked first at Leeds and later at Birmingham during this period, contributed to theoretical discussion with his *Key Problems of Sociological Theory* (1961). This was the first book to deal in such an explicit way with sociological theory in Britain for a very long time (some might even say since Herbert Spencer), and was particularly noticeable for its discussion of Weber and for introducing students to the social action perspective and ideal-type analysis. He went on to make substantive contributions to the field of race relations within a neo-Weberian conflict perspective. With Robert Moore he wrote *Race, Community and Conflict* (1967), a study of Sparkbrook in Birmingham. This drew upon the Weberian concepts of life-chances and market situation in its exploration of the housing situation for immigrants in Sparkbrook. But it also reflected other influences – Park and Wirth on the city, Marshall on citizenship and Myrdal on race. Rex explicitly endorses Myrdal's position on the relationship between social science and questions of value. The Sparkbrook study can fairly be regarded as a seminal contribution to the study of race relations in Britain. Rex did not confine himself to the British scene, as reference to *Race Relations in Sociological Theory* (1970) and *Race, Colonialism and the City* (1973) makes plain. The second of these is dedicated to 'Nelson Mandela and all of those of my fellow countrymen who lie in gaol'. We are thus sharply reminded that ethical neutrality in sociology is not the same as moral indifference. The point is strongly made at the beginning of *Race Relations in Sociological Theory*:

> The problem of race and racism challenges the conscience of the sociologist in the same way as the problem of nuclear weapons challenges that of the nuclear physicist. This is not to say that sociology can dictate to men and nations how they should behave to

one another any more than the nuclear physicist has some special competence to advise the American President whether or not he should drop the atom bomb on the Japanese. But it is to say that insofar as whole populations have been systematically discriminated against, exploited and even exterminated, the sociologist might legitimately be asked to lay the causes of these events bare. (Rex, 1973, p. 1)

Race and ethnic relations has continued to be an important area of sociological study. Its national and international dimensions are well represented in the more recent work of Cohen (1987) and Miles (1987). Some of this naturally engages with work in the sociology of development and underdevelopment, of which Peter Worsley's *The Three Worlds* (1984) stands as an impressive work of synthesis and originality. His purpose is clearly stated:

My main hope is that I may have thrown some theoretical light on ethnicity and nationalism and their relationship to class, because of the inadequacy of theorising about these important forms of social life, particularly in Marxist materialism, which has had such dire consequences. (pp. xii–xiii)

Most of Worsley's career was spent at Manchester, and this, together with his earlier and important works (1964 and 1968), a productive blend of sociology and social anthropology, reminds us of another provincial strand to which Halsey had alluded.

I want now to turn to the interesting case of Leicester and its contribution to the development of sociology in Britain, where I have some personal experience to draw upon. I was a student at Leicester University from 1954 to 1959. When I went there, Leicester was still a satellite of London University, in that we did external London degrees. The sociology teaching staff consisted of Ilya Neustadt and Norbert Elias, with occasional help from outside – notably, for a short but memorable period, from Ernest Gellner. There is something remarkable and significant about the growth of the sociology department at Leicester, from such a small nucleus to one which, during the 1960s and 70s, contained between twenty and thirty staff. In 1982, Giddens and Mackenzie (both former Leicester people) edited *Social Class and the Division of Labour: Essays in Honour of Ilya Neustadt*. Other former students and colleagues of Neustadt's from Leicester who contributed were: Sheila Allen, Richard Brown, John

Goldthorpe, Paul Hirst, Geoffrey Ingham, Terry Johnson, Ali Rattansi, Graeme Salaman, Richard Scase and John Scott. This list in itself represents a considerable spread of talent and influence in British sociology. When I add that the other contributors, T. H. Marshall, Tom Bottomore, Ely Chinoy and David Lockwood, were all long-standing friends and supporters of Leicester's activity, something of the respect with which Neustadt was held is reflected in the volume. And if we were to add to the list former students such as Bryan Wilson, Kenneth Thompson, Roy King, Chris Bryant and Bert Moorhouse, we can see that Leicester was indeed a very important seedbed for the development of the subject in Britain.

In his foreword to *Social Class and the Division of Labour*, T. H. Marshall drew particular attention to Neustadt's merits as a teacher. It was no accident that the title of his inaugural lecture was 'Teaching Sociology'. He was especially stimulating in small group discussions with, as Marshall put it, his 'relentless questioning and Socratic probing'. His enthusiasm for and joy in his subject were contagious and left their imprint on large numbers of students, not only those who were to enter the profession.

Neustadt, who went to Leicester in 1949, was joined three years later by Norbert Elias. Both were refugees from Europe and had spent some time at LSE before moving to Leicester, and both these cosmopolitan men brought with them their wide and scholarly knowledge of the European tradition in social thought. The story of the impact of Elias's *The Civilising Process* on an English-speaking readership has been told before, but it is extraordinary how a book first published in 1939 and which appeared in English translation in 1978 (vol. 1) and 1982 (vol. 2) has been received with such enthusiasm – some indeed are still catching up with the fact that it is much more than a history of manners and actually offers us a challenging theory of state formation. Elias received a *Festschrift* on his eightieth birthday – *Human Figurations: Essays for Norbert Elias* (Gleichman *et al.*, 1977); more remarkable is the fact that the journal *Theory, Culture and Society* devoted a double number (vol. 4, 1987, nos 2–3) to Elias on his ninetieth birthday, to which Elias himself contributed three articles. This is something to celebrate and take pleasure in.

I would refer the reader to Richard Brown's piece in *Theory, Culture and Society* (1987) – 'Norbert Elias in Leicester: Some Recollections'. Brown rightly reminds us how much writing Elias did in his Leicester period, though much of it did not see the light of day until much later, except of course in lectures and seminars, where his ideas were much discussed. One of the few papers of his that was published at that time was 'Problems of Involvement and Detachment', which appeared in the *British Journal of Sociology* in 1956. A more extended version of that paper has now been republished in *Involvement and Detachment* (Elias, 1987b) by Blackwell, together with other essays. This represents a subtle and impressive attempt to consider the problem of objectivity in social science and the similarities and differences between the natural and social sciences. The practical importance of theory, even if it appears to be divorced from immediate action, is clearly expressed at the end of that essay.

> How far is it possible under present conditions for groups of scientific specialists to raise the standards of autonomy and adequacy in thinking about social events, and to impose upon themselves the discipline of greater detachment, only experience can show. Nor can one know in advance whether or not the menace which human groups on many levels constitute for each other is still too great for them to be able to bear, and to act upon, an overall picture of themselves which is less coloured by wishes and fears and more consistently formed in cross-fertilisation with dispassionate observation of details. And yet how else can one break the hold of the vicious circle in which high affectivity of ideas and low ability to control dangers coming from people to people reinforce our work (Elias, 1987, p. 34).

Elias, in various ways, enunciates the view that sociologists can obtain knowledge that is reality congruent. This is well expressed, for example, in *What is Sociology?*

> If a sociological theory of knowledge is to be based not on the postulation of scientific utopias but on the investigation of sciences as observable social processes, then it must focus on the nature of the cognitive processes in the course of which first a few, then more and better organised groups of people, succeed in bringing human knowledge and thought into ever closer agreement with an ever more comprehensible range of observable data. (Elias, 1978, p. 53)

For Elias this entailed a teaching programme that was comparative in the manner of a Weber or a Hobhouse and which, by virtue of a historical dimension, was also developmental in its orientation – using that term not in a unilinear evolutionary sense, or in any teleological manner, but pointing nonetheless to real processes taking place in actual societies (cf. Brown, 1987).

One more reference to Elias must suffice, which I will use for bridging purposes. This is to his essay, 'The Retreat of Sociologists into the Present' (1987a). He argues that, unlike Marx and Weber, who used comparative and historical analysis to illuminate the problems of their own time, sociologists since the Second World War have tended to focus on short-term problems in a short time perspective rather than to give serious attention to long-term social processes.

Some qualification of this point may be made, thinking particularly of the British context of sociological work with which this chapter is concerned. There is, after all, evidence of work which does operate with wider time perspectives and comparative horizons. T. H. Marshall's *Citizenship and Social Class*, first delivered as a series of Cambridge lectures by a scholar who was originally a historian, was published as long ago as 1950. It has rightly been pointed out in a recent article by Michael Mann that the thesis only references Britain in its discussion of the development of civil, political and social aspects of citizenship, and he is, I think, correct to caution sociologists against too easy and Anglophile extrapolation to other societies. His own paper, 'Ruling Class Strategies and Citizenship' (Mann, 1987b), provides a valuable corrective when he suggests that we should distinguish between five types of regime strategies which have different implications for citizenship – liberalism, reformism, authoritarian monarchy, fascism, and authoritarian socialism. Mann uses his comparative approach to criticise what he regards as the over-simplistic and over-optimistic picture of citizenship implied in Marshall's model and also to advance his own view of the importance of geo-political factors. Again, perhaps this leads us to consider the relevance of sociology from a perspective that is not simply about short-term problem-solving. Mann's article concludes:

> Warfare at the highest level would now destroy society. Therefore, the war-assisted pattern of change dominant in the first half of the century cannot be repeated. The emergence of the superpowers and of nuclear weapons both indicate that the future of citizenship will be different from its past. Our assessment of its prospects must combine domestic with geo-political analysis. (Mann, 1987b, p. 352)

Mann has of course been involved in an extremely ambitious

project, with a wide remit. The first volume of his *The Sources of Social Power* is subtitled *A History of Power from the Beginning to AD 1760*. Volume 2 will bring his study up to the present and volume 3 is intended to present the theoretical conclusions of the whole work. Working with the concept of societies as organised power networks he seeks to show that a history of power will seek to identify and explain the inter-relations between the four sources of social power: ideological, economic, military, and political. Thus he writes:

> The four sources of social power offer alternative organisational means of social control. In various times and places each has offered enhanced capacity for organisation that has enabled the form of its organisation to dictate for a time the form of societies at large. My history of social power rests on measuring sociospatial capacity for organisation and explaining its development. (Mann, 1987a, p. 3)

The critical appraisals of Mann's work have yet to be fully assembled. It remains to be seen, for example, whether he will seek to relate his theorising on social power to Elias, whose work does not appear to be explicitly discussed in volume 1. It is interesting to notice that in another recent publication by a geographer, Robert S. Dodgshon's *The European Past: Social Evolution and Spatial Order* (1987), considerable attention is paid to Elias and other sociologists, which prompts me to observe, if only in passing, that the connections between geography and sociology have come very much into focus in the last few years. The Marxist perspective of David Harvey was one contributing factor, but on the sociologists' side, theoreticians such as Giddens (1984) have worked through the implications of spatial order and social space for the explanation of social change. Incidentally, whilst Giddens can be cited as taking the view that sociology is that branch of social science which focuses particularly on the 'advanced' or modern societies, this particularity does not denote exclusiveness. The most notable example of his own readiness to work on a wider canvas is *The Nation-State and Violence* (1985). Indeed, I think this is a book which can profitably be read alongside Mann (1987a). Giddens's wide-ranging study is ultimately concerned with teasing out what is different about our present situation and with the meaning of modernity. The theoretical and practical significance of this is nicely encapsulated in his contention that:

> There are four 'institutional clusterings' associated with modernity:

heightened surveillance, capitalistic enterprise, industrial production and the consolidation of centralised control of the means of
violence. None is wholly reducible to any of the others. A concern
with the consequences of each moves critical theory away from its
concentration upon the transcendence of capitalism by socialism as
the sole objective of future social transformations. (Giddens, 1985,
p. 5)

There is, then, a recognition of the usefulness for sociology of the
longer view. A few more examples must suffice, which I select as
indicative of fruitful accomplishments. Poggi's *The Development of the
Modern State* (1978) contains many insights and challenges the
adequacy of general theories of the state. His discussion of what he
calls the 'type switch' from feudalism to the *Ständestaat* is particularly
illuminating and can, I think, be helpfully read alongside his percep-
tive commentary on Weber's *Protestant Ethic*, namely, *Calvinism and
the Capitalist Spirit* (Poggi, 1983). The causes and consequences of the
rise of the west is no less a theme in John Hall's *Powers and Liberties*
(1985). It is somewhat unnerving to see such a master theme dealt with
in a mere 272 pages, but we have Ernest Gellner's word for it that the
book is a brilliant and decisive contribution to the re-thinking of the
history of human society. Hall's preface makes interesting reading. He
reveals that as a history undergraduate at Oxford he noted that
'Oxbridge' historians were prone to dismiss, out of hand, analyses that
treated of social structures. Barrington Moore's *Social Origins of
Dictatorship and Democracy* (1969) was therefore something of a
turning-point for Hall and took him back to the great classical
sociologists. And yet, turning to modern sociology he found it a
disappointment:

> It was a desert of arid concept-chopping where some sort of
> multiplier ruled; among the various theoretical recipes to our ills and
> supposedly as guides to social reality were ethnomethodology,
> structuralism, structuralist Marxism, hermeneutics, phenomen-
> ology, functionalism, exchange theory, phenomenological
> Marxism, hermeneutics plus Marxism, linguistic philosophy,
> network analysis, and so on, and so on. Poincáre's observation, that
> natural scientists discuss their results, social scientists their methods,
> seemed horribly true. This theoretical extravagance scarcely ad-
> vanced the subject at all for the banal but forceful reason that
> theories *can* only develop in the process of trying to explain reality.
> (Hall, 1985, pp. 1–2)

With the thrust of this I have much sympathy, although I think it is an overstatement of what has been happening in the British context at least.

Gellner's work, of course, is a continuing delight, unless one happens to be on the receiving end of his barbed and provocative attacks, as many have over the years – Wittgenstein and his followers, Winchean idealists, and ethnomethodologists, assorted Marxists and relativists and even the later Popper. Gellner himself has written widely, often in telling essay form, not only on social philosophy but ethnographical social anthropology, as well as broad sociological concerns with the nature and significance of social change. Important examples of the last-named are *Thought and Change* (1964), *Legitimation of Belief* (1974) and *Nations and Nationalism* (1983). Here I simply draw attention to his preoccupation with the significance of the scientific revolution – in terms of its cognitive power and therefore as a challenge to unlimited relativism, and the practical consequences of the scientific revolution – in terms of the possibilities of control over nature. It is indeed this relationship between thought and change that leads Gellner to point out the significance of Weber's work – its discussion of rationality and disenchantment sociologises Kant by putting the capacity for particular kinds of cognitive achievement into a distinctive social and historical context. To unpack that would demand at least an extended essay in its own right.

Historical Sociology (1982) was Philip Abrams's last book, and in a series of essays he sought, as he put it, to celebrate the meaninglessness of the separation of history from sociology. Two of his former colleagues, Philip Corrigan and Derek Sayer, in their book *The Great Arch: English State Formation as Cultural Revolution* (1985), have acted on this premise. The study is extremely wide-ranging. They offer a narrative account stretching from the eleventh to the nineteenth century, with a distinctive argument that state formation is itself a cultural revolution. It is worth recording that a leading historian of English history, G. E. Aylmer, in his foreword to the book, remarks:

This is a work of courage, scope and immense thoroughness. Moreover, the argument is presented lucidly and cogently, while the difficulties and limitations of the evidence are seldom if ever concealed or glossed over. The sheer quantity of material assimilated compels respect (p. viii).

That kind of informed judgement speaks well of the rapprochement which now exists between the practice of history and sociology in Britain. As Aylmer also makes clear, the intellectual debts of the authors include Marx, Weber, Durkheim, Christopher Hill, E. P. Thompson, Raymond Williams, Philip Abrams, Norbert Elias and Michel Foucault. These figures on the intellectual landscape do, I think, give a good representation of the influences that impinge on the practice of historical sociology in Britain.

I want now to shift focus and discuss some of the institutional elements in the development of post-war British sociology and to comment on the changing political context. Whatever reservations there may have been about the subject in Oxbridge circles (though we were not without friends there), sociology was written into the growth and development of the university sector during the 1960s and, indeed, the polytechnic sector as well. Those of us who went into the 'greenfield' new universities, for example, found a situation open with possibilities.

It was a period of intellectual ferment and excitement – although, given the administrative and practical problems of getting new teaching courses off the ground, it was not that easy to make space for research. I think that the nature of this ferment can be variously illustrated. For example, York became the home base of the deviancy symposium – initiated by young academics including Laurie Taylor, Stan Cohen and Jock Young. It emerged partly in response to what was felt to be an inadequate positivist orthodoxy in criminology at Cambridge. It contained within it elements that focused on neo-Marxism, others that emphasised the importance of symbolic inter-ationism and were much impressed by Becker's labelling perspective and Matza's views on delinquency and drift. This was mixed with a practical, humanistic concern for the casualties of the welfare state and the long-term imprisoned and was to have some influence on the teaching and practice of social work as well as the sociology of deviance. The interest in reaching a wide public was well reflected in the still available *Images of Deviance* (1971) edited by Stan Cohen, and in Cohen and Taylor's *Long-Term Imprisonment* (1972). When Ian Taylor, Paul Walton and Jock Young published *The New Criminology* (1973), complete with a laudatory foreword by Alvin Gouldner, this represented a codification from a neo-Marxist perspective of the intellectual concerns of what was later to be known as the National Deviancy Conference. But I think the most notable production of that period was Stan Cohen's *Folk Devils and Moral Panics* (1973), which continues to be re-published. Cohen himself has offered important critiques of the work and activities of the deviancy symposium, but it is out of such reflections that he has been able to write such a fine book as *Visions of Social Control* (1985).

But, of course, there was not only a new sociology of deviance, but a new sociology of education, of industry, of science, of urbanism, of development; there was even, however ironically intended, Giddens's *New Rules of Sociological Method* (1976). This emphasis on newness, while it signified different things to different people and groups, is, I think, worth bearing in mind. Though at times it must have looked like an anarchistic notion of letting a thousand flowers bloom in a rather eclectic way, at other times it seemed to represent a great deal of intellectual in-fighting, which may have seemed important to the participants and absorbed a great deal of energy, but mystified the spectators. So we were indeed surrounded by debates about theoretical perspectives – systems theory, social action theory, symbolic interaction and labelling theory, ethnomethodology, neo-Marxism, neo-Weberianism and the rest. Once we have discounted for fads and fashions, which can give a faded look to clothes once proudly worn, I think there are a number of positive features to be noted.

What happened in British sociology was anything but parochial. For example, the sociology of education owes much to Basil Bernstein and A. H. Halsey in Britain, but, early on, the work of Pierre Bourdieu was taken seriously into account. This is notably illustrated in Michael F. D. Young (ed.) *Knowledge and Control* (1971), which itself grew out of a BSA annual conference. To that extent the familiar British Fabian agenda for the sociology of education was challenged and augmented. In the field of urban sociology, we can see not only the older tradition of community studies and the contribution of researchers such as Ruth Glass, Margaret Stacey and Ray Pahl, but also the engagement with French urban sociology. A good example of what is involved is found in C. G. Pickvance (ed.) *Urban Sociology: Critical Essays* (1976) which contains contributions from Manuell Castells, François Lamarche, Jean Lojkine and José Olives (though they are not, of course, all French nationals). This represents a particular attempt to apply an historical materialist approach to urban processes. This has not been received uncritically but has been a source of intellectual stimulation and a challenge to research activity.

The field of industrial sociology serves as another good illustration. The 'affluent worker' studies directed by David Lockwood and John Goldthorpe became a justifiably celebrated landmark in industrial sociology and, more generally, social stratification (Goldthorpe *et al.*,

1968, 1969). But, without question, we can clearly see the ways in which the American studies, particularly of assembly-line workers, were drawn upon, as well as the work of Touraine, Willener, Popitz and others from Europe concerning matters such as social imagery, project, action, and also debates about the new working class. A good representation of these issues is found in M. Bulmer (ed.) *Working Class Images of Society* (1975). Since then, there has been another kind of debate centred around Braverman and questions of the labour process. In passing, we might recall that Braverman treated as an important point of reference the work of Joan Woodward, whose pioneering contributions on management and technology helped to shape the research strategy of much post-war research in British industrial sociology. Debates around Braverman are well illustrated in Craig Littler's *The Development of the Labour Process in Capitalist Societies* (1982) and Stephen Wood's (ed.) *The Degradation of Work?* (1982), and indeed, in the last few years, annual conferences on the labour process have taken place at UMIST and Aston University. In his edited book, *Capital and Labour* (1980), Theo Nicholls acknowledges that the collection was put together in train of 'this welcome "rediscovery" of the labour process' (p. 15). But what is noteworthy about the book is its wide-ranging approach in terms of authors, as varied as Ernest Mandel and Donald Roy, and in terms of the location of the studies, including Nazi Germany, the United States, Italy and Southern Rhodesia (as is then was) as well as Britain.

All of these developments were helped by certain material arrangements, networks and activities which served to create a healthy infrastructure. Much credit must surely go to the British Sociological Association. Its annual conferences have covered most of the major themes of sociology over the years. Many of these have led to published volumes. The Association has promoted publications through reputable publishing houses, and, perhaps most important, established a journal, *Sociology*, now in its twenty-second year, that has earned international respect and recognition. There are, in addition, a plethora of study groups. These are based on specialist interests – Sexual Divisions and Society, Religion, Mass Communications, Theory, are some examples. One of the most recent groups to be formed is the Sociology of War and Military Organisation, which was given some impetus by the 1985 conference on the sociology of war and peace. Such groups have their own cycles of activity, but some have had long and profitable lives with publications ensuing, as is the case for example with Medical Sociology and the Sociology of Work and Industrial Relations.

Through its conferences, study groups and publications, and also in its organisational practice, the BSA has served as a facilitating mechanism for those who have sought to place feminist issues on the sociological agenda. A very useful reference to some of the dimensions of this process is found in Angela Hale Glasner's review article, 'Gender, Class and the Workplace' (*Sociology*, 1987). *Sociology* has itself published a number of important papers on gender issues, and was the arena for a vigorous debate between John Goldthorpe in defence of the conventional view of women and class analysis in stratification theory and those who were critical of it. In any event, gender is now in the mainstream of sociological work and no longer treated as marginal or even trivial. In 1974, in *The Sociology of Housework*, Ann Oakley had a convincing opening chapter entitled 'The Invisible Woman: Sexism in Sociology'. Although many of the empirical inequalities to which she pointed clearly remain, within sociological work there is now a much greater measure of visibility. Glasner, in her paper, puts the matter thus:

> By the beginning of the 1980s, the data on women's participation in the formal, public arena had increased, as had their overt visibility, and for a number of reasons the debate began to accelerate. The growth and consolidation of a strong British Women's Caucus, itself an outcome of the confrontation between the established elders of British sociology and the newer, visibly female, junior ranks, was but one impetus. In 1982, the BSA annual conference specifically focused on gender, and in the following three years several further conferences were held. In many cases these have resulted in publications, the most substantial and, I believe, potentially the most important in terms of the debate within the field of social stratification, is the edited collection by Rosemary Crompton and Michael Mann, *Gender and Stratification*, published in the middle of 1986 (Glasner, 1987, p. 295).

In the main, British sociology has been extremely well served by the major publishers. The 'blue tombstones' of the famous Routledge and Kegan Paul International Library of Sociology and Social Reconstruction, whose first editor was Karl Mannheim, are particularly worth a mention, as is Polity Press, started in 1984 by Anthony Giddens. So too are the course materials and edited books published by the Open University and the series of discussion papers which a number of sociology departments produce.

Sociologists do not simply speak to one another. This is true in the obvious sense that sociologists often need to learn from the subjects of their investigation – sociologists of science from scientists, medical sociologists from health professionals and patients, sociologists of religion from religious adherents, and so on. But it is also true in terms of inter-disciplinary communication. The case of cultural and media studies serves as a significant illustration. The Centre for Cultural Studies at Birmingham, led first by Richard Hoggart and later by Stuart Hall, proved to have fruitful implications for sociology. In the work of the Centre was a mixture of literary and social criticism, interests in social history and the idea of community, extended discussions of Marxist theory, studies of popular culture and education and explorations of the cultural apparatus – particularly the mass media. The work of Stuart Hall has certainly been influential, both at the Centre and, more recently, at the Open University. His co-authored *Policing the Crisis: Mugging, the State and Law and Order* (1978) clearly drew upon sociology (notably Cohen's *Folk Devils and Moral Panics*) and contributed to it (particularly in its discussion of how the media define deviant events). His theoretical papers on 'Encoding and Decoding in Television Discourse' (1980) and 'The Rediscovery of "Ideology": The Return of the Repressed in Media Studies' (1982) constitute elegant contributions to a critical theory of media. The influence of cultural studies on the sociology of the media is there for all to see – in publications from Leicester's Mass Media Centre, Glasgow University Media Group and the work of scholars such as Philip Schlesinger and James Curran. In particular, Raymond Williams has exerted a considerable intellectual influence, and more generally, from beyond Britain, the work of Bourdieu, Eco and Barthes has been seminal. What media sociologists have done in Britain is to give a more empirical basis for answering the question, What do the media do when they mediate? This is particularly true for studies of media production and output – issues of message reception and decoding have been less explored, but there is no shortage of ideas.

I have referred to a number of features of the infrastructure of sociology which have contributed to its life and vitality over the post-war period, more particularly the last twenty years. I have deferred discussion of the Social Sciences Research Council, now called the Economic and Social Research Council. The Council was set up in 1965 in a mood of considerable optimism about the potential and importance of social science research when the need to establish adequate research funding and post-graduate awards was clearly recognised. The first Chairman of the Council, Michael Young, was himself a sociologist who had conducted community studies with colleagues such as Peter Wilmott and Peter Townsend. He was also the author of the satirical *Rise of the Meritocracy* (1958) and I think brought a creative, even playful, sense of what the SSRC could accomplish. His immediate successor was Andrew Shonfield, an economist of wide-ranging interests, who wrote impressively on the British economy and on the nature of modern capitalism.

It is an exercise in instant nostalgia to re-read some of the early Annual Reports, when new possibilities were being explored by the disciplinary committees and panels set up for explicit purposes, such as the Panel on Race Relations in 1968, or the Mass Communications Panel, which presented its report in 1970. The 1968–69 Annual Report referred to the programme of 'action research' in Educational Priority Areas:

> This arose out of the decisions prompted by the *Plowden Report on Children and their Primary Schools* about the special treatment to be accorded to children in places where the total environment was disadvantageous to the process of education. The Council decided to support two schemes which would monitor results in five areas as remedial action proceeded, and do so on a common basis applying uniform criteria of measurement to a wide spread of geographical experience (Social Science Research Council, 1969, p. 14)

There was, almost from the beginning, a tension between those who thought the Council should be responsive to research proposals and those who thought it should initiate them. In the Annual Report for 1969–70, there is a very good summary in the Economic and Social History Committee's Report:

> There are considerable differences of opinion on the Committee as to how far the Committee should adopt a *dirigiste* policy in respect of research. There are those who believe that initiative is best left to individual scholars who know their own fields of interest and would resent direction, and some members are also impressed by the difficulty of reaching agreement on gaps in research. On the other hand there are those who believe that depending on 'market forces' alone would produce an irrational and unsatisfactory pattern of research; that large projects and programmes will not be undertaken without central initiative and that such programmes help to prevent

the dispersal of good research workers to places where working alone they are less productive.

There is agreement that the Committee should attempt to exercise a somewhat greater degree of influence on research than in the past, but those who are nervous of a *dirigiste* policy would hope to do this by drawing attention to gaps in research by e.g. inter-University conferences, discussion with individual scholars. Those who are impressed by the size of the existing gaps and in particular by the absence of large-scale programmes would like to see the Committee take the initiative in identifying the areas where research is most needed and in inviting groups of scholars to submit proposals for a programme of research in a specified field. (Social Science Research Council, 1970 pp. 34–5)

Note the even tenor of the discussion and the assumption of committee autonomy. But consider too what the Sociology and Social Adminstration Committee were concerned about in the same Annual Report:

There are . . . the anxieties, often expressed by politicians and others who were well-disposed towards the Council, about the need to demonstrate its usefulness by greater concentration on 'applied' or 'problem-oriented' research. The Committee took the view that such anxieties or complaints were misdirected and ill-founded. (pp. 50–1)

Two reasons were advanced for this opinion. The first was that social research over the previous fifteen years had become a cumulative process and that the main thing was to make sure relevant people in government and the professions knew about this. Not only could existing social research be better utilised but this would be improved when trained social scientists were in senior positions in organisations, which would then be able to make better use of social science. But secondly, and here I quote from the report again:

the committee took the view that there was an ultimate conjunction of interest between the preoccupations of academic researchers and those of groups and organisations seeking answers to 'social problems'. Research judged worth supporting on its merits in terms of theoretical contribution and methodological rigour was precisely that which, in the long run, could help most in the solution of problems which were seen as demanding attention in society at

large. Investigation directed to the solution of problems encountered by administrators concerned with the design or reform of
services, or with the identification of inadequacies or needs (so-
called 'administrative research') was another matter, which seemed
best dealt with by governmental and other agencies concerned.
(p. 51)

Although differently expressed, this view is not dissimilar to the
position advocated by Norbert Elias, which I drew attention to early in
this chapter. It is, however, one of the ironies of the SSRC's
subsequent history that, in a period of new right politics of the
conservative administrations of recent years, it has become more, not
less, *dirigiste*.

The hostility of the incoming Conservative government of 1979 to
social science was scarcely a secret – not least, one supposes, to the 364
economists who wrote to the press some years later to question the
efficacy of the government's economic policies. But sociology also was
on the receiving end of criticism from the right, for its alleged left-wing
tendencies and 'Marxist bias'. I have discussed the kind of criticisms
that were advanced, including some from within the ranks of
sociology, in my paper 'Images of Sociology' (Eldridge, 1981). The
attack on the SSRC was not therefore surprising. Leaked documents
of correspondence between Sir Geoffrey Howe and Sir Keith Joseph
indicated that they hoped the inquiry into the SSRC, headed by Lord
Rothschild, would provide grounds for closure. In that they were
disappointed, since Rothschild recognised the importance of the
Council's work and argued that its funding base had already been
pared to the bone (Rothschild, 1982). But the Council was instructed
to change its name to the Economic and Social Research Council by Sir
Keith Joseph, on the grounds that it was inappropriate to talk of social
science. This, of course, was not the produce of epistemological debate
but of political fiat.

The Council has clearly felt itself to be in a back-to-the-wall
position. Although I am not in agreement with the kind of decisions it
has taken on restructuring and research management, I am naturally
very sympathetic with the dilemmas it has faced. It has quite simply
been on the receiving end of enormous political pressure. In 1987 it
issued a document entitled *Research Horizons and Opportunities in the
Social Sciences* (Economic and Social Research Council, 1987), the
outcome of discussions with social scientists here and abroad (mostly
in the USA). The document points out that most of our social science,

including sociology, is held in high regard abroad, but that there is a very serious funding and resource problem if this reputation is to be sustained.

One small indication of the problems we now face can be given with reference to postgraduate studentships. In the years 1969–70, 1970–71 and 1971–72 the total number of postgraduate training awards made available for all social science was 1192, 1521 and 1526 respectively. For sociology and social adminstration the numbers were 190, 218 and 214. In the coming session (1988–89) it has recently been announced that the total number of awards for all social science postgraduate work will be 250. There will be no quotas against any individual discipline. Relate that to the number of social science disciplines and higher education outlets and we can see that selectivity is a mild word to describe what is going on.

Following discussions with the BSA and the SSRC, in which it was recognised that the SSRC could not always speak for social science with an independent voice, soundings were taken with the whole gamut of social science associations and in the early 1980s the Association for the Learned Societies in the Social Sciences (ALSISS) was established. ALSISS, on the basis of small resources but considerable commitment by its executive, has sought to ensure that the case for the social sciences in our society is not neglected. A Parliamentary all-party committee on social science has been set up which meets regularly. Annual conferences are held in which senior politicians, civil servants and educators are able to explain what each does to a sometimes critical audience. And a certain amount of lobbying activity has taken place on both sides of the binary divide. The Association met Dr Roberta Miller in 1986 to hear of the work she had accomplished as Director of the Consortium of Social Sciences Associations in the USA (COSSA). It is still actively trying to raise funds to carry out comparable lobbying activity.

At the time of writing there are two features of the present institutional arrangements which are under scrutiny and have a bearing on the future practice of sociology. The first is the uncertain future of the ESRC. Having been saved from abolition by a favourable Rothschild report it is currently in some organisational difficulties as a result of a decision to relocate it from London to Swindon. The Chairman-designate, Professor Peter Hall, has resigned in protest, and two-thirds of the staff are leaving.[1] This has raised fears that the organisation will either die from atrophy or be swallowed up by another research council and become the poor relation of the natural sciences.

The second is that university departments of sociology are to be evaluated by the University Grants Committee, shortly before the UGC itself is transformed into a University Funding Council as part of the government's Education Bill which is now before Parliament.[2] It should be made clear, however, that such inquiries are by no means confined to social science subjects. The British Sociological Association and the University Professors and Heads of Sociology Group (which came into existence in the 1980s) have played a proactive rather than reactive role in this matter. In contrast to the UGC evaluation of the research activities of sociology departments in 1986, the assessors to the committee are known and acceptable to the profession.[3] They are Emeritus Professor John Westergaard of Sheffield, Professor Anthony Giddens of Cambridge and Ms Jennifer Platt of Sussex, the current President of the BSA. In the light of the inquiry uncertainties necessarily remain, given the continuous cuts in university funding over the past decade, both for teaching and research, in the sciences, arts and social sciences. In an institutional sense the future of sociology in Britain is related to the future of higher education in general. That future has been diminished by a political perspective which treats higher education as a cost and not as an investment, and which sees academic freedom as an obstructionist nuisance rather than an intrinsic part of our democracy. This problem is much larger than particular hostility to sociology whose practitioners, along with many other groups in our society, may be regarded as the enemy within. In such a situation we need to keep a cool head to meet the demands of the day.

Notes

1. In 1988 Howard Newby, a sociologist, took over as chairman of ESRC. (Eds)
2. As this volume goes to press the report of the UGC Review of Sociology is still awaited. (Eds)
3. The evaluation of research in all subjects is being repeated in 1989. The names of the sociology assessors for this second 'Research Selectivity Exercise' will not be made known by the new UFC until the final report is published. (Eds)

References

*Abrams, P. (1968) *The Origins of British Sociology 1834–1914* (Chicago: University of Chicago Press).
—— (1982) *Historical Sociology* (Shepton Mallet: Open Books).

——, Deem, R., Finch, J. and Rock, P. (eds) (1981) *Practice and Progress: British Sociology 1950–1980* (London: Allen & Unwin).

Banks, J. A. (1954) *Prosperity and Parenthood* (London: Routledge & Kegan Paul).

Banks, O. (1955) *Parity and Prestige in English Secondary Education* (London: Routledge & Kegan Paul).

Bernstein, B. (ed.) (1971 and 1973) *Class Codes and Control* (London: Routledge & Kegan Paul).

Brown, R. (1987) 'Norbert Elias in Leicester: Some Recollections', *Theory, Culture and Society*, vol 4, pp. 533–9.

Bulmer, M. (ed.) (1975) *Working Class Images of Society* (London: Routledge & Kegan Paul).

*—— (ed.) (1985) *Essays on the History of British Sociological Research* (Cambridge: CUP).

Cohen, R. (1987) *The New Helots* (Aldershot: Avebury Gower).

Cohen, S. (ed.) (1971) *Images of Deviance* (Harmondsworth: Penguin).

—— (1973) *Folk Devils and Moral Panics* (London: Paladin).

—— (1985) *Visions of Social Control* (Cambridge: Polity Press).

—— and Taylor, L. (1972) *Long–Term Imprisonment* (Harmondsworth: Penguin)

Corrigan, P. and Sayer, D. (1985) *The Great Arch: English State Formation as Cultural Revolution* (Oxford: Blackwell).

Crompton, R. and Mann, M. (eds) (1986) *Gender and Stratification* (Cambridge: Polity Press).

Dahrendorf, R. (1959) *Class and Class Conflict in an Industrial Society* (London: Routledge & Kegan Paul).

Dennis, N., Henriques, F. and Slaughter, C. (1956) *Coal Is Our Life* (London: Eyre and Spottiswoode).

Dodgshon, R. A. (1987) *The European Past: Social Evolution and Spatial Order* (London: Macmillan).

Economic and Social Research Council (1987) *Research Horizons and Opportunities in the Social Sciences* (London: HMSO).

*Eldridge, J. (1980) *Recent British Sociology* (London: Macmillan).

—— (1981) 'Images of Sociology', *Department of Sociology Discussion Paper* (Glasgow: University of Glasgow).

Elias, N. (1956) 'Problems of Involvement and Detachment', *British Journal of Sociology*, vol. 7, pp. 226 ff.

—— (1978 and 1982) *The Civilising Process* (2 vols) (Oxford: Blackwell).

—— (1978) *What is Sociology?* (London: Hutchinson).

—— (1987a) 'The Retreat of Sociologists into the Present', *Theory, Culture and Society*, vol. 4, pp. 223–47.

—— (1987b) *Involvement and Detachment* (Oxford: Blackwell).

Gellner, E. (1964) *Thought and Change* (London: Weidenfeld & Nicolson).

—— (1974) *Legitimation of Belief* (Cambridge: CUP).

—— (1983) *Nations and Nationalism* (Oxford: Blackwell).

Giddens, A. (1976) *New Rules of Sociological Method* (London: Hutchinson).

—— (1984) *The Constitution of Society* (Cambridge: Polity Press).

—— (1985) *The Nation State and Violence* (Cambridge: Polity Press).

—— and Mackenzie, G. (eds) (1982) *Social Class and the Division of Labour: Essays in Honour of Ilya Neustadt* (Cambridge: CUP).

Glasgow University Media Group (1976) *Bad News* (London: Routledge & Kegan Paul).
—— (1980) *More Bad News* (London: Routledge & Kegan Paul).
—— (1985) *War and Peace News* (Milton Keynes: Open University Press).
Glasner, A. H. (1987) 'Gender, Class and the Workplace', *Sociology*, vol. 21, pp. 295–304.
Gleichman, P. R. *et al.* (eds) (1977) *Human Figurations: Essays for Norbert Elias* (Amsterdam: Amsterdam Sociologisch Tijdschrift).
Goldthorpe, J. H., Lockwood, D., Bechofer, F. and Platt, J. (1968, 1969) *The Affluent Worker in the Class Structure* (Cambridge: CUP).
Hall, J. (1985) *Powers and Liberties* (Harmondsworth: Penguin).
Hall, S. (1980) 'Encoding and Decoding in Television Discourse', in S. Hall, *et al.* (eds), *Culture, Media and Language* (London: Hutchinson).
—— (1982) 'The Rediscovery of "Ideology": The Return of the Repressed in Media Studies', in M. Gurevitch, T. Bennett, J. Curren and T. Woollacott (eds), *Culture, Society and Media* (London: Methuen, 1982).
——, Critcher, C., Jefferson, T., Clarke, J. and Roberts, B. (1978) *Policing the Crisis: Mugging, the State and Law and Order* (London: Macmillan).
Halsey, A. H. (1985) 'Provincials and Professionals: The Post-war Sociologists', in M. Bulmer (ed.) (1985).
Littler, C. (1982) *The Development of the Labour Process* (London: Heinemann).
Marshall, T. H. (1950) *Citizenship and Social Class* (Cambridge: CUP).
Mann, M. (1987a) *The Sources of Social Power* vol. 1 (Cambridge: CUP).
—— (1987b) 'Ruling Class Strategies and Citizenship', *Sociology*, vol. 21, pp. 339–54.
Miles, R. (1987) *Capitalism and Unfree Labour* (London/New York: Tavistock).
Moore, B. (1969) *Social Origins of Dictatorship and Democracy* (Harmondsworth: Penguin).
Nichols, T. (ed.) (1980) *Capital and Labour* (Glasgow: Fontana).
Oakley, A. (1974) *The Sociology of Housework* (London: Martin Robertson).
Pickvance, C. G. (ed.) (1976) *Urban Sociology: Critical Essays* (London: Methuen).
Poggi, G. (1978) *The Development of the Modern State* (London: Hutchinson).
—— (1983) *Calvinism and the Capitalist Spirit* (London: Macmillan).
Rex, J. (1961) *Key Problems of Sociological Theory* (London: Routledge & Kegan Paul).
—— & Moore, R. (1967) *Race, Community and Conflict* (London: OUP).
—— (1970) *Race Relations in Sociological Theory* (London: Weidenfeld & Nicolson).
—— (1973) *Race, Colonialism and the City* (London: Routledge & Kegan Paul).
—— (1974) *Approaches to Sociology: An Introduction to Major Trends in British Sociology* (London: Routledge & Kegan Paul).
Rothschild, Lord (1982) *An Enquiry into the Social Science Research Council* (London: HMSO).
Schlesinger, P. (1978) *Putting 'Reality' Together* (London: Constable).

Social Science Research Council (1969) *Annual Report 1968–69* (London: HMSO).
—— (1970) *Annual Report 1969–70* (London: HMSO).
Taylor, I., Walton, P. and Young J. (1973) *The New Criminology* (London: Routledge & Kegan Paul).
Weber, M. (1948) *The Protestant Ethic and the Spirit of Capitalism* (London: Allen & Unwin).
Wood, S. (ed.) (1982) *The Degradation of Work* (London: Hutchinson).
Worsley, P. (1964) *The Third World* (London: Weidenfeld & Nicolson).
—— (1968) *The Trumpet Shall Sound* (London: MacGibbon & Kee).
—— (1984) *The Three Worlds* (London: Weidenfeld & Nicolson).
Young, M. D. (1958) *The Rise of the Meritocracy* (Harmondsworth: Penguin).
Young M. F. D. (ed.) (1971) *Knowledge and Control* (London: Collier/Macmillan).

10   What Has Sociology Achieved? The French Paradox

Philippe Bernoux

1 INTRODUCTION: THE PARADOXICAL INSTITUTION OF SOCIOLOGY

It is curious that in France, the land of Le Play, Durkheim, Mauss and Halbwachs, to name but a few of the more celebrated members of the sociological Pantheon, the institutionalisation of the teaching of this discipline did not occur until the beginning of the 1960s. Before then, certainly, sociology had been taught in faculties of letters, but the sociology degree appeared only towards the end of the 1950s at the prestigious Sorbonne, in Paris; it then spread progressively into the provincial universities. As for the National Centre for Scientific Research, the CNRS, created by statute in 1948, though it was to be a driving force in the development of research, this did not become perceptible until about fifteen years after the end of the war.

To say that sociology did not begin until after the Second World War is at the same time true and false. It was in 1898 that Emile Durkheim founded *L'Année Sociologique*. In the same period, he directed the Institut Français de Sociologie. Thus there have existed, since the start of the century, an institutional foundation and an intellectual milieu which have ensured the existence of French sociology and its dissemination around the world. But the institution remained academic, and the milieu very hermetic, serving rather more to promote internal discussion than the diffusion of sociology outside the university debate (except for the influence on primary school teachers). Durkheim and the members of his school (among others the ethnologists Marcel Mauss and Lucien Lévy-Bruhl, the economist François Simiand, the sociologists Célestin Bouglé and Maurice Halbwachs) are considered today throughout the world among the founders of sociology – even though they proved incapable of laying an enlarged foundation for their discipline in their own country.

The weakness of the influence of sociology is also to be sought in its origin, philosophy. French sociology had difficulty in detaching itself from a certain theoretical, all-embracing vision, more suited to reflection on society than action in it. The source of this type of outlook is to be found in the philosophical method, which is less concerned than the social sciences with the application of concepts to social reality.

This double origin – academic and philosophical – of sociology ensured its detachment from society in general: sociology played no important social role, for example in terms of intervention or of guidance; while, on the part of society, demand for it was all but non-existent. Up until the end of the Second World War, public authorities, firms, local organisations and other public or private bodies almost never had recourse to sociologists, or to their knowledge. During the first fifty years of the twentieth century, no major study was commissioned by them. Never, during this period, did sociology in France play the active, counselling role that it did, for example, in the United States.

In short, although teaching and reflection in this country began at the end of the nineteenth century, they hardly extended beyond university and academic circles. Georges Gurvitch, summing up the orientation of French sociology between the wars, notes that 'the categories of Durkheimian sociology are flexible and refined . . . But the sociologist's attention remains fixed, by choice, upon archaic societies or upon the reform of the spirit of particular social sciences' (Gurvitch, 1963, p. 2). It may be added that, outside the universities, sociology, at that time, was taught in highly academic institutions, such as the Collège de France, the Ecole Pratique des Hautes Etudes and the Ecole Normale Supérieure, where its academic image could hardly be other than reinforced.

In the sense that a body of knowledge arises as a response to a social demand, it is thus true to say that French sociology did not begin to exist in society until after the Second World War. And even then it came about in a very particular way, compared with what had happened in other countries. It was as a result of State intervention, through the universities (and particularly the CNRS), that sociological research and teaching of relevance to contemporary France came into being.

2 EARLY RESEARCH AND ITS ENVIRONMENT

Not being directly linked to, or dependent on, social demand, sociological research became oriented towards a general investigation of the problems of society as it was evolving before the eyes of the sociologist. It may be recalled that the post-war period was one of considerable economic and social upheaval; economic growth in France was – up to about 1970 – among the highest in the world; the population was expanding faster than at any time for more than a century; and the agricultural world was modernising, with the break-down of its old structures and a considerable exodus from the countryside. Most important, perhaps, the dominant classes were changing. The old landed aristocracy was disappearing, and socio-economic power was being partly withdrawn from the hands of industrialists, passing into those of a new planning-conscious admin-istrative system which felt responsible for putting France back on its feet.

At the same time, there existed few models of social analysis. Did the young sociologists perhaps look for them in the USA in the already famous system of Parsons and Merton? Alain Touraine (1986) affirms as much, and it is true that the influence of American thinkers on certain French researchers was strong. But this influence was quali-fied, and was certainly contested. The qualification arose from an outlook that was more pessimistic, and more attentive to 'the forces of disintegration than to the mechanisms of integration' (Touraine, 1986, p. 134) and also, in the humanist perspective of Georges Friedmann (1973), more anxious in the face of the development of technology. The contest, which had a political character, was prosecuted in particular at the CNRS, where power no longer remained almost exclusively in the hands of the founding academics but was shared between them and the delegates of the staff (*les élus syndicaux*) who were by then oriented towards a theoretical, militant critique of the capitalist mode of development of industrial society – a critique highly influenced by Marxism.

The starting phase of empirical research occurred as a result of pres-sure from the two founding fathers, Georges Friedmann and Jean Stoetzel, and young researchers such as Henri Mendras, Edgar Morin, Jean-Daniel Reynaud and Alain Touraine. (The great in-fluence of Raymond Aron and Georges Gurvitch was essentially theoretical, while Paul-Henri Chombart de Lauwe was a man apart.) Georges Friedmann, especially, launched certain of these young researchers in fields chosen according to their own projects, each one of them coming from a non-sociological discipline such as history, philosophy (most common of all – which is not surprising given that the philosophy degree programme was the only one in which sociology was taught), law and business studies. Empirical sociology after the war was set up by non-sociologists, for the very good reason that there were no sociologists. More and more, however, the pressure of the orientations noted above led to the carrying-out of empirical inquiries in a perspective where the accent was placed on theoretical criticism of society and the weight of its structures. A large number of researchers distanced themselves from the desire for rigour in the analysis of facts, preferring instead to devote themselves to their militant interpretation. Without altogether stifling the former, this latter perspective dominated the 1960s and 1970s, particularly in the sociologies of the school, work and urbanism – the fields to which the present analysis will be necessarily limited. The major thinkers were philosophers who were Marxist, or close to Marxism:

> The power of this current of thought was greater in France than elsewhere, but this sociology of suspicion and its structuralist foundation managed to cross the seas, and exert a profound influence in the United States, and still more in Latin America, where Althusserian Marxism . . . attained quite dominant positions. (Touraine, 1986, p. 136)

An example will illustrate this perspective: Paul Sweezy, the author of the foreword to Harry Braverman's work, *Labor and Monopoly Capital*, found a response in France when he wrote:

> Harry Braverman's book is to be considered an invitation and a challenge to a younger generation of Marxist economists and sociologists to get on with the urgent task of destroying bourgeois ideology and putting in its place an honest picture of the social reality within which we are forced to live. (Sweezy, 1974, p. xii)

Resolutions of this kind bore heavily upon sociologists' work during this period, through their permeation of the circles charged with directing, orienting and selecting research themes, and with assessing researchers' work, particularly in university or CNRS commissions. This type of gloss on the works of major authors distorted the spirit in which they had been written. Its proliferation distorted the spirit of research.

This last statement must of course be qualified. Though Lévi-Strauss's ethnology-based structuralism greatly influenced interpretive theories, it would be unjust and ridiculous to hold it responsible for the lack of rigour mentioned above. Though it was certainly difficult to apply the methods and hypotheses used in the analysis of Bororo societies to our own industrial societies, the fault lay not with the author of *Tristes Tropiques*. Nor could one lay at Michel Foucault's door an interpretation denying to the human sciences any rigour and any right to analyse social phenomena using as a pretext his own historical analysis of the relations between power and knowledge. It finally required a rather feeble return to Marx to deny sociology any ambition to objective knowledge. That all analysis is socially situated, that it is important to know the social conditions of theoretical production, these obvious facts justify neither the conclusion that there is no possibility of any scientific analysis, nor the consequent rejection of all research that is not 'committed'. This was unfortunately all too frequently the case in French sociology during the 1960s and 1970s.

3 THE SOCIOLOGY OF THE SCHOOL: FROM PIERRE BOURDIEU'S 'HABITUS' TO RAYMOND BOUDON'S INTERACTIONISM

The school became a problem for French society, and its control an issue, when the 'baby boom' generation of the fifteen years that followed the end of the war reached school age, beginning in the 1960s. Never, at least since the nineteenth century, had France experienced such an explosion in the birth rate. The primary schools and the first years of secondary schools developed at that time without too much difficulty, but the same could be said neither of the later secondary classes nor of higher education, hence the impassioned debate which opened up among sociologists. This debate began with the important researches of Alain Girard (1961) and the publications of the Institut National d'Etudes Demographiques (INED) including the review *Population*.

It was in 1964 that P. Bourdieu and J. C. Passeron published *The Heirs*. Their central thesis was that, contrary to what had been hoped by its founding fathers, the secular, free, obligatory education system was no longer a factor for the democratisation of society but, on the contrary, a factor for the reproduction of social inequalities. Let us recall that the Third Republic, proclaimed in 1870, had had difficulty in imposing itself against the conservative parties which wanted the return of the monarchy. One of the points of conflict had been the school and, more generally, teaching, which up to then had largely been in the hands of the Catholic Church. This led to the accusation that the Church had made education an instrument for maintaining its influence and for moulding youth in the support of social order, the monarchy and conservatism. At that time, to be republican was equivalent, in the public mind, to fighting the Church and the monarchy, and to being in the party of progress. This ideology, and this struggle, were to be promoted by the education of youth in schools removed from the influence of the Church, open to all, and, in this way, on the side of the egalitarian ideal. The 'secular, obligatory' school was – and remains in large measure – the symbol of egalitarianism against elitism, of the active defence of a milieu where the children of the people could at last accede to the knowledge and culture that the conservative ruling classes had refused them. Undoubtedly the stake represented by the secular school is no longer so important in 1988 but it was still quite important when Bourdieu and Passeron first published in 1964.

This latter was felt to be an event. The author argued the thesis that we have just presented, analysing the correlation between social origin and success in school for secondary pupils and students. The results of these correlations were indeed convincing: the higher the social origin, the greater the success at school. Though schools were open to all, and though they were effectively free, they set up, Bourdieu argued, a selection process which eliminated the children of the less privileged classes. This selection operated through a system of sanctions which favoured the children of other classes, in particular through the mastery of language, and through falsely democratic examinations and competitive examinations.

Bourdieu's argumentation was gone through with a fine-tooth-comb, and highly criticised (Paradeise, 1988, pp. 79 ff; in this paragraph we make use of this article and discussions with the author.) If it is true that the pedagogical apparatus translates social origins into success at school – those who get on best at school being, overall, the children of privileged classes – can one, for all that, infer that success at school is an instrument of reproduction? Three conditions would have to be met for such reasoning to be valid. First, the 'failures' of the system must be accounted for. Bourdieu is content to speak about them in terms of a residue, whereas, in a rigorous explanation, they represent a serious dysfunction of the school system. Next, the effect of success at school on social destination requires serious analysis; it is inexact to make the possession of diplomas a simple determinant of social destination. The latter is equally dependent on other individual characteristics, like family history, parent's social status, etc. Many French heads of business are autodidacts, for example, and one obviously cannot treat this problem as residual. Lastly, deformations of the social structure over time also require explanation, but Bourdieu omits them. He postulates that the structure of social destinations can be deduced from the supply of education, as though this alone weighed upon individual destinies, whereas these structures become deformed over time. Individual behaviour is not only the product of such structures, and does not necessarily tend to reproduce them.

The methodological error in Bourdieu's reasoning arose from his exaggeratedly structuralist perspective. In insisting on the influence of structures, he overstated their importance at the expense of the autonomy of the actor. He acknowledged, however, that it could not be eliminated completely; indeed, this awareness explains the evolution of the concept of 'habitus' in his work. *Habitus* is defined, to begin with, as the 'product (within the individual) of the structures, the producer of (individual) practices', and thus also as 'the reproducer of structures', which allows individual action to depend on one's place in the social structure. Subsequently the *habitus* becomes a 'predisposition to act' in which dependence on structure is no longer a necessity (Paradeise, 1988, p. 86).

This thesis was contested by Raymond Boudon. A philosopher by training, influenced also by Paul Lazarsfeld with whom he had prepared his PhD thesis at Columbia University in the USA, Boudon vigorously criticised structuralism – a class of theories whose specific character is that they claim to give an account of the systematic character of the objects which they consider (Boudon, 1968) – and the use of the concept of structure. He attempted to construct a scientific sociology based on a rigorous methodological apparatus, which he presented in one of his first works (Boudon, 1967), and which was the source of his theory of 'methodological individualism' according to which a social phenomenon can be understood only 'as the consequence of the behaviour of the individuals belonging to the social system in which this phenomenon is observed' (Boudon, 1982, p. 286). Every phenomenon of this type must therefore be explained as the result of individual actions, and not interpreted as that of global correlations. While it may be true that individual action is subject to social constraints, one cannot deduce from this that it is determined by them. 'These constraints mark out the field of the possible, not the field of the real . . . [and do not have] . . . any signification unless one refers them to the intentions and plans of the actors' (ibid, p. 287). This opens the way to interactionism, understood as the necessity, in order to understand an action, of defining the actor's intentions and the means which are, or which he believes to be, at his disposal, and of identifying the field of possibilities in which his situation of interaction with other actors is located.

The sociology of education provided Boudon with a privileged domain of demonstration, since it lent itself to the interpretation of overall correlations, like those between social origin and success at school, or between success at school and social destination, in a model where it was possible to 'take account fully of the relative autonomy of the institutions and the agents' (Paradeise, 1988, p. 85). In particular, it required these correlations to be interpreted not in terms of the rigidity of social structures but as a 'complex effect of a set of factors' (Boudon, 1982, p. 352), factors which were not to be conceived of independently of one another, and which had to be interpreted in the framework of a systemic analysis. The key to this analysis was the idea that a school system could be assimilated to a series of points of bifurcation, with which one could associate a space for decision that varied with each type of social position. It was thus necessary to construct a formalised model which included at the same time the constraints of the social system and the multiple decisions which would orient the individual's behaviour en route to an aggregation of these individual behaviour patterns. Boudon's methodological grasp permitted him to construct this model, including the effects of a large number of factors. The models and studies used in demography and in economic studies were very helpful in the construction of this theory.

At the time of the debate on the school, Boudon developed concrete applications of his theory of interactionism and methodological individualism. Let us add that he also made greater use of historical comparisons than did the exponents of the structuralist interpretation.

The sociological debate on the school was not confined to Bourdieu and Boudon but they do indicate its parameters. It is also worth noting that Bourdieu launched the non-specialist review, *Actes de la Recherche en Sciences Sociales*, in 1975.

4 THE CASE OF THE SOCIOLOGY OF WORK

Georges Friedmann gave the initial push. His work was not limited to the critical dissemination of other work (essentially American, on Taylorism, the human relations school and the socio-psychology of work), and the introduction thereby, in France, of a discipline which reflected this work. This he did do, but also much more. His main work was twofold: on the one hand, a humanist reflection on man at work; on the other, the professionalisation of sociology in France. The humanist asks himself, as a priority, questions concerning the becoming of man projected into the industrial mechanism; he proposes to probe 'the intellectual and moral repercussions . . . of the mechanical adventure into which man has thrown himself, and in which he risks sinking' (Friedmann, 1946, p. 12). The sociology which he promoted set itself the task of observing these consequences in order to act upon them. He was *a priori* neither an optimist nor a pessimist. 'The effects of mechanisation do not justify any abstract value judgements on the concrete circumstances in which the problems are posed, and in particular on economic and social conditions in industry' (Friedmann, 1946, p. 390). It was thus advisable to set up as many concrete studies of work as possible.

The importance of work and the firm derived from the fact that, according to Friedmann, they are the sources of socialisation in a society in which technology, industrialisation and the figure of the industrial worker predominate. This has been contested by D. Monjardet (in *Collectif*, 1985, pp. 117–18). The issue is twofold. First, is work the central focus of the way in which our society is constituted? Second, is the corresponding sociology a sociology of work, or indeed of the worker, or is it a sociology of industrial society? We feel that, for Friedmann, who was marked by Marxism in his youth (he distanced himself from it after the rejection by the French communists of his work *From Holy Russia to the USSR*, 1938), our society is firstly a society of work and industrialisation, and the worker is its central figure.

Young researchers set to work by Friedmann thus received a mandate to seek knowledge without the latter corresponding to any very precise social demands. The sociology of work became a kind of sociology of changing crafts and jobs which was, so to speak free-forming (*gratuite*) – the response to an anxious humanist enquiry. The researchers were to explore the centres of production, and observe work and the workers, with the aim of finding solutions – or at least of opening up paths which would lead to an improvement in the condition of man at work – to making work more human, where up till then it had been Taylorised, and little improved by the theorists of the human-relations school. They were to study the work environment, and workers' reactions to technical change and to modernisation. It was not a question of offering answers but, to begin with, of knowing and of making known.

These researchers thus came from a background which was neither that of the academic nor that of the private consultant. Nor were they trained in sociology. Two things resulted from this absence of roots in a tradition: first, the absence of unified doctrine was accompanied by the carving up of the domain into different fields whose rationality was not really apparent, being closer to empiricism than to a well-structured doctrine. These fields were disparate, and there was no theory to bring them together. The *Treatise on the Sociology of Work* (edited by Friedmann and Naville in 1962) includes few references to the major authors, the founders of sociology, apart from the relatively large impor- ance given to Marx. The researchers whom Friedmann inspired were forced to constitute for themselves their theoretical frames of reference; two examples will be given below. It was hardly surprising that they should afterwards have found themselves going their separate ways.

Second, the links between these sociologists and public bodies, and also certain socio-professional organisations (in particular trade unions like the CGT and, perhaps even more, the CFDT) were close, and remained so. The sociology of work set itself up as a profession whose paying clientele was the public authorities, in the form of the major administrative bodies, particularly the General Planning Com- missariat. This sociology appeared as the focus of expertise and advice for such administrative bodies, albeit an expertise very free in its choice of fields of study and in analyses which were more often turned towards a radical critique of the system than a scrupulous examination of the terrain – at least for some members of the research milieu, and up to the end of the 1970s.

The fields covered, and the problems studied, may be grouped round a few large themes. To begin with, there were the division of labour, working conditions (with the creation under the influence of a sociologist, Y. Delamotte, by law in 1974, of the Agency for the Improvement of Working Conditions, which today covers a much larger field, including, in particular, the introduction of new tech- nology and the organisation of work), salaries, and everything concerning qualifications. Social classes and trade-union affairs oc- cupied an important field, in which attention must be drawn to Serge Mallet's work (Mallet, 1963). According to Mallet, technicians and engineers, who are becoming more and more numerous in the industries of the future, belong in fact to the working class – this contributed to an exceedingly sharp debate at the time – since they are excluded from possession of the means of production, and from power in the firm. But their claims, which find expression in the trade–union movement, are no longer a simple contestation of the owners' power, like that of the traditional working class. They have to do instead with control over the organisation of production and with the management of the firm. Such themes found a place in the review *Arguments*. The sociology of social conflict gave rise to many monographs on conflict, and to some more synthesising works (Adam and Reynaud, 1978; Reynaud, 1982).

Another important area in the sociology of work has been the firm, both its organisation and the participation of the employees. This theme was often termed 'reformist', in opposition to the previous manner of treating it. It gave rise to a group of important works, critiques of theses which, like those of human relations or of motivations, ignored power and its conquest. Some participant observation studies of the working environment (Bernoux, Motte and Saglio, 1973) adopted an original approach to the struggle for the appropriation of power as experienced by workers' groups themselves.

In these domains of social movements and of the organisation of the firm, special mention must be made of two authors who, in their different ways, have dominated the debates.

4.1 Alain Touraine's Actionism

In 1965, Alain Touraine published his thesis, *The Sociology of Action*. In 1984, *The Return of the Actor*, one of his best works, came off the press. Here he posed once again, in greater depth, the question which, twenty years earlier, was already at the heart of his thought and of his activity: how, and with what tools, to construct a new sociology? (cf. Bunel, 1983, upon whom we draw heavily). According to Touraine, this task is today a priority. Since the time of the pioneers of sociology, the world has been turned upside down. It is thus urgent that we re-think our sociological approach, and 'replace a representation of social life founded on the notions of society, of evolution and of role, by another, in which the notions of historicity, of social movement and and of subject will occupy the same central position' (Touraine, 1984, p. 13). Today, our societies are no longer concerned with questions of Progress or of the meaning of History; they have become secularised, or disenchanted, as Max Weber had it. Does there then exist a central principle of explanation, taking the place of the old notions? And if so, how is it to be used to analyse this society?

Touraine gives the name Historicity to this central concept. It is an ensemble of principles which defines a society at a given moment in its history, which allows it to construct itself and to define its practices, and which guides the orientations of its actors. The domains where these principles are put to work, and which are central for our societies and perhaps for all societies, are those of knowledge, culture, production and their accumulation. They have changed profoundly since the first period of industrialisation, in the sense that they are no longer given, nor imposed on our societies from outside, as Progress or the meaning of History were imposed. Today, for the first time, it is men who make their history in what was called first post-industrial, and now the programmed, society, since it possesses a capacity for action upon itself, for programming its own development.

Historicity is apprehended through the attempts at control made by social actors, which is the reason why sociology must make it a priority to look into the study of social movements, 'the weave of our society. Their study is not a particular domain of sociology, a specialty; it is the flag of the sociology of action, which is itself at the head of the whole of sociology' (Touraine, 1978, p. 46). Our societies themselves are at issue in the struggle which is being waged between the ruling and the working classes – the social movements – for control of the production of knowledge, of culture and of accumulation. This struggle is also called Historicity.

This is why Touraine's approach is important. It is thus necessary to study the struggles for control of the three instruments which make societies, and also the struggles for their conquest. The difficulty is that the immediate categories of social practice, and the concrete struggles, most often of an offensive or reactive kind, conceal social movements; but it is through these that social movements and Historicity must be made to appear. Within this perspective, Touraine has studied several social movements, including the trade-union, feminist, ecological and anti-nuclear movements, and the student revolt, using an original method which consists of bringing together the actors in a group and putting them, in the presence of the sociologist, in a situation of auto-analysis. It is necessary, in effect, to reject the classical method, which consists of questioning actors and relating their answers to an economic or socio-professional situation, because this method separates a given situation from the consciousness which actors have of it. Contrary to appearances, one needs to understand, not how actors react to situations, but how they produce them and, in doing so, produce action.

An immense ambition! If the results of his studies of social movements often appear disappointing – perhaps on account of their excessive ambition or their use of a new and difficult method – the particular place of Touraine in French sociology is also linked to this ambition. His work unceasingly calls on sociologists to broaden their horizons by questioning societies on what they are becoming. These societies are, for the first time in the history of humanity, capable of orienting their future, of destroying themselves or of constructing something else. Humanity is giving birth to its destiny; actors are producing societies. Sociologists, who are also to some extent philosophers, must help them to be aware of this and, knowing better what they are doing, to become capable of acting with more lucidity.

4.2 Michel Crozier: From Bureaucratic Culture to Strategic Analysis

Michel Crozier was led to reflect on the functioning of bureaucracy by concrete studies of two large French administrative bodies, and within a framework elaborated at, among other places, the Center for Advanced Study in the Behavioral Sciences in Stanford, California. The work which resulted from this (Crozier, 1963) has retained its impact.

From observation of the functioning of these public enterprises, Crozier draws the following features into a theory of the bureaucratic phenomenon: the compartmentalisation of impersonal rules, the centralisation of decisions, and the isolation of different hierarchical categories. A bureaucratic enterprise is characterised by relations of this type, where unforeseen problems in the regulations, the zones of uncertainty, are at stake in the development of parallel power relations – a fourth feature of bureaucratic functioning. There are no methods for dealing with these problems other than the reinforcement of impersonality and centralisation; the only possible ways of reducing conflicts also increase dysfunctioning. So one falls into a vicious circle.

This type of analysis was not absolutely new, though Crozier's synthesis was, in many respects, very original, in particular in emphasising that the logic of the system renders it incapable of correcting itself. Change requires external pressure – the system is incapable of auto-correction – but this only reinforces already existing dysfunctions. Change can only come through crises which call in question the previous equilibrium, but these crises can only have lasting results if the organisation has prepared itself for change by learning a new set of rules, which is impossible in the bureaucratic structure. Change is the central problem, its resolution being envisageable only through the appearance of crises whose outcome is uncertain.

What is new in Crozier is the identification in the functioning of French society of features of the bureaucratic model, namely the identification of the bureaucratic model and culture, the isolation of the individual, the absence of informal activities, the fear of face-to-face relations which transforms every authority relationship into impersonal rules, and finally the weakness of the central power. The most famous application of the bureaucratic model to society is that of industrial relations:

> The fundamental problem posed by industrial relations in France concerns the difficulties experienced by workers and unions in communicating with the employers. But such problems can be considered as the exact replica of those created by the fear of face-to-face relations in our bureaucratic model. (Crozier, 1963, p. 315)

How have they been resolved?

> The centralisation of negotiations, State intervention, and the elaboration of more and more detailed impersonal rules have constituted the essential elements in the French response to the problem of communications between employers and employees. (ibid, p. 316)

This analysis has had a major impact on those in charge of French politics, economics and social matters. It has shaped a number of reflections and political decisions, in particular in the world of the planners.

Fourteen years after the publication of *The Bureaucratic Phenomenon*, there came *The Actor and the System* (1977). The object, construction of theory of organisations, is new. The authors, Crozier and Friedberg, want to distance themselves from the previous structural-functional theses, challenging, on the one hand, the rational aspect of roles and, on the other, the almost natural conformity of the occupants of a role with the expectations of their partners. (This critique is also aimed at the the interactionist school, of the Goffman type for example; see chapter 9). They put forward the following postulates:

——people never accept being treated as a means, in the service of the aims of the organisers. Each has his goals, his own objectives.

——in an organisation, the actor is free and autonomous. The role and the function assigned to him leave him a certain freedom of interpretation, which can extend as far as transformation of the initial definition of the role.

——the strategies of actors – the term 'actor' is retained, displacing that of 'individual' – are always rational, but of a limited and contingent rationality. Each sees the organisation in the light of his objectives (commercial personnel emphasising the importance of their function at the expense of those in production, who do likewise, etc. One cannot but defend one's territory; one is conditioned by day-to-day practice).

The concept of strategy is thus central, as long as it is not reified; the actor only rarely has clear objectives or coherent plans. His behaviour is active and rational, but his rationality is defined with respect more to the opportunities presented by the organisation, and by the behaviour of other actors, than to coherent objectives and plans. He may take an offensive line, seeking opportunities to improve his situation, or a defensive one, maintaining his margin of freedom and his capacity to act. To understand an actor's strategy, it is important to take into account his behaviour pattern. The three concepts to which the analysis of this behaviour is articulated are: power, uncertainty, and the system of action. These concepts, put into circulation by the exponents of strategic analysis, have been, and are, much used by management and by all those concerned with the functioning of organisations. One may say that their use typifies the current generation of managers.

From *The Bureaucratic Phenomenon* to *The Actor and the System* there is a distance, ignorance of which has caused numerous errors concerning Crozier's thinking. One might say, schematically, that it has gone from determinist culturalism to a model which places the actor's freedom at the centre of the system. The actor is seen as the site, and the condition of exercise, of games which reinforce, rather than constrain, his freedom. By placing the concepts of power, uncertainty and the system of action at the centre of the analysis, he gives great intelligibility to the concrete functioning of organisations, and confers great importance on strategic analysis today.

5 URBAN SOCIOLOGY

The history of urban sociology from the post-war years to the present day can be described in three phases, corresponding to the three above-noted periods in the history of sociological research:

> Three main reference models appear to us to have marked urban thinking in France during the last two or three decades, and these determine, in a sense, three phases of urban studies: after the technical phase of town and country planning, in the 1950s and 1960s, there came, at the end of the 1960s and in the 1970s, a period centred on the study of the economic and political determinants of the town. These overall perspectives are now avowedly in the process of replacement by a return devoted to everything that is 'local'. (Ganne, 1980, pp. 3–4)

This section draws heavily on Ganne's 1980 article in particular, and more generally, on the issue of the review *Economie et Humanisme* devoted to 'The Town and the Urban Question' in which it appeared.

5.1 The Technical Phase of Town and Country Planning

This was defined with regard to several phenomena whose effects converged; post-war reconstruction, a higher birth rate, the rural exodus, industrial growth, and finally, in France, the start of reflection on urban problems. It was necessary to build quickly, massively, and without a previous accumulation of theoretical experience. The beginnings of reconstruction were carried out in an anarchic way, towns spreading out without apparent logic or thought about development. Very quickly, this anarchy began to appear nonsensical to the decision-makers; order had to be imposed, and developmental perspectives decided upon. This was done in two directions. First came the organising of urban growth, starting with recognition of a town's different functions, and the more rational location of projects. Then – the politicians and administrative appointees having been struck by large disparities, like those between Paris and the provinces, or the case of certain regions which were becoming unbalanced, to the advantage of a few industrial or urban centres, etc. – an attempt was made to classify, order and list towns and their functions. This was the period of the typologies of towns in terms of their major variables; growth, industrial or other commercial functions, regional importance, etc.

The figure who dominated this period, and who impressed upon it a certain theoretical perspective, was Pierre-Henri Chombart de Lauwe (1965 and 1973). Heir to Marcel Mauss and his anthropological approach to social phenomena, he refused all determination of the latter by material factors, postulating instead that the urban framework is the reflection or image of society. The role of the sociologist is then to announce the needs of the population – needs to which the town must respond. He is the expert charged with enumerating, then ranking, these needs, and it is to his expertise that technicians of town planning and construction must submit. 'Against the hegemony of architect-planners, P. H. Chombart de Lauwe defends the rights of urban sociology' (Amiot, 1986 – the source for much of this paragraph). Architects tend to usurp the sociologists' educative role; yet it is the latter who have the skills necessary to define 'real needs', not the architect-planners and certainly not the economic planners and town planners who succeeded them. Architects must at least collaborate with the sociologists, whose metier it is. There is in Chombart de Lauwe 'a utopia of interdisciplinary cooperation, under the direction of the specialist in aspirations and needs-values' (Amiot, 1986, p. 40).

This proposal to transfer urban expertise to specialists in the human sciences brought Chombart de Lauwe into protracted conflict with the planning administrations, as well as with the national, regional and local political powers. In the end he resigned his official functions, contending that his voice had not been heard, while the urban experts and town planners were won over by a perspective of adaptation: 'Modernisation of the economy and its structures, carried out under the impetus of technical progress, presents the national consciousness with delicate problems of adaptation and accommodation' (Girard, in Reynaud, 1966, p. 460). The powers-that-be should adapt and accommodate, not direct.

During this period, specific measures were taken to extend a centralising policy inaugurated before the war, and continued under the German occupation. They included the Town Planning Delegation (DATA – Délégation à l'Aménagement du Territoire), the strengthening of legislation on urbanism, increased powers for central and regional bodies and local administrative bodies. But the most important position was granted to the State, itself a comment on the failure of 'municipalism' compared with other European countries. This failure may be attributed to the facts that, in France, real conflicts were, and are, dealt with in Paris, and that the 'influence of the lower middle class and of the self-employed agricultural population', who defended the interests of landed property (Duby, 1985, p. 76) meant that the task of making fundamental social choices, and of resisting social constraints, fell to the State.

The task devolved upon this centralising policy of urbanism, and put into operation through these bodies and this legislation, still remains that of 'unifying the urban framework by bringing out the different functions to be taken care of in a complementary way between towns over the country as a whole' (Ganne, 1980, p. 8). One is dealing here with organicist and functionalist perspectives, which ignore the role that the sociologists could, or would like to, have played. The intervention of the authorities was limited to technical domains, the urban phenomenon having, in these perspectives, an ineluctable character that one could do no more than organise. Urban sociology, in retreat after the failure of Chombart de Lauwe's proposals, no longer contested this technicist character, which is presented as self-evident once the previous orientation had been abandoned.

5.2 The Town Seen Through Its Economic and Political Determinants

The preceding double perspective (part ethnological, culturalist, and founded on the needs of the sociologists; part technicist, and that of the planners) was to be radically called into question at the end of the 1960s. Without doubt one can date the change from a highly documented article by Manuell Castells (Castells, 1968). In this article, having critically reviewed French and other work on the subject, and, in particular, having rejected the notion of urban culture (which was particularly aimed at the work of the Chicago School), Castells defined his own analytical perspective on the urban phenomenon: 'What we hold is that the fundamental features of this urban culture are the direct consequence of the industrialisation process and, for certain among them, of capitalist industrialisation' (p. 87). The author hopes that studies will be conducted on what he calls 'the urban institution' where the town is studied as an element of society as a whole in such a way that it disappears 'as a scientific object . . . as a real object itself' (p. 88). Four years later he entitled his book-manifesto *The Urban Question* (1972).

In Castells' analysis, urbanisation is not something to be taken for granted; on the contrary the urban raises questions, Ganne comments, 'insofar as it proves to be indissociable from the overall economic and political structures which, by regulating society, at the same time regulate the distribution of the activities from which urbanisation arises' (Ganne, 1980, p. 5). Hence the town cannot be understood without referring to economic determinants brought into play, in our capitalist society, by big economic interests and by the State apparatus. For example, the transfer of large steelworks from the iron-mining regions where they had been set up (in France, the eastern Lorraine region) to maritime sites (Fos-sur-Mer, near Marseille, and Dunkirk in the North) was decided according to criteria of industrial efficiency, and towns were thus developed or transformed for politico-economic reasons, the State apparatus supporting the logic of capitalist profitability.

This Marxist perspective gave rise to a series of reflections and analyses that had a certain impact in France and elsewhere, to the point where one could speak of a 'French school of Marxist urban sociology' (Godard, 1980). Urban researches carried out within this perspective were numerous and in general well documented; they were either done at the request of public administrative bodies, or were financed by them. The guideline for analyses was provided by the search for economic determinants transmitted by public bodies. The term 'local hegemonic systems' (Lojkine, 1980) was applied to the system of decision-making resulting from the co-ordination effected by the central power – which was always necessary to major urban projects – or the influence of economically powerful local notables and classes. Good examples of this type were provided by studies such as that done on major building projects in Lyon (the new commercial and business centre of the Part-Dieu, the decision to build Satolas International Airport, the creation of industrial development zones forty kilometres from the town centre, etc.). The study of these choices resulted in 'the observation that local policy was completely subordinated to the central State power and the dominant classes' (Lojkine, 1980, p. 5). In this perspective, the social effects of these choices on urban questions led to a reinforcement of class cleavage between the social stratum which benefited – the monopolistic upper middle class (*grande bourgeoisie*) – and the dominated social strata – the working class and the local middle class *(bourgeoisie locale)*, which were in any case, according to this analysis, in the process of decomposition. Finally, the local was swallowed up in the global, a term which has to be taken as referring to an alliance between the State apparatus and the monopolistic middle class (*bourgeoisie monopolistique*).

This type of analysis was also meant to elucidate the relations between industrialisation (public and private sectors taken together) and the administrative bodies charged with the general interest. The planners in charge of the economic management of society, and the industrialists who supported the idea of long-term management, were no longer opponents:

> A liberal like V. Giscard d'Estaing has completely accepted the conceptual tools and techniques of the new form of State intervention . . . Rigid opposition between liberalism and interventionism is merely superficial. To revive private initiative and to improve public intervention are two sides of the same policy of national power . . . (Amiot, 1986, p. 63).

The Marxist urbanists set out to condemn this osmosis.

5.3 The Return to Localism

The one-dimensional aspect of this analysis led to questions about the specificities, the particularities, of the town. If the previous reasoning was valid, urban particularisms were simply a residue of the past. This was an excessive suggestion, and was challenged by some of those selfsame people who had supported the previous thesis. Lojkine, in the article quoted above, explained that the renovation of the centre of Lille, carried out by a socialist authority with a view to the continued presence of, and support for, the less privileged classes, was absolutely inexplicable in terms of capitalist logic. It had to be admitted that other factors played a role, if the evolution of towns, and the fact that the urban was not the same as the global, were to be understood. In the same way, when Castells and Godard analysed urban movements in: *Monopolville* (1974), they ran up against the inability of the labour movement to relate to the demands of the urban movement. It is a feature of the urban phenomenon that one must study everyday life, and accounts of this life, in order to understand that which according to the previous theory should have happened, but did not.

From this there has sprung a body of research which takes the local as a central principle of analysis. But if the rejection of previous perspectives is clear, due to their 'too exclusively general, economic and political' form, the choice of the local is not free from ambiguities. What do sociologists mean by 'local'? It is a question of lifestyles, sociability networks, and local actors' strategies. But these perspectives are still incompletely thought through, and are not at all, or only poorly, integrated into a theory of the town and of the urban.

However, it is not without interest to analyse the degrees of freedom left to local actors, and the way in which they influence the decisions of the central power, or of national and local agents. Capitalising on the experience of the two previous periods of French urban sociology may allow a synthesis; but, though it pleases some to see signs of this, for the moment the construction of such a synthesis is not really apparent.

6 CONCLUSION: SOCIOLOGY AND SOCIETY – A NEW RELATIONSHIP

As may be seen, sociology's situation of isolation and absence from the social field, which characterised the 1950s, has been changing for some time; let us say, since the end of the 'Thirty Glorious Years'. The reasons for this are multiple (Bernoux, 1985, pp. 9 ff). Many represent a reversal of those which had given rise to the original situation. Firstly, a certain body of knowledge has grown up. The group of researchers and teachers who launched sociology in the field has come to maturity, the first sociology graduates of the 1960s having now almost thirty years of practice and experience. The research environment is well established; it may be reckoned that there are around five hundred sociologists at the CNRS, about the same number in universities and public bodies, plus another five hundred in private bodies. These fifteen hundred individuals constitute a stable, not very mobile, milieu, in the majority Parisian. During the same time, teaching has developed. Even though French universities have difficulty in giving a thorough training to a student body which is too large for the means at their disposal, a few respected professors maintain a high reputation. The results of empirical studies have accumulated, and are beginning to be analysed in a critical way. And finally the institution of sociology, less impassioned by politico-theoretical debates, but more realist, is beginning to produce rather than merely reproduce.

In this way, sociology's relationship with society is more objective. It is beginning to give a frankly positive, sometimes even too positive, response to the question of the utility of the social sciences. It sometimes asks researchers for applications which are very, or even excessively, concrete. This would tend to turn these researchers into producers of studies with a short-term purpose, which could not fail to create debate in the scientific community. It seems to us, however, that researchers are better equipped than before to distance themselves from the pressure of a social demand that is too concerned with applications.

This closer proximity to society, together with a change of attitude on the part of the social actors – particularly the public bodies which finance the universities and the CNRS – risks the introduction of an era of profound upheaval. Now that the period of economic prosperity is over, the institutionalisation experienced by research in the preceding period will probably be called into question. The expansion of the CNRS is unlikely to continue in the coming years, and another mode of development will have to be found, without giving up theoretical and basic research. The utility of sociology has been recognised but it has occurred in a changing world, and one which will perhaps try to attribute to it a new status. It is thus in a situation which will change, but whose contours are as yet difficult to discern.

6.1 The New Theory of the Socio-Economic

A final point: a team of researchers from different disciplines – sociology, economics, statistics – some of whom are, or have been, members of the INSEE (National Institute of Statistics and Economic Studies), has been working for several years on what some people feel might be called a new theory of the social. Rejecting as an ultimate explanatory principle the opposition between the individual and the social, which has for long been superimposed on the opposition between economics and sociology, they are looking for ways to construct the social through the choice of the 'rule of agreement, the reference to a universal form which goes beyond the particularities of persons' (Boltanski and Thévenot, 1987, p. 4). The concept of 'agreement' refers to the need in all societies to harmonise the different principles to which individuals and groups appeal in the course of their action. Of special importance here is the question of the constraints born of these indispensable agreements.

Each of the scientific explanations offered by the founding disciplines demonstrates 'the reality of a possible form of agreement between persons' through the social, or through the market. They:

> cannot treat of the relations between men in society, which is their aim, without taking into account the forms of *agreement* which men have fashioned. However, each of the disciplines from which we started out treats this agreement as a natural law, so that its construction becomes, automatically, impossible to grasp.

This construction is the object which we propose to study; it presupposes taking seriously the demand for agreements that a social order prescribes. We will seek to link up the regularity of observed behaviour, notably collective behaviour, or that of vested interests, not with positive laws like those of social facts (in the Durkheimian sense) or commercial exchanges, but with an obligation of agreement between people. (Boltanski and Thévenot, 1987, p. 8)

One can see how ambitious this project is. To understand it better, let us give two examples. The first is drawn from an article by Thévenot (1985), which had a large impact. Here he analyses Taylorism, putting the accent on the conditioning (*mise en état*) of the workers, to bring them to espouse the general forms on which the Taylorist model rests. This model is characterised by a form of imposed agreement, observable for example in Taylor's insistence on the exclusion of understandings which the workers might be able, or tempted, to make for themselves. The originality of Taylorism lies in the inability to see at the outset, as often happens, the oppression of the worker, or social control, or again the surplus value extorted by the owner. The essence of Taylorism can be seen in the study of the instruments on which the model is based; various instruments (from the deskilling machine to intimate collaboration between management and staff via time-clock, bonus, and workers' education) which are integral to the whole, considered as a form. This analysis is neither purely economic nor purely sociological, tending rather to go beyond the explanations given by these two disciplines, in order to offer an analysis in terms of the agreement which underlies the whole model.

Another historical example is that of workers' representatives in firms, and their manner of designation (for example, the case of safety delegates in coal-mines at the end of the nineteenth century). Union members always attempted to obtain a procedure in which the union would have a voice, while the owners took up contrary positions, for example that of direct elections without regard to union membership. A controversy of this type is defined as a point of contention, resulting in a question of order based on antagonistic general principles (Boltanski and Thévenot enumerate six) which are the basis for different legitimacies. Each justifies his action with reference to certain of these general principles – and sometimes the same ones – in order finally to reach an agreement.

The authors' attempts to theorise the social must not, they say, be interpreted in the perspective of a consensus theory, or a theory of the functional type. It is rather an analysis and a classification of the critical points of social life, and of ways of resolving them; how is one to understand conflict and negotiation in a society if not through their legitimation on the basis of general principles? They have attempted to classify – as is the nature of any science – and thereby provide a principle of intelligibility.

This perspective (should one speak of a 'new theory'?) is developing within an active group which possesses an instrument of dissemination, the *Cahiers du Centre d'Etudes de l'Emploi* (Notebooks of the Centre for Employment Studies). It is certainly to be followed attentively.

References

Adam, G. and Reynaud, J. D. (1978) *Conflits du travail et changement social* (Paris: Presses Universitaires de France).
Amiot, M. (1986) *Contre l'Etat, les sociologues* (Paris: Ed. de l'Ecole des Hautes Etudes en Sciences Sociales).
Bernoux, P. (1985) *La sociologie des organisations* (Paris: Seuil).
——, Motte D. and Saglio, J. (1973) *Trois ateliers d'O.S.* (Paris: Les Editions Ouvrières).
Boltanski, L. and Thévenot, L. (1987) *Les économies de la grandeur* (Paris: PUF, Cahiers du Centre d'Etudes de l'Emploi no. 31).
Boudon, R. (1967) *L'analyse mathématique des faits sociaux* (Paris: Plon).
—— (1968) *A quoi sert la notion de structure? Essai sur la signification de la notion de structure dans les sciences humaines* (Paris: Gallimard).
*—— and Bourricaud, F. (1982) *Dictionnaire critique de la sociologie* (Paris: PUF).
*Bourdieu, P. (1980) *Le sens pratique* (Paris: Minuit).
—— and Passeron, J. C. (1964) *Les héritiers* (Paris: Minuit).
Bunel, J. (1983) 'L'intervention sociologique et les mouvements sociaux de la société programmée', *L'Année sociologique*, pp. 489–507.
Castells, M. (1968) 'Y-a-t-il une sociologie urbaine?', *Sociologie du Travail*, no. 1, pp. 72–90.
—— (1972) *La question urbaine* (Paris: Maspero).
—— and Godard, F. (1974) *Monopolville* (Paris and The Hague: Mouton).
Chombart de Lauwe, P. H. (1965) *Essais de sociologie* (Paris: Les Editions Ouvrières).
—— (1973) *Des hommes et des villes* (Paris: Payot).
Collectif (1985) *Le travail et sa sociologie* (Paris: L'Harmattan).
Crozier, M. (1963) *Le phenomène bureaucratique* (Paris: Seuil).
*—— and Friedberg, E. (1977) *L'acteur et le système* (Paris: Seuil).
Duby, G. (ed.) (1985) *Histoire de la France urbaine*, vol. 5 (Paris: Seuil).
Duclos, D. (ed.) (1985) *Les sciences sociales dans le changement sociopolitique* (Paris: Economica).

Economie et Humanisme (1980) no. 252, *La ville et la question urbaine*.

Friedmann, G. (1938) *De la Sainte Russie à l'URSS* (Paris: Gallimard).

—— (1946) *Problèmes humains du machinisme industriel* (Paris: Gallimard).

—— (1973) *Où va le travail humain?* (Paris: Gallimard) 1st edn, (1950).

—— and Naville, P. (1962) *Traité de Sociologie du travail* (Paris: A. Colin).

Ganne, P. (1980) 'De l'aménagement du territoire aux études de quartier ou les avatars de la question urbaine', *Economie et Humanisme*, no. 252, pp. 3–12.

Girard, A. (1961) *La Réussite sociale en France* (Paris: PUF).

Godard, F. (1980) 'Sociologie urbaine?', *Economie et Humanisme*, no. 252, pp. 13–23.

Godelier, M. (1982) *Les sciences de l'homme et de la société en France*. Rapport au Ministre de la Recherche et de l'Industrie. See chapter on 'Sociologie. Bilan et perspectives' by J. C. Passeron, esp. p. 190.

Guillaume, M. (ed.) (1986) *L'état des sciences sociales en France* (Paris: La Découverte).

Gurvitch, G. (1963) *La vocation actuelle de la sociologie*, vol. 1 (Paris: PUF).

Le Bras, G. *et al.* (1966) *Aspects de la sociologie française* (Paris: Les Editions Ouvrières).

Lojkine, J. (1980) 'Le marxisme et les recherches urbaines', *Economie et Humanisme*, no. 252, pp. 24–32.

Mallet, S. (1963) *La nouvelle classe ouvrière* (Paris: Seuil).

Paradeise, C. (1988) 'Acteurs et institutions: la dynamique du marché du travail', *Sociologie du travail*, vol. 1, pp. 79–105.

Reynaud, J. D. (ed.) (1966) Tendances et volontés de la société française (Paris: SEDEIS., Futuribles).

—— (1982) *Sociologie des conflits du travail* (Paris: PUF).

Sweezy, P. (1974) 'Foreword' to H. Braverman *Labor and Monopoly Capital* (New York: Monthly Review Press).

Thévenot, L. (1985) 'Les investissements de forme' in *Conventions économiques* (Paris: PUF, Cahiers du Centre d'Etudes de l'Emploi, no. 29).

Touraine, A. (1965) *Sociologie de l'action* (Paris: Seuil).

—— (1973) *Production de la société* (Paris: Seuil).

*—— (1978) *La voix et le regard* (Paris: Seuil).

—— (1984) *Le retour de l'acteur* (Paris: Fayard).

—— (1986) 'Sociologies et sociologues', in Guillaume (ed.) (1986) pp. 134–43.

11   Sociology in Germany: Institutional Development and Paradigmatic Structure
Ansgar Weymann

INTRODUCTION

The German Sociological Association (Deutsche Gesellschaft für Soziologie/DGS) was established in 1909. Its first meeting was held in Frankfurt in 1910. Both dates indicate a longish history of German sociology. That history also signals a typically German problem: this chapter is in fact not about sociology in all Germany nor about all sociology in German. First, sociology in the German Democratic Republic is excluded. After a late start and a time of troubled recovery in the late 1960s and early 1970s, which included conflicts with the official doctrine of Marxism-Leninism (Weymann, 1972), it may now be experiencing an interesting development. Second, sociology in Austria (and German-speaking Switzerland) is also excluded, although separate national sociological associations were only founded very recently and mutual memberships as well as common annual meetings continue – for example, 5th meeting Vienna, 1926; 6th meeting Zurich, 1928; 24th meeting Zurich, 1988 (see Lepsius, 1981a; Knoll *et al.*, 1981; Käsler, 1981). Third, this article will not deal with the impact of Nazism, which forced about 80 per cent of sociologists to emigrate or to retire and caused some other scholars to collaborate with the regime (Lepenies, 1981; Lepsius, 1981b; Mertens, 1987). Thus it is basically my aim to describe sociology in the Federal Republic of Germany, with the history of sociology in Germany as the broader frame of reference (König, 1987; Lepsius, 1981a; Lüschen, 1979a).

INSTITUTIONAL DEVELOPMENT

Sociology has been one of the most rapidly expanding academic disciplines. In 1953–4, staff (professors and others in full-time teaching and research positions) included some fifty scientists (Busch, 1956). Around 1977 the number of professorships had gone up to 279, the number of other teaching and research positions to 551. By that time the academic staff was 830 in total and sociology was offered as a major degree (M.A./Ph.D) in forty-one universities (see Lüschen, 1979a). According to Ludger Viehoff, of the German Science Council, in 1981 sociology was offered as a major degree in forty-three universities. Viehoff counted 425 professors and 865 other senior teaching and research positions – 1290 scientists in all (Viehoff, 1984, p. 266). By 1986 the number of professorships had reached 484 (Landmeier, 1987). This exceptional increase was accompanied by a rapidly growing number of students and graduates. The number of students with sociology as a major grew from 1086 in 1960 to as many as 21 705 in 1981 (Viehoff, 1984, p. 267). (There are, of course varying ways of counting students numbers; Hofmann, 1986; Lepsius, 1979.)

Sociology grew faster than most other academic disciplines. Whereas the academic staff in total increased at a rate of 595 per cent between 1960 and 1981, the comparative figure for sociology is 2481 per cent (Viehoff, 1984, p. 265). The growth was extremely unevenly distributed over university departments. For example, the number of professors is 30 in Bielefeld, 22 in Frankfurt, 15 at the Free University of Berlin; other research and teaching positions total 48 at the Free University of Berlin, 40 in Bielefeld, and 20 in Frankfurt. On the other hand, universities with only one or two positions in sociology can be found as well: for example, Passau, Eichstätt, Kiel, Würzburg (Hofmann, 1986). The number of students enrolled range from 2299 at the Free University of Berlin to 3 in Eichstätt (Viehoff, 1984, p. 265). Both factors – extreme expansion and uneven distribution – have issued in severe problems today. For about one decade, successful university careers were too easy to achieve. A large cohort of graduates took advantage of this situation, and have occupied positions for a long time. The replacement rate is low. The uneven distribution brought into being too large as well as too small departments. Today, in the late 1980s, the situation has changed considerably. The number of student enrolments in sociology stagnates or decreases. All too often vacant positions are not refilled but are cut out. It is somewhat random which positions remain and which positions are eliminated. In the longer run some departments might be closed down.

This brief description of the ups and downs of sociology resembles the situation in other countries represented in this volume. In some respects, however, the German situation is more specific. In addition to sociological departments in universities, a large number of non-university research units exist. These institutions are maintained in different ways. Growth and welfare depend on research, labour market or social policy, etc., not on educational policy. Furthermore, the financing is different. Whereas universities are basically financed by the states (Länder), other institutions are mainly financed by the Federal Government, or by other sources. The Länder differ greatly with respect to financial capacity and educational policy. This situation exerts specific impacts on universities, but not on other institutions. The latter deserve separate comment.

First of all the Max-Planck-Gesellschaft maintains two institutes where relevant sociological research is carried out: the Max-Planck-Institut für Bildungsforschung in Berlin (Max-Planck-Institute for Human Development and Education) and the Max-Planck-Institut für Gesellschaftsforschung in Cologne (Max-Planck-Institute for Research on Society). Another important and large non-university institution is the Wissenschafszentrum Berlin (Berlin Science Centre), mainly financed by the Federal Government, the Senate of Berlin, grants, etc.; sociological research on labour policy, management, consumers, and new technologies is a major component of its programme. The Wissenschaftszentrum (Zapf) as well as the two Max Planck Institutes (Mayer and Mayntz respectively) are headed by sociologists as president or director. A third large institution of independent and/or 'pure' extra-university research is the Gesellschaft Sozialwissenschaftlicher Infrastruktureinrichtungen (GESIS) in Mannheim. GESIS incorporates three different institutes: Zentrum für Umfragen, Methoden and Analysen (Centre for Surveys, Methods and Analysis/ ZUMA) in Mannheim, Informationszentrum Sozialwissenschaften (Social Sciences Information Centre/IZ) in Bonn, Sozialarchiv Köln (Cologne Social Archive). GESIS supplies an infrastructure of social science service institutions. In the fourth place, 'joint ventures' between universities and the Deutsche Forschungsgemeinschaft (National Science Foundation/DFG) are of interest. Besides offering individual grants to applicants, the DFG finances Special Research Programmes (*Sonderforschungsbereiche*/SFB) and Focused Research Programmes (*Schwerpunktprogramme*/SPP). These programmes give substantial support to larger interdisciplinary groups of scientists from one individual university (SFB) or from several universities (SPP). 'Sociological' programmes are currently underway, for example, at the Universities of Bremen, Bielefeld, Frankfurt, Mannheim and Munich.

These programmes run for five to fifteen years. I will conclude this outline of the institutional development of sociology with some remarks on the German Sociological Association (Deutsche Gesellschaft für Soziologie/DGS) and on the Association of Professional Sociologists (Berufsverband der Soziologen/BDS). The DGS, founded in 1909, had 834 members in 1983 (Ziegler, 1984). Membership is restricted to sociologists who have graduated with a PhD. (Being German or German-speaking is not required.) The DGS is strictly an association of academics; the BDS was additionally established in the 1970s. The BDS brings together professionals. Its existence reflects the perceived need for a professional association representing the estimated fifteen thousand sociology graduates.

TEACHING, GRADUATES AND THE LABOUR MARKET

In 1949–50 a total of 148 courses in sociology were being offered by twenty three universities. Twenty-five years later, in 1975, thirty-nine universities offered 2571 courses in sociology per semester. This is an increase of 1673 per cent (Klima, 1979). Although sociology lost prestige and public support in the next decade, the number of courses still grew. According to Heitbrede, seventy universities offered sociology and the number of courses per semester had reached 5682 (Heitbrede, 1986, p. 121). The extremely uneven distribution of courses over the various university departments should be noted. On the one hand there are departments with over 300 courses per semester, on the other hand small departments offer as few as three courses (ibid, p. 109). In terms of topics or sociological subject matters things have not changed very much over the same period from 1949 to 1985. In rank order: Research Methods are most frequently offered; next is General Sociological Theory; in third place Sociology of Labour/Economy/Industry; in fourth position we find Social Psychology/Socialisation/Life-course and Biographical Research (ibid, p. 111). General Sociological Theory today is most often represented by the 'interpretative-hermeneutic paradigm'; by contrast the previously important Marxist paradigm is now in a marginal position. We will not go deeper into details of rank orders of various subject-matters, but would point out the chronic differentiation. Fragmentation and over-specialisation of curriculum are now more of a problem than ever. The policy of the 1970s which aimed to concentrate professional sociological *knowledge* on a very restricted number of longstanding social problems did not meet with success. Professionalisation today is about applicable *skills*. It requires one to be familiar with methods of empirical research, data processing, statistics; to be intensively trained in the application and implementation of research; and to use general sociological theory as a means of observing and analysing problems and developing strategies of intervention.

Continuity and change in teaching sociology reflect the labour market situation and public support. With the transformation of sociology from an 'orchard' to a professional discipline, graduating in sociology as a major became possible. The 'diploma' was introduced in the 1960s. The diploma supplemented or replaced the traditional MA degree. Whereas *Diplom* in German terms is perceived as indicating a professional training, MA is seen as testifying liberal arts skills. The introduction of the *Diplom* as the regular, compulsory degree in sociology went along with university expansion, rapidly growing student numbers, and belief that sociology would become one of the most important tools for social analysis, political planning and sophisticated intervention in social problems. It is worth recalling that in 1969 the board of the German Sociological Association warned against the introduction to a specific diploma in sociology as a major subject – but to no effect (DGS, 1969). During the 1970s it transpired that the demand for professional sociologists was much lower than had optimistically been expected. The unemployment rate increased. Nowadays it is one of the highest among university graduates. Nevertheless approximately 15 000 sociologists are now working in a professional position (according to estimates). The labour market has accepted professional sociologists, but the ratio of graduates to vacant positions is very unfavourable. Sociologists graduating nowadays have as many or as few employment possibilities as anybody else in the humanities. They have to be enterprising and find their own way in a difficult labour market. The type of personality required is unfortunately not widespread among sociologists among whom social engagement, empathy and a civil service orientation prevails. The average student is interested in social problems and social policy, willing to help the underprivileged, but is less interested in the research, methods, statistics, data processing and general theoretical competence which would give him or her the necessary general professional skills. These difficulties and contradications have caused stagnation or decline in enrolment. However, new developments can be observed. Students choosing sociology today have a more realistic orientation towards study and professional work. They are well aware of the problems they are going to face, but trust their own ability to find a way. They are basically interested in sociology as a subject and are willing to accept the necessary components of training. Therefore the gap between supply and demand might become smaller over the years to come, in terms of both quantity and quality. For the present a large number of surveys conducted by various university departments of sociology indicate the following: approximately one-third of graduates are immediately appointed to appropriate positions, another third fill acceptable professional positions after a period of intensive search and extensive applications; the final third faces long-term problems which are not solved, or at least not solved in an acceptable way (Grühn, 1985; Tessaring, 1982; Backes, 1983; Brusten *et al.*, 1983; Ebbighausen *et al.*, 1982; Kärner and Giegler, 1985).

UTILISATION

The decline of student enrolment, the labour market problem of graduates, and the end of the period in which sociology penetrated other disciplines are disturbing; they undermine confidence in the usefulness and applicability of sociology. At the same time other university disciplines have successfully incorporated sociological methods and theoretical concepts. Hostility towards the 'leftist' subject of sociology may have almost ceased to exist but attitudes have turned instead to an even more threatening indifference and neglect. The public, politicians, the administration and employers perceive sociology as not really powerful in terms of its capacity to solve old and new problems by means of scientific innovation and practical improvement.

The usefulness of sociology is questioned in two ways. On the one hand, teaching and learning and student skills are criticised. This development may limit the acceptance of sociology in university departments and will result in a revision of the curriculum and standards, but will not extinguish or radically diminish the discipline as an academic subject. In any case, sociology shares this fate with other social sciences and humanities. More of a threat, on the other hand, is the criticism of sociological research. Whereas the public interest in education is generally relatively low and financial spending stagnates, efforts to support research are still great. Research policy has kept its public support and budgets increase. The legitimacy of an academic discipline is probably more dependent on the perceived prestige of its

research than upon its esteemed or non-esteemed contribution
to education. Being well aware of this fact the National Science
Foundation (DFG) launched a large-scale Focused Research
Programme (SPP) on the utilisation of social sciences in the early
1980s. This programme combined over forty single projects, covering
a large variety of fields in applied sociology. To summarise the purpose
of this programme, I will quote the National Science Foundation's
(DFG) council:

> There is evidence that social science has influenced policy and
> society extensively in the last fifteen years. At the same time it
> cannot be claimed that systematic research on utilisation is pursued.
> Therefore, we do not always know which findings are selected and
> implemented by users, and which factors determine the utilisation in
> various institutions. Research on utilisation can produce some
> insight into the usefulness of findings from the point of view of
> scientists and it can allow the correction of prejudices on the part of
> users. Furthermore, it may define the potentialities and boundaries
> of applied social science in general. (The President, German
> Research Community, grant no. 322 144, 1981, p. 3.)

It is impossible to give a detailed overview on the results of this large-
scale programme. As a general outcome it can be stated that utilisation
in a number of fields is largely underestimated (Weymann, Ellerman
and Wingens, 1986; Wingens and Weymann, 1988). Utilisation is too
exclusively conceived as a technical procedure of planning, consulting
and the implementation of policies. Utilisation no doubt happens (or
not) in this way as a process of implementing legal and fiscal
procedures or of improving organisational structures. But the use of
sociological knowledge might just as readily take the form of a change
of public opinion via the media; or utilisation happens when new
generations get a different education which includes knowledge of
social science, as even larger parts of the population pass through
institutions of higher education and come into touch with the social
sciences. This utilisation largely takes place as a slow and latent
process which effectively transforms culture, values and perceptions.
Looking on utilisation in a broader sense and over longer periods one
has to recognise a penetrating impact of the social sciences on culture
and society (Beck, 1982; Bonss and Hartmann, 1985; Tenbruck, 1984;
Beck and Bonss, 1988).
    Confidence in the usefulness of social research and applied soci-

ology is indicated by stable financial support from the National Science Foundation (DFG), the Volkswagen Foundation, and other sources. It is also indicated by continuing grants from the Federal Government. In this case it is interesting to observe how much support of social research depends on public interest in 'trendy' social problems. Whereas the quantity of research money does not change very rapidly, what it is spent on changes fundamentally. Thus the Ministry of Education and Science (BMBW) was the most important support institution in the 1960s, the Ministry of Labour and Social Order (BMA) took over this role in the 1970s, whereas today the Ministry of Research and Technology (BMFT) is the most important institution in financing (contracted) social research. Public interest sets up a hierarchy of political relevance, and this determines the willingness of politicians to support social science research selectively. Utilisation cannot be analysed the other way around: the influence of social science on the media, public opinion, policy, and their conceptions of relevant problems, is very small. Applied sociology is often a useful tool for backing arguments in public debates; it is less influential on the internal decision-making process (Weymann and Wingens, 1988a and b). The steady situation of social research, as well as the thematic dependence of sociology on changing political and public frames of reference, is also reflected by the installation of several large semi-independent institutes of applied social research in the last two decades. To name just a few: the German Youth Institute (Munich), the Institute on Labour Market and Occupational Research (Nuremberg), the Federal Institute of Vocational Training (Berlin), the University Information System (Hanover), Woman and Society (Hanover), and many others. All of them are involved in research, analysis, counselling, and consulting. These institutes are predominantly financed by the Federal Government, but also by the *Länder*. Also other institutes exist, but they are being maintained by trade unions, political parties, private foundations, etc. This illustrates how extensively applied social research is used in day-to-day political life to collect information and/or to back political arguments and positions.

SOCIAL REFORMERS, PROFESSIONALS AND THE SCIENTIFIC COMMUNITY

In 1973, Joachim Matthes published an introduction to the study of sociology. In his preliminary remarks he described the 'state of the art' in a way which is still to the point: theoretical weakness, divergent curricula, lack of public prestige, exaggerated service expectations on the part of other departments, shortage of brilliant young scholars (in a time of high demands), fragmentation and particularism, and lack of practice, applicability and utilisation. According to Matthes, 'Sociology as an academic discipline presented a picture of misery at the beginning of the 1970s' (Matthes, 1981, p. 24).

In giving an explanation for the misery, Matthes argues that sociology was traditionally located in departments of economics and/ or philosophy until well into the twentieth century and had difficulty subsequently in separating itself successfully. The process of becoming a separate discipline was disrupted by the Nazi terror from 1933 to 1945. Later, in the 1950s, sociology was dominated by 'grand old men' and developed a structure of 'schools': Frankfurt (Horkheimer, Adorno), Cologne (König), Hamburg/Münster (Schelsky)and Berlin. The seclusion of schools prevented the development of a competitive market of scholars and ideas. The lack of a forceful scientific community of sociologists caused another problem, which is still pertinent: a sociologist's academic career is not exclusively dependent on his or her being accepted within the scientific community and on meeting its standards. A career can just as well be based upon conformity to the expectations and standards of lay constituencies: for example, media, politicians, unions, employers, parties, administration, social movements, etc. Reviewing Matthes's outline of the state of the sociological art, one has to agree with most of his critical remarks, but I will suggest an additional element in the present situation: the scientific community itself is split into a number of subgroups. On the one hand, theorists and methodologists endeavour to purify the discipline in terms of analytical and methodological strength; on the other, scholars, working in applied sociology, are basically interested in improved utilisation. For the latter the accumulation of knowledge, the institutionalisation of data-based research, and co-operation with the administration and other social forces in the implementation and evaluation of policies and politics, are the main points of interest. Although logically the two strategies are not mutually exclusive, separation along the lines 'purified basic research versus sophisticated applied research' does happen. This situation is different from the one observed by Matthes. His lay public orientation towards social action and action-research is less important to sociology today, because sociology is no longer a sinecure for journalists, politicians, social workers and social reformers looking for social prestige, a reliable income, reduced professional risks and the aura of a scientific background as they pursue their causes.

PUBLICATION

The depression of the market for scientific books is a general phenomenon, but for some disciplines, including sociology, the downward tendency is so strong that publishers have gone bankrupt or changed their programmes. Today it is more difficult than before for a young scholar to get work published or to get acceptable contract terms. There is simultaneously a decline in the reading public on the one hand and a steady increase in the number of authors on the other. The *Soziologische Revue* (Sociological Review) is offered as many as 1000 to 1200 items per year to review. This massive (over)production reflects the impact of the 'publish or perish' principle as well as the weakness of an effective selection procedure within sociology as a scientific community (Borkenau and Kammer, 1988; Matthes, 1988). The scope of literature is affluent, pluralistic, and diffuse in structure. With respect to sociological journals, the most prestigious still are: *Kölner Zeitschrift für Soziologie, Zeitschrift für Soziologie* and *Soziale Welt*. But besides these long-respected journals, a growing number of other journals which specialise in a certain field of applied sociology or which have an interdisciplinary profile have come into being. These journals reflect the multi-paradigmatic and diffuse structure of sociology. It is worth mentioning that none of them is printed in English, or simultaneously in German and English, given that in the natural sciences and some other social sciences German journals printed in English do exist. More than other social sciences, sociology is tied to the German language and to national traditions of society, culture and history. Of course sociology has in all countries an ethnocentric bias; and this general circumstance or problem is naturally true for German sociology with its long tradition and its institutional strength.

PARADIGMATIC STRUCTURE AND APPROACHES

In their Introduction to this volume Bryant and Becker develop a paradigmatic framework of sociological approaches which mainly covers empirical-analytical, hermeneutic, and historical-institutional sociology. In this final paragraph we will follow their typology but will also suggest some elaboration. It should be noticed too that we will not try to submit scholars to this categorical framework exhaustively. We will simply give examples without pretending that our selection is the only possible one.

The category *empirical-analytical sociology* includes neopositivism, rational-choice theory (utilitarianism), critical rationalism, and data-based sociology. It largely overlaps what we earlier called applied sociology, but is not identical with it in so far as applied sociology can also make use of other methodological approaches. A traditional stronghold of empirical-analytical sociology is the department of sociology at the University of Cologne (formerly von Wiese, König, Scheuch, Neidhardt, Esser) and the Sozialarchiv (Scheuch). Cologne was and still is a centre of empirical-analytical methodology in sociological research. New institutes to be mentioned are: The Max-Planck-Institut für Gesellschaftsforschung also situated in Cologne (Mayntz, Scharpf), and the Wissenschaftszentrum in Berlin (Zapf). Other centres of empirical-analytical sociology are the department of sociology at Mannheim University (Müller, Ziegler) and the nearby Zentrum für Umfragen, Methoden and Analysen (Mohler, Esser, Küchler, Mayer, Kaase). Also the Max-Planck-Institut für Bildungsplanung (Human Development and Education) in Berlin must be mentioned in this respect (Mayer). Several other non-university research units fall within this category including two leading institutes on industrial sociology: Soziologisches Forschungsinstitut in Göttingen (Schumann; Baethge), and the Institut für Soziologische Forschung in Munich (Lutz). The majority of special research programmes (*Sonderforschungsbereiche*) might be best covered by this category too, but may also follow other paradigmatic approaches. Applied sociology in general makes use of different methodological approaches of which the empirical-analytical approach is probably the mainstream one, but it is not the only choice. For the same reason it does not make much sense to identify sections of the German Sociological Association with specific approaches. However, there are two exceptions: the sections on Methodology and Social Indicators fall overwhelmingly within the empirical-analytical category – for example, Allerbeck (Frankfurt), Friedrich (Hamburg), Glatzer (Frankfurt), Ziegler (Munich), Zapf (Berlin).

A different situation is found in the case of the *hermeneutic paradigm* because a comparable research infrastructure does not exist. Scholars committed to this approach are less provided with comparable institutional support. However, hermeneutic sociology has a long and well-known tradition in Germany (for example, Schütz, Husserl, Scheler, and other phenomenologists). With the decline of Marxist sociology, which had predominated in the 1960s, this approach was 'rediscovered'. The fresh interest in everyday life, knowledge, meaning, and the theory of action, directed attention to related interpretative approaches like symbolic-interactionism, ethnomethodology, ethnotheory, and the sociology of language/ sociolinguistics. A consequently greater interest was also taken in research on life-events, human development, biographical studies, etc. It is difficult and somewhat arbitrary to connect names to this approach, because it cannot be done via an institutional structure, and there is sophisticated scholarship in abundance. Having said that the sociology of language/sociolinguistics is represented by Soeffner (Hagen), Grathoff (Bielefeld), Oevermann (Frankfurt) and Schütze (Kassel) among others; sophisticated biographical studies are carried out by Matthes (Erlangen), Kohli (Berlin), Fuchs (Hagen), Hörning (Berlin); theoretical work in symbolic interactionism and the interpretative paradigm in general is found in Matthes (Erlangen), Joas (Erlangen), Luckmann (Konstanz), Oevermann (Frankfurt), and a former Bielefeld group of sociologists, the Arbeitsgruppe Bielefelder Soziologen (for example, Weymann, Matthes, Schütze, Bohnsack, Meinefeld, Springer). Just recently another traditional field of sociological investigation and theorising has attracted fresh attraction: culture (interest in culture and society having for a time been biased in favour of society). Studies on culture are associated with the names of Matthes (Erlangen), Stagl (Bonn), Weiss (Kassel), Lepsius (Heidelberg), Lipp (Würzburg), Sprondel and Seyfarth (Tübingen), Neidhardt (Cologne), and others.

In several contributions to this volume the *historical-institutional paradigm* is associated with Elias's work. Unlike the Netherlands, no 'Elias School' has emerged in Germany, but his work is well known and appreciated. For example, the University of Bielefeld awarded him an honorary doctorate. (Elias was a fellow of Bielefeld's Centre for Interdisciplinary Studies.) Other scholars within this approach are Korte (Bochum) and Gleichmann (Hanover). Historical-institutional sociology in the German tradition should also be traced back to the works of Weber, who continues to inspire sociological investigations today. The Weberian tradition is reflected and continued in the work of Winckelmann (formely Munich), Schluchter (Heidelberg) and Tenbruck (Tübingen), to mention only a few eminent scientists within this approach. Most comparable to work in the sociology of modernity and culture which evokes widespread interest in the contemporary United States (for example, Riesman, Bell, Bellah, Sennet and others), are the historical-institutional studies on the theory of modernisation by, for example, Beck (Bamberg) or Berger (Bielefeld). A specific variation of the modernisation theory, the pessimistic view on civilisation held by Schelsky (formerly Münster) or Tenbruck (Tübingen), is both interesting and, perhaps, very German. A final comment should be given on the relationship between sociology and history. Sociology replaced the traditional historical perspective in German universities and schools in the 1960s and 1970s. The dominance of a sociological point of view on society and history, however, did not last for long. The historical perspective soon recovered among teachers and with the public. Scholars working in historical sociology are, for example, Lepenies (Berlin), or Jonas (formerly Mainz) or, as a historian, Wehler (Bielefeld).

As was mentioned at the beginning of this section, the paradigmatic structure of German sociology does not fit in completely with the categorical framework developed by Bryant and Becker. The Frankfurt School of Critical Sociology (Horkheimer, Adorno, Habermas) has a specific tradition and approach of its own which does not really fit any of the three categories above. The Critical School incorporates hermeneutic and historical-institutional sociology, political economy, economics, and aspects of political science and psychoanalysis, for example. It should be treated as a paradigmatic type in its own right. Another inspiring contribution to German sociology, and one influential in theoretical discourse, is the work of Luhmann, who took up Parsons's structural-functional theory and turned it into a very sophisticated theory of social systems. The Luhmann (Bielefeld) – Habermas (Frankfurt) controversy fascinated sociologists in the 1970s.

We will not trace in detail other approaches which can be found within German sociology, like, for example, the interest in the sociology of social movements which momentarily enjoys great popularity. Instead we will conclude with a general statement on the paradigmatic structure of sociology in Germany. It took sociology about one hundred years to emancipate itself from 'mother disciplines', originally philosophy and economics. During the 1960s and 1970s sociology gained such an intellectual hold and institutional strength that an independent institutionalisation became possible and the subject exercised a fundamental influence on other disciplines.

The sociological point of view more or less effectively penetrated economics, law, medicine, psychology, history, philosophy, pedagogics, linguistics and political science, etc. After having incorporated sociological concepts, however, these disciplines proved impervious to further influence from sociology, treating it as a junior partner only. This new and at the same time classical status must be faced without resentment. There remain possibilities of interdisciplinary collaboration.

Close co-operation between sociology, political science and law can be found within administrative science; sociology, psychology and medicine work together within therapies and education; sociology does interdisciplinary work with engineering and natural sciences in various areas of technological innovation and impact; together with economics sociology investigates problems of social policy, employment, etc.; sociology is participating in research on contemporary social problems and social movements like AIDS, the environment, women's liberation, minorities, immigrants, etc. These kinds of interdisciplinary co-operation in applied research create a variety of specific, specialised theoretical and methodological approaches. They are too small to fit in with the typology of paradigms, and are often short-lived, but they can be inspiring too. Components of what emerges here eventually, after a long selection process, become part of sociology's mainstream paradigmatic structure. On the other hand, it cannot be excluded that all this indicates instead the subject's progressive dissolution.

ACHIEVEMENTS?

Yes, achievements definitely have been made in terms of quantitative growth and institutionalisation: staffs have grown, student enrolments have increased, and departments of sociology or sociological institutes exist at almost every university. Book production and production of a great variety of journals has accelerated. A considerable number of research units have been established. Sociology graduates can be found widespread in a diversity of professions.

But severe problems remain; non-achievements have also to be acknowledged. There is no balance between supply and demand in the number of graduates and the fit between the qualifications offered by employees and the skills sought by employers is inadequate. Even though this is not a new problem it still has not been solved. Then, too, the research situation is weakening. A split between research and teaching has opened up. Specialised research units have come into existence in large numbers outside, and even inside, the university system; research and teaching units are increasingly differentiated. While teaching facilities depend on usually small university budgets, research is largely dependent on fresh money from various extra-mural sources. No doubt this is welcome because university research funds are too small and their supplementation or replacement is necessary. Even so, the *raison d'étre* of teaching and research is disintegrating; Humboldt's idea of their unity is more and more a historical memory.

References

Backes, R. (1983) 'Projekstudium: Situation Saarbücker Diplomsoziologen in Studium and Beruf', *Soziologie*, vol. 11, pp. 137–51.

Beck, U. (1982) *Soziologie und Praxis* (Göttingen: O. Schwartz).

—— and Bonss, W. (1988), *Verwendung, Verwandlung, Verwissenschaftlichung* (Franfurt: Suhrkamp).

Bonss, W. and Hartmann, H. (1985) *Entzauberte Wissenschaft* (Göttingen: O. Schwartz).

Borkenau, P. and Kammer, D. (1988) 'Publizieren oder resignieren? Subjektive Perspektiven und Bewaltigungsstrategien des Mittelbaus der Universität Bielefeld', *Zeitschrift für Soziologie*, vol. 17, pp. 72–9.

Brusten, M. *et al.* (1983) 'Arbietsmarkt und Berufserfahrungen Wuppertaler Sozialwissenschaftler', *Soziologie*, vol. 11, pp. 152–76.

Busch, A. (1956) 'Stellenplan und Lehrkörperstruktur der Universitäten und Hochschulen in der Bundesrepublik und in Berlin (West) 1953/54', in H. Plessner (ed.) *Untersuchungen zur Lage der deutschen Hochschullehrer*, vol. 3 (Göttingen: Vandenhoek & Rupprecht).

DGS (1969) 'Erklärung des Vorstandes der Deutschen Gesellschaft für Soziologie zum Hauptfachstudium der Soziologie vom 11.4.1969', *Kölner Zeitschrift für Soziologie und Sozialpsychologie*, vol. 21, pp. 444–5.

Ebbighausen, R. *et al.* (1982) 'Soziologen in der Grauzone? Erste Ergebnisse einer empirischen Untersuchung uber Studium, Berufsverbleib, Arbeitslosigkeit and Ausweichstrategien Berliner Diplomsoziologen', *Soziologie*, vol. 10. pp. 17–60.

Grühn, D. (1985) 'Sozialwissenschaften zwischen Akademikerarbeitslosigkeit und Deprofessionalisierung', *Soziologie*, vol. 13, pp. 95–119.

Heitbrede, V. (1986) 'Identifikation einer Disziplin. Stand und Entwicklung der westdeutschen Soziologielehre 1975–1985', *Soziale Welt*, vol. 37, pp. 107–42.

Heitbrede-Florian, V. (1985) 'Praxis auf Rezept? Angewandte Soziologie im amerikanischen Lehrbetrieb', *Soziolgie*, vol. 13, pp. 39–48.

Hofmann, G. (1986) 'Die methodologische Ausbildung von Soziologen', *Soziologie*, vol. 14. pp. 37–51.

Kärner, H. and Giegler, H. (1985) 'Berufskarrieren Giessener Sozialwissenschaftler', *Soziologie*, vol. 14, pp. 120–42.

Käsler, D. (1981) 'Der Streit um die Bestimmung der Soziologie auf den deutschen Soziologentagen 1910–1930', in Lepsius (1981a) pp. 199–244.

Klima, R. (1979) 'Die Entwicklung der soziologischen Lehre an den westdeutschen Universitäten 1950–1975. Eine Analyse der Vorlesungsverzeichnisse', in Lüschen (1979a) pp. 221–56.

Knoll, R. *et al.* (1981) 'Der österreichische Beitrag zur Soziologie von der jarhundertwende bis 1938', in Lepsius (1981a) pp. 59–101.

König, R. (1987) *Soziologie in Deutschland. Begründer/Verächter/Verfechter* (München/Wien: Hanser).

Landmeier, R. (1987) 'Die unbekannte Fachgemeinschaft. Materialien zur Socialstruktur der Soziologen der Bundesrepublik Deutschland', *Soziale Welt*, vol. 38, pp. 379–407.

Lepenies, W. (1981) *Geschichte der Soziologie*, 4 vols (Frankfurt: Suhrkamp).

Lepsius, M. R. (1979) 'Die Entwicklung der Soziologie nach dem Zweiten Weltkrieg 1945–1967', in Lüschen (1979a) pp. 25–70.

—— (ed.) (1981a) 'Soziologie in Deutschland und Österreich 1918–1945', *Kölner Zeitschrift für Soziologie und Sozialpsychologie*, Sonderheft 23 (Opladen: Westdeutscher Verlag).

—— (1981b) 'Die Soziologie der Zwischenkriegszeit: Entwicklungstendenzen und Beurteilungskriterien', in Lepsius (1981a) pp. 7–23.

Lüschen, G. (1979a) 'Deutsche Soziologie seit 1945', *Kölner Zeitschrift für Soziologie und Sozialpsychologie*, Sonderheft 21 (Opladen: Westdeutscher Verlag).

—— (1979b) 'Anmerkungen zur Entwicklung und zum Praxisbezug der deutschen Soziologie', in his (1979a) pp. 1–24.

Lutz, B. (1986) 'Warum jetzt die Frage nach der Zukunft der Soziologenausbildung stellen?', *Soziologie*, vol. 14, pp. 153–62.

Matthes, J. (1973; 3rd edn, 1981) *Einführung in das Studium der Soziologie* (Opladen: Westdeutscher Verlag).

—— (1988) 'Quo vadis litteratura sociologica?', *Soziologische Revue*, vol. 11, pp. 253–56.

Mertens, L. (1987) 'Die personelle Enthauptung der deutschen Soziologie', *Soziologie*, vol. 15, pp. 120–32.

Neidhardt, F., Lepsius, M. R. and Weiss, J. (eds) (1986) 'Kultur und Gesellschaft', *Kölner Zeitschrift für Soziologie und Sozialpsychologie*, Sonderheft 27 (Opladen: Westdeutscher Verlag).

Schelsky, H. (1977) *Die Arbeit tun die anderen. Klassenkampf und Priesterherrschaft der Intellektuellen* (Opladen 1975: Westdeutscher Verlag; hier München 1977: dtv).

Tenbruck, F. H. (1984) *Die unbewältigten Sozialwissenschaften oder die Abschaffung des Menschen* (Graz: Styria).

Tessaring, M. (1982) 'Anmerkungen zur Beschäftigungssituation von Gesellschaftswissenschaftlern', *Soziologie*, vol. 10, pp. 15–17.

Viehoff, L. (1984) 'Zur Entwicklung der Soziologie an den Hochschulen der Bundesrepublik Deutschland 1960–1981', *Zeitschrift für Soziologie*, vol. 13, pp. 264–72.

Weymann, A. (1972) *Gesellschaftswissenschaften und Marxismus. Zur methodologischen Entwicklung der Gesellschaftwissenschaften in der DDR* (Düsseldorf: Westdeutscher Verlag).

——, Ellerman, L. and Wingens, M. (1986) 'A Research Programme on the Utilisation of Social Sciences', in F. Heller (ed.), *The Use and Abuse of Social Science* (London and Beverly Hills: Sage) pp. 64–73.

—— and Wingens, M. (1988a) 'Soziologisches Wissen in der AFG-Politik', *Zeitschrift für Rechtssoziologie*, Sonderband 1988 (in press).

—— (1988b) 'Die Versozialwissenschaftlichung der Bildungs- und Arbeitsmarketpolitik', in Beck and Bonss (1988).

Wingens, M. and Weymann, A. (1988) Utilization of Social Sciences in Public Discourse: Labeling Problems', *Knowledge in Society*, vol. 1 (Pittsburgh and New Brunswick: Transactions).

Ziegler, R. (1984) 'Die Entwicklung der Mitgliedschaft in der Deutschen Gesellschaft für Soziologie seit 1955', *Soziologie*, vol. 12, pp. 5–11.

12   What Dutch Sociology Has Achieved

Leo Laeyendecker

Before trying to describe and analyse the possible achievements of Dutch sociology, I will briefly indicate the main lines of its development and some of its distinctive characteristics. This is necessary for two reasons. First, one cannot assume that the history and character of Dutch sociology are well known to foreign sociologists, since most Dutch sociologists write and publish only in their native language. Second, achievements depend on both the internal and external functioning of the sociological system. Therefore I will describe the latter first.

Leaving aside the forerunners who published around the turn of the century, the first period of Dutch sociology can be said to have run from about 1920 until the early 1950s. The work was largely descriptive. This has been called the period of *sociography*. The main object was the description of social life in all its aspects and in various settings: villages, neighbourhoods and regions as well as specific groups. These activities were comparable with the work of the Chicago school. Both suffered from a lack of theoretically guided analysis.

The second period lasted until about 1969. A number of younger sociologists became dissatisfied with description only, and wanted a type of sociology that offered explanation too. They leant strongly on American sociology with its combination of theory and empirical analysis. These sociologists were less interested in a grand theory (such as that of Parsons) than in theories of the middle range (in the style of Merton). One of the leading figures in Dutch sociology remarked that:

> This preference is in harmony with the Dutch dislike of the sweeping gesture, the overall design, our predilection for prudent limitation, for careful restriction and going the middle way. (den Hollander, quoted by Berting, 1985, p. 11)

These sociologists were seriously convinced of the relevance of sociology for the post-war reconstruction of Dutch society and the building of a welfare state. They saw sociology as a method of

221

intervention, to echo Comte. The positivistic search for laws and regularities had to be pressed into the service of society in general and the government in particular. Sociology had a very pronounced policy orientation at that time.

This orientation was appropriate to the specific Dutch situation. The Netherlands is a very crowded country, needing to utilise every inch of space for agriculture, industry, housing and recreation. In the postwar period new polders were endyked and these were an excellent sphere for planning. There was a planning-mood in the Netherlands and this turned out to be a stimulating climate for social scientists in general and sociologists in particular.

One of the consequences was that the number of students rose rapidly. In the 1960s the number of freshers increased from about 75 to about 400 a year. This level was maintained until the mid–1970s, although, as we shall see, that was for another reason. The growing number of students necessitated an enlargement of the sociological institutes and an accompanying recruitment of teachers on different levels. Here one of the reasons for later decline becomes manifest already. There simply was not enough quality to fill the vacancies.

It has to be said also that the ideal of the angry young men, the effective combination of theory and research, was only half realised. Most of the studies were of a descriptive nature. Something else has to be mentioned too. In contrast to the sociologists of the previous period, who were more or less worried about the way in which socio-cultural changes affected the traditional institutions, the 'new' sociologists were 'modern'. They believed in progress, acclaimed the modernisation process and tried to stimulate it with the help of research and advice.

THE STUDENT REVOLT AND ITS CONSEQUENCES.

An apparently radical change took place at the end of the 1960s. Strongly influenced by a Marxist and 'critical' mood, students pressed for basic change in the way of doing social sciences; a not insignificant number of staff-members joined them. It was suggested that so far the social sciences had functioned as a lubricating oil of the societal system but from now on these sciences had to contribute to changing society in the direction of liberty, equality and social justice. This could only be done with the help of Marxism, which was considered by many students as the only acceptable way of doing social science. It has to be noted, however, that this mood did not go along with any substantial knowledge of Marxism. It nevertheless had its effects.

A number of developments have to be indicated very briefly. First, revolting against the existing hierarchy of power, students and staff-members demanded effective participation in decision-making and that was what they obtained. A new law was enacted, by which councils were established, at both the university level and that of the faculties. In these councils, which had the right to decide on matters of teaching programmes and research projects, students and young members of staff were sometimes able to overrule the professors. Several professors avoided participation in these councils and went their own way as much as possible. They no longer accepted responsibility for the overall policy, in a sense waiting for better times.

Second, the teaching programmes were influenced by the Marxist mood and the critical theory of the Frankfurt school. This does not mean Marxism dominated all along the line. But the least one can say is that radical students and staff-members claimed an equal place for Marxism alongside the more traditional teaching. It is worth mentioning that this development stimulated the so-called pluralism debate. Having started in the early 1960s, with the consensus-conflict debate, it now received new impetus with the battle between 'positivists' and 'critical theorists'.

The third point concerns the research being done. It is no exaggeration to say that it stagnated. Greater autonomy for younger staff-members did not lead to successful research projects. The anti-positivistic climate was another factor in inhibiting empirical investigations. Statistics and methodology were not very well developed and received little attention, because students were inclined to under-estimate these courses. Of course, this does not mean that there was no research at all. But the overall level of academic sociology was declining relatively rapidly.

At the same time the number of freshers in all the Dutch university departments of sociology increased to a maximum of about 480 a year. They had a different motivation from that of earlier generations: a lot of them wanted to change society, preferably overnight. Its natural counterpart, the expansion of the institutes, continued. These quantitative developments resulted in a high density of sociologists in the Netherlands. In 1981 their total number was about 7000. The rate of increase was higher than in the United States and reached several times that of West Germany (Creemers and IJzerman, 1985, p. 81). Nearly 50 per cent had a job in governmental institutions or in the social services and 20 per cent were employed by the universities. The absorptive capacity of Dutch society was still sufficient to prevent unemployment.

These developments were a curse in disguise. There were too many sociologists and many of too low quality. This became apparent inside and outside the universities by the end of the 1970s and the beginning of the 1980s. Inside the universities a growing number of sociologists realised that something had to be done about it. But that was not easy, for at least two reasons. First, for every change in, for example, teaching programmes, approval of the councils was needed. And a lot of its members were eager to defend their own interests. Second, university teachers, as government employees, were difficult to dismiss, even if they had not accomplished any academic output.

In this situation the teachers inside the institutes, concerned about academics standards, were in need of external assistance. This assistance came primarily from the boards of the universities. In several universities the state of research became an object of concern. This resulted in effective quality control. Only those projects that could stand evaluation by competent judges could count on personnel and money. With these measures the boards appeared to anticipate governmental measures in the 1980s.

REORGANISATION

The assistance came from outside the universities too. The government tried to get a grip on the universities. Already in 1960s the government had tried to evolve plans for a reorganisation of the universities. The rapid increase of the total number of students, together with the long time they used to spend at the university, required a stricter regulation of the 'input' and 'throughput' of students. But these plans met with relatively little success in the 1970s. For that, an economic recession was needed and a more forceful government. Both 'conditions' came to be fulfilled in the 1980s.

Successive governmental measures in that period aimed at a more strict organisation of teaching programmes and research. The first measure to be mentioned was aimed purely at economising. The university courses were reduced to the present length of four years. Only a very small percentage of graduate students is allowed to continue another four years in order to prepare a doctorate. Because of this the average quality level of graduates is in danger of going down. Second, the government has taken several measures to re-organise research. On the assumption that the research programmes were too fragmented (for another view, see Leeuw and van Gageldonk, 1984), the government wanted to finance only such programmes as would answer some new criterion of size, in terms of internal consistency and number of participating sociologists.

A third measure affected some disciplines only, including sociology, and had to do with another development. The increase in the number of enrolments for sociology came to a standstill at the end of the 1970s and changed into a severe decrease in the course of the 1980s. This development led to a surplus of staff – and an opportunity for the government to cut budgets for the universities in general, and the humanities and the social sciences in particular. As far as sociology was concerned, the government decided to close down some institutes and to merge others. Moreover, the budgets of the remaining institutes were cut back severely.

Given the carefully guarded autonomy of the universities, this was a unique policy, but the government had no cause to fear extensive political resistance or even protest. The universities in general and social sciences in particular had suffered from a heavy loss of prestige in society. This is not easy to explain but is worth considering.

In the first place, it may be due to rising scepticism about science in general. With respect to the natural sciences, this has to do with the growing awareness of the heavy risks connected, for example, with the enormous expansion of modern (nuclear) technology. Although it is absurd to stigmatise sociology for exactly this reason there is another reason for scepticism. Sociology may not be seen as a source of problems but it also appeared to be of little help in solving social problems. The expectation that sociological knowledge could be used to change society in any desired direction could not be substantiated. This disillusion went hand in hand with a decreasing belief in the possibility of steering and planning society.

But the problem may also be seen from a different angle. In a paradoxical way the loss of prestige may partly be ascribed to a certain measure of success achieved by sociology. The sociological perspective on social processes and some ways of thinking unexpectedly became widely accepted in society. Sociological concepts such as 'system', 'role', 'mobility', 'ideology', 'consensus model' and 'conflict model' by now belong to everyday language. Sociological interpretations help people to interpret their own situation. They assume, for example, that they are victims of the system or that their private problems are really public issues. Social movements, such as the feminist movement, legitimise their strivings with – more or less sophisticated – pieces of sociological analysis, by claiming to be striving, for example, towards 'a new division of male and female roles' in society. This is the process of social 'scientification' of daily life and it is indeed a success. But the perverse effect is that the specificity of the social contribution is not recognisable any longer.

A rather trivial factor is relevant too. The university is no longer the closed world it used to be. The public was able to witness all the quarrels and fights that took place in that sacred institution and the sociologists especially did not try very hard to hide their problems. They had a tradition of debunking, and in the late 1960s and the 1970s they were debunking their own situation by saying in interviews, for example, that the way sociological departments were governed was a mess, and that something should be done about it. Other faculties, although not very different, showed a more prudent attitude.

Finally, the demand for problem-solving had led to the development of new disciplines which were partly derived from sociology and partly grew on the basis of experience of all those who had gone into practical jobs. Freshers are more interested in these new disciplines: management science, organisational counselling, educational counselling and administrative sciences. These *kundes* have a more practical orientation and seem to promise a better chance of a job.

One has to consider the possibility that these developments may bring about a return to a more realistic situation. It may be said that sociology was for a while too popular and that the expectations with respect to its practical potential were too high. From that point of view there is no reason for alarm, although such a period of crisis involves a lot of problems on the personal level.

SOCIOLOGISTS AT WORK

As far as internal functioning is concerned there is no doubt that we are now definitely advancing after a period of crisis in the 1970s. There is no reason to deny the positive influence of some (not all) of the pressures from outside the sociological institutes. But it is equally true that sociologists themselves have reorganised their teaching and research in a most promising way. Therefore it is now time to look more closely at the theoretical and empirical achievements of Dutch sociology.

Three preliminary remarks are in order. The first one is a warning against a possible misunderstanding. In the foregoing exposition I have spoken about the problems in the internal and external functioning of sociology as a social system. That does not mean, however, that there were no achievements at all. In the period before 1969 and in the subsequent period of troubles, a number of excellent pieces of research were published. It must be noted too that the upheavals have called attention to neglected areas of concern, such as deprived groups, the role of women and ethnic minorities, as well as methods of investigation based on interactionist and conflict approaches to social processes. I will mention a few of the programmes.

In the field of agrarian sociology a nice and impressive research programme was carried out in the 1960s dealing with the modernisation process. It concentrated on changes in cultural patterns and in attitudes of farmers. This programme of the Wageningen School – an agricultural university – was well-founded theoretically, empirically sound, and highly relevant for policy-makers. Some of its results were a more precise insight into selective adaptation of new patterns of behaviour, into the tension with old traditions, into the role of information services and into the introduction of new methods of farming (Benvenuti, 1961).

Another important research programme originated in the University of Leyden. Already in the 1950s a strong research tradition in stratification and mobility had come into being under the direction of one of the most important Dutch sociologists in the postwar period, F. van Heek. In the 1960s this programme as such came to an end, but it found a continuation in the field of educational sociology also under the direction of van Heek. That 'new' programme concentrated on the problem of inequality in pupils' performance. It turned out that such an inequality was not due to differences in natural abilities, but to differences in the opportunity-structure, more particularly language differences, in various social settings (Kuiper, 1978).

Mentioning only these two bigger programmes does not mean that other work in the form of projects was unimportant. Interesting work has been published, for example, on religious pillarisation, on the behaviour of religious groups, on organisational sociology and on policy-oriented research. But it is not possible to be exhaustive here.

In the second place it must not be concluded that the research activities of the 1980s are a direct result of pressures from outside. Already in the 1970s new programmes were launched in a number of places, and these received unexpected support from the governmental measures, fighting the supposed fragmentation of sociological research.

My third preliminary remarks concerns the fact that the three most important research programmes in the late 1970s and 1980s are connected with different paradigms in the Kuhnian sense. This is an important difference with earlier programmes. The programmes on stratification or on rural modernisation are not easy to classify in terms of paradigms. It is empirical research in the Mertonian sense, testing hypotheses of the middle range. Such empirical programmes which have no explicit connection with any specific paradigm are still present in modern Dutch sociology. An example is the extensive programme now in progress on Society and Religion in the Netherlands. But I will here confine myself to three programmes which are not only empirically oriented, but have an explicit interest in theory formation and paradigm development as well. The selection of these programmes is not a matter of personal 'taste', but is in line with the results of some inquiries into 'the state of the art' of Dutch sociology that have been initiated by the government (Ellemers, 1982; van der Kaa, 1987). These reports give more complete information regarding specific tendencies, numbers of students and academic output.

The three programmes are connected with figurational sociology, with structural-individualistic sociology and with data-based sociological practice. Before starting the description it is advisable to say something about their origin and infrastructure.

Their origin is connected with the organising activities of certain individuals. The figurational sociology stems from N. Elias, of course, and is propagated in the Netherlands by J. Goudsblom of the University of Amsterdam, who has gathered a number of students around him. The structural-individualistic approach came into being as an organised phenomenon, when:

> a small number of sociologists, scattered over several Dutch universities and isolated in their own departments, formed a joint working-group. They shared a strong dissatisfaction with the prevailing emphasis on metatheoretical topics (such as 'paradigms' and 'theoretical perspectives') and with the ubiquitous gap between theorising and empirical research. Besides this community, they all shared a positive concern for sociology as an explanatory science. (Wippler, 1978, p. 138).

The leading figures are R. Wippler and S. Lindenberg from the

Universities of Utrecht and Groningen. The data-based sociological practice stems in its specifically Dutch form from M. van de Vall (University of Leyden) who developed 'a professional paradigm' in several publications and who founded the Leyden Institute for Social Policy Research. The two first groups are characterised by a kind of 'closure' and this becomes apparent in citation networks and the use of favourite journals (Hagendijk and Prins, 1984). The figurational sociologists publish in *Sociologisch Tijdschrift*, edited in Amsterdam. As a matter of fact, most of the articles of that journal are written in a figurational vein. The structural-individualists find their home in *Mens en Maatschappij*. However, this latter relation is less compelling. The 'data-based' group do not have a specific journal at their disposal. This group seems to be less coherent, not only for lack of a journal and an extensive citation network, but also because its orientation is a more restricted one.

ACHIEVEMENTS

Figurational sociology seems to be an orientation rather than a systematic complex of premises, models and hypotheses. Reacting against two characteristics ascribed to modern sociology – that is to say, too strong a distinction between man and society and a neglect of process and change – figurational sociology focuses on 'figurations'. The assumption is that one can get an adequate idea of social reality only if one starts with the concept of interdependence. People are dependent on each other for, among other things, emotional, political or economic reasons and enjoy relative autonomy only. Together they form figurations, 'structures of interdependence'. The concept of figuration is applicable on different levels, that of the small group, the organisation, the national society or the international community. The smaller figurations form part of the bigger ones and every higher level is relatively autonomous over against the lower levels. This whole complex of figurations forms a 'process'; it is constantly moving. In simple figurations the direction of the process is strongly influenced by power relations, for example between the 'established' and the 'outsiders', but in the more complex figurations nobody has the capacity to control the direction of the process. Actions by people in figurations have effects that are unforeseen and unintended.

This general idea finds its most fruitful application in the analysis of long-term processes. Figurational sociology is a kind of historical sociology. Elias is particularly interested in the interdependent processes of differentiation, integration (state-formation in particular) and civilisation (increasing restrictions on behaviour). In other words, sociogenetic processes are interdependent with psychogenetic processes and vice versa.

This 'orientational frame' has been used for research on a great variety of topics, and a great many studies have been published in this vein. They include, for example, studies on property relations in the nineteenth century (Wilterdink, 1984); on the civilising of workers between 1870 and 1940 (de Regt, 1984); on taboo, power and morality in Dutch society (Kaptein, 1980); on the development of the welfare state (de Swaan, in press); on the informalisation process (Wouters, 1977); on the sociogenesis of the psychoanalytic setting (de Swaan, 1977); on the establishment of Freudian psychotherapy in the Netherlands (Brinkgreve, 1984); on the development of art in the Renaissance (Kempers, 1987); on the use and control of fire from the early beginnings of history to the present (Goudsblom, 1984, 1985a, 1985b, 1986a, 1986b).

It is possible to continue for a while but since this is not a bibliography of figurational sociology it is time to stop here and assess the achievements. But why talk of achievements at all? This question cannot be answered without taking into account the ideas of figurational sociologists about the functions of sociology. They especially accentuate its enlightenment function. One of its representatives considers sociology

> an intellectual tradition, an inheritance of theoretical literature, a more or less continual discussion about a number of interdependent themes. In his view the sociologist is a well-read and trained spectator of society for general use . . . and has to have the disposal of a broad erudition and an encompassing insight in societal developments in their interdependency. One cannot expect a sociologist to make a direct contribution to the improvement of society, to say nothing about a contribution to the control of society. It is the task of sociology to contribute to the improvement of the discussion about society. (de Swaan, 1985, pp. 101–2)

It is significant in this context that Elias and his followers speak about 'means of orientation'. (See also van Benthem van den Berg, 1980, pp. 176–206.) People are in need of such means in a society that is characterised by an ever-growing complexity. It is the task of the sociologist to develop and refine such means of orientation and to show how in a variety of situations changes in human behaviours are accompanied by changes in social figurations, and how people form an active part of processes that are difficult to control or to foresee. Formulated this way it is difficult to avoid the accusation of triviality, and in some cases the studies are trivial indeed. But to express a well-founded opinion it is necessary to look at the better studies, which were mentioned above. They help people to get a better view of the dynamics of personal and social life in their interdependency.

Some problems are involved, however. The first problem concerns the identity of sociology. Reading the publications it is sometimes difficult to distinguish between sociology and history. That frequently is the case in historical sociology. Those who make a plea for an integration or at least a very strict co-operation between the two disciplines are probably not impressed by such a remark. In agreement with Elias they will point to the fact that the distinction between the two is a historical product itself, institutionalised in the academic world. In this view there is no sense in splitting up disciplines which share an object that is essentially historical.

That is indeed true. But since this development has taken place and since there are advantages too in the division of labour it may be useful to keep to the distinction. One cannot have the best of both sides combined in one person, and it can certainly not be learned in the short time of academic training.

Another problem is related to the enlightenment function. In my view it is remarkable that, as far as I can see, the figurational sociologists, who like to contribute to the discussion about society, show very little interest in 'moral problems'. Of course, they are interested in morals as a historical phenomenon and try to understand why morals have changed. But that is different from taking part in a discussion about the 'right' choices in personal and social life. Mostly the attention is focused on problems in past centuries which is beyond doubt important for understanding life at the end of the twentieth century. But understanding is one thing, responsible action another, and enlightenment implies reflection on both.

I admit that this problem is a product of my conviction that sociologists have to engage themselves in the clarification and possible solution of actual social problems. This personal point of view will be disputed by others. It is true that a value-free *sociology* does not and cannot formulate standpoints about moral problems, but *sociologists* can and have to. It is not easy to understand why figurational sociologists disapprove of a division of labour between sociology and history, while maintaining that division between sociology and/or history on the one hand and ethics on the other.

The last comment concerns the problem of the accumulation of knowledge and is connected with the internal coherence of the programme. The great variety of topics in figurational sociology is a serious hindrance to accumulation. Accumulation of knowledge supposes, in my view, continuous research on the same subject-matter. But the connecting element in figurational sociology seems to be only its specific perspective, its approach. It would be advisable instead to concentrate on a restricted number of substantive problems if any illuminating view on present society is to result from the studies.

The structural-individualistic approach contrasts heavily with its figurational counterpart. Explanation and accumulation of inform-ative statements are its ideals. Both programmes, however, have one thing in common: they both try to bridge the micro-level and the macro-level. But figurational sociology tries to do so with the help of a new concept, that of 'figuration', and the structural-individualistic approach does so by a strict explanatory frame of reference. The assumptions of this programme as formulated by Wippler (1978, 1985) may be summarised as follows. (i) The explanatory strategy is the deductive-nomological one or DN-explanation. (ii) In accordance with the principle of methodological individualism the universal statements are formulated on the individual level (this implies a rational choice theory or learning theory). Structural and institutional conditions are taken into consideration as initial and boundary conditions. (iii) The complexity of social phenomena necessitates the construction of models, that is to say the utilisation of simplifying assumptions. These models 'will successfully be replaced by more realistic assumptions' (Wippler, 1985, p. 66). (iv) The question now is 'how individual action (or effects) which are explained by general propositions about individuals and initial conditions referring to social settings, are to be related to these collective "phenomena"?' This 'problem of transformation' has to be resolved by the formulation of transformation rules – a set of rules specifying how and when particular individual actions produce a particular collective effect. 'These transformation rules fulfil, in the context of explaining collective phenomena, the same function as general propositions about in-dividuals do in the context of explaining individual effects.' (v) In conclusion, Wippler states:

the structure of explanation of collective phenomena can be schematically described as a twofold argument. First from laws about human nature and initial conditions referring to social situations, statements about different courses of individual action under varying social circumstances can be derived (so called individual effects). Secondly: Transformation rules, together with given individual effects and various boundary conditions (referring to institutional or social-structural arrangements) allow the deduction of statements about collective phenomena. (1978, p. 143)

(vi) And finally, it is said that the approach is opposed to psychological reductionism and is not satisfied with macro-sociological description without explanation; i.e. it is concerned with a theoretically powerful macro-sociology.

The sociologists working on this programme have concentrated on a small number of themes. In the last ten years attention has shifted from theoretical and methodological to substantive problems, while the variety of topics has decreased. Examples to be mentioned are: deviant behaviour (Vos, 1976); culture and the processing of information (Ganzeboom, 1984); conflict, loyalty and violence (Flap, 1988); oligarchic tendencies in democratic organisations (Wippler, 1986); and social mobility (Ultee, 1986).

It is beyond doubt a strong research group and a strong programme as well. The group is systematically planning its activities and effectively striving for national grants. Its productivity is high. The researchers utilise sophisticated methods of investigation and a good co-operation with data-theorists is guaranteed. It is worth mentioning also that they attempt to reconstruct classical theories such as Durkheim's theory of suicide (Lindenberg, 1975) and Michels's iron law of oligarchy (Wippler, 1986).

Nevertheless, there is a problematic point in this approach. One may well say that the explanatory method has many merits. But the correctness of the explanations provided depend on the possibility of connecting universal laws of human behaviour with specific social and cultural conditions. An interesting question is whether and to what extent such an explanation becomes invalid or non-comparable with others if these conditions change. Let me elaborate this a little. If there are parliamentary rules with respect to legislation and if members of parliament vote according to these rules and the conditions for passing a law are fulfilled, then a collective phenomenon, such as this new law, has come into existence. (Here the behaviour of individuals leads to a fact on the level of the collectivity and this can become clear by virtue of a transformation rule). This transformation rule, however, is valid only because of the existence of an institution which, of course, is changeable on the one hand, and varies from country to country on the other. It is questionable, therefore, how these transformation rules can be applied to accumulated observations on the behaviour of individuals in different times and at different places.

This problem – leading to a 'devaluation' of sociological knowledge – has led some Dutch sociologists, also non-figurationists, to drop the pursuit of the accumulation of explanatory statements and to plead for a sociology as an art of commenting on the societal situation and social developments. It is understandable that this horrifies the structural-individualists. And not only them, because the position and 'professional identity' of the sociologists are at stake here.

The third research group is engaged in 'data-based sociological practice'. This programme has a much smaller focus, since it is not oriented to society as an object of research, but to meta-research as has been mentioned above. It is analysing data and constructing theories as well as methods of applied social research and it is developing procedures for the diffusion of research results. It also tries to design policy alternatives and to implement policy programmes (van de Vall and Leeuw, 1987).

In its policy-orientation this programme is not very new, since one of the characteristics of Dutch sociology has traditionally been exactly such a policy-orientation. But there are now important differences from the traditional policy-oriented research. The first difference concerns the claim to take into account two parameters, the implemental and the strategic, in addition to that normally considered, namely the epistemological. The second lies in the importance these researchers attach to systematic (re)construction of policy theories. For the clarification of both differences, I will follow the exposition that two of the leading figures of this approach have recently given.

Social policy research aims 'at facilitating organisational decisions'. It

caters to a more complicated value context that besides rigorous epistemological standards, also includes two additional require- ments . . . [it] consists of a sequence of transformation processes in terms of three different value parameters. (a) The epistemological parameter: translating a social policy problem in terms of epistemo- logically sound research operations; valid, reliable, representative and exact. (b) The implemental parameter: translating the research results in terms of manipulable variables and conditions to facilitate the design and development of policy alternatives. (c) The strategic parameter: translating the manipulable variables into a strategy of problem reducing policy action. (van de Vall and Leeuw, 1987, p. 192)

'Policy theory' is 'defined as a deductive system of hypotheses about certain problems that underlies policy measures and that deals with cause-effect relationships' (Leeuw, 1984, p. 2). All policies 'rest on theories about human and social behaviour', and policy-makers use them consciously or even unconsciously. It is the task of policy-oriented research to (re)construct these theories and to judge them in terms of epistemological, implemental and strategic parameters.

The (re)construction can be done as follows. (i) Collect statements of policy-makers with respect to a particular problem; (ii) write down the intended effects of the policy as exactly as possible; (iii) differentiate the policy in terms of policy-proposals, policy-intentions and policy-practices on the one hand and types of steering mechanisms on the other; (iv) trace the means-ends relations and translate them into hypotheses about causes (planned means) and effects (intended goals); (v) add, with the help of argumentation analysis, the missing of implicit links in the claim of reasoning; (vi) bring the results of the operations (iv) and (v) together in a deductive system (Leeuw, 1986, p. 35). It has to be noted that this concept of theory is on a different level. It refers to the theories policy-makers have in mind with respect to the problems considered. When these theories have been reconstructed, they can be 'checked' against the scientific theories about these problems.

So far, the programme has resulted among other things in the development of methods for policy research in the Third World, a procedure for social policy research planning or 'programming' and methods for assessing 'policy theories' underlying programme implementation (van de Vall and Leeuw, 1987, p. 194). Besides pertinent publications in the field of meta-research, reports have been published in which specific policies were analysed, such as the population policy (Leeuw, 1984) and research policies with respect to the supposed fragmentation of the research in the social sciences (Leeuw and van Gageldonk, 1984).

In my opinion this programme is a promising and effective one, precisely because of the two innovations in policy-oriented research

236   *What Dutch Sociology Has Achieved*

mentioned above. The implemental and strategic parameters facilitate
the effectiveness of application; the reconstruction of policy theories
invites a fundamental discussion about the implicit or explicit assumptions of the policy-makers. The relation between policy and sociology
can be improved that way.

At the end of the 1980s we may say that Dutch sociology has
overcome its temporary setback in the 1970s. Although the external
conditions are not yet favourable, the theoretical and empirical
performance and potentialities are strong enough to be optimistic
about the future.

References

Berting, J. (1985) 'Continuities and Changes in Dutch Sociology', *The Netherlands Journal of Sociology*, vol. 21, pp. 4–19.
Benthem van den Berg, G. van (1980) 'De sociale wetenschappen als orientatiemiddel', in his *De staat van geweld* (Amsterdam: Meulenhoff).
Benvenuti, B. (1961) *Farming in Cultural Change* (Assen: van Gorcum).
Brinkgreve, C. (1984) *Psychoanalyse in Nederland* (Amsterdam: de Arbeiderspers).
Creemers, W. J. G. and IJzerman, T. J. (1985) 'De beroepsperspectieven van sociologen in Nederland', *Mens en Maatschappij*, vol. 60, pp. 79–90.
*Doorn, J. A. A. van (1956) 'The Development of Sociology and Social Research in the Netherlands', *Mens en Maatschappij*, vol. 31, pp. 189–264.
Ellermers, J. E. (1982) 'Sociologisch onderzoek in de jaren tachtig', in *Visies op onderzoek in enkele sociale wetenschappen. Pre-adviezen ten behoeve van een beleidsnota maatschappij- en gedragswetenschappen* ('s-Gravenhage: Staatsuitgeverij) pp. 179–99.
Flap, H. D. (1988) *Conflict, Loyalty and Violence. The Effects of Social Networks on Behaviour* (Frankfurt and Bern: Lang).
Ganzeboom, H. B. G. (1984) *Cultuur en informatieverwerking* (Utrecht: Sociologisch Instituut).
Goudsblom, J. (1984, 1985a, 1985b, 1986a) 'Vuur en beschaving. De domesticatie van vuur als een beschavingsproces', pts 1–4, *De Gids*, vol. 147, pp. 227–43: vol. 148, pp. 3–27; vol. 148, pp. 714–22; vol. 149, pp. 640–52.
—— (1986b) 'Vuur in de wereld van het Oude Testament', *De Gids*, vol. 149, pp. 784–802.
Haan, H. J. de and Nooy, A. T. J. (1985) 'Rural Sociology in the Netherlands', *The Netherlands Journal of Sociology*, vol. 21, pp. 51–62.
Hagendijk, R. P. and Prins, A. A. M. (1984) 'Referenties en Reverences. Onzekerheid, afhankelijkheid en citeernetwerken in de Nederlandse sociologie', *Mens en Maatschappij*, vol. 59, pp. 226–50.
Heek, F. van (1968) *Het verborgen talent* (Meppel: Boom).
*Hofstra, S. (1967) 'Die gegenwaertige Situation der neiderlaendischen Soziologie', in G. Eisermann (ed.), *Die Gegenwaertige Situation der Soziologie* (Stuttgart: Enke) pp. 140–81.

Kaa, D. J. van der (1987) 'Advies Sociale Wetenschappen', *Uitleg*, vol. 2, no. 70, pp. 4–11.

Kaptein, P. (1980) *Taboe, macht en moraal in Nederland* (Amsterdam: de Arbeiderspers).

Kempers, B. (1987) *Kunst, macht en maecenaat* (Amsterdam: de Arbeiderspers).

Kuiper Hzn, G. (1978) 'Stratificatie in Nederlands: De Leidse School', in J. L. Peschar and W. C. Ultee (eds), *Social Stratificatie* (Deventer: van Loghem Slaterus) pp. 13–26.

Leeuw, F. L. (1984) *Overheid en bevolkingsgroei: een evaluatie en beleidstheorie* ('s-Gravenhage: Vuga).

—— (1986 'Beleidstheoretisch onderzoek, toen en thans', *Beleid en Maatschappij*, vol. 13, pp. 27–39.

—— and van Gageldonk, A. (1984) *Differentiatie in sociaal en geesteswetenschappelijk onderzoek* ('s-Gravenhage: Staatsuitgeverij).

Lindenberg, S. (1975) 'Three Psychological Theories of a Classical Sociologist', *Mens en Maatschappij*, vol. 50, pp. 133–53.

*Peype, D. C. J. van (1979) 'Ontwikkeling van de sociologie in Nederland', in L. Rademaker (ed.), *Sociologie in Nederland* (Deventer: van Loghem Slaterus) pp. 22–66.

Regt, A. de (1984) *Arbeidersgezinnen en beschavingsarbeid. Ontwikkelingen in Nederland 1870–1940* (Meppel-Amsterdam: Boom).

Swaan, A. de (1977) 'On the Sociogenesis of the Psychoanalytic Setting', in P. R. Gleichmann *et al.* (eds), *Human Figurations* (Amsterdam: Amsterdams Sociologisch Tijdschrift) pp. 281–313.

—— (1985) 'Kleine sociologie van de sociologie', *Kennis en Methode*, vol. 9, pp. 90–104.

—— (in press) *In Care of the State.*

Ultee, W. C. (1986) 'Intergenerational Standard of Living Mobility in the E.E.C. Countries', *European Sociological Review*, vol. 27, pp. 1–18.

Vall, M. van de and Leeuw, F. L. (1987) 'Unity in Diversity: Sociology in the Netherlands', *Sociological Inquiry*, vol. 57, pp. 183–203.

Vos, H. de (1976) 'Groepsgrootte als randwoorwaarde voor twee theorieen over afwijkend gedrag', in W. A. Arts *et al.* (eds), *Gedrag en strucktuur* (Rotterdam: U.P.R.) pp. 177–93.

Wilterdink, N. (1984) *Vermogensverhoudingen in Nederland* (Amsterdam: de Arbeiderspers).

Wippler, R. (1978) 'The Structural-Individualistic Approach in Dutch Sociology: Toward an Explanatory Social Science', *The Netherlands Journal of Sociology*, vol. 14, pp. 135–56.

—— (1985) 'Explanatory Sociology. The Development of a Theoretically Oriented Research Programme', *The Netherlands Journal of Sociology*, vol. 21, pp. 63–74.

—— (1986) 'Oligarchic Tendencies in Democratic Organisations', *The Netherlands Journal of Sociology*, vol. 22, pp. 1–17.

Wouters, C. (1977) 'Informalisation and the Civilising Process', in P. R. Gleichmann *et al.* (eds), *Human Figurations* (Amsterdam: Amsterdams Sociologisch Tijdschrift) pp. 437–55.

13 Strategies for Future Achievement in Sociology
Wil A. Arts and Henk A. Becker

1 INTRODUCTION

In this chapter we will search for strategies that could stimulate future achievement in sociology. This task requires finding an answer to three questions.

1. What is the situation in sociology with regard to the stimulation of achievement, both national and international?
2. Which are the social actors available for carrying out strategies, and what are the constraints confronting them?
3. What strategies are available, and what are their most likely consequences?

In this chapter we will have to concentrate on the enhancement of knowledge and methodology in sociology and on their application. Equally important subjects like the education of students will be dealt with marginally only.

2 SOCIOLOGY AS AN OPEN SOCIAL SYSTEM

When sociologists are looking for strategies to reach achievement in their discipline they often look at their discipline as a rather autonomous system of theoretical ideas and research methods. From this point of view growth of knowledge in sociology can be obtained by just elaborating, against the background of the philosophy of science, better rules of method and a critical analysis of sociological traditions with the help of those rules (Ultee, 1980). This viewpoint often goes hand in hand with the idea that achievement in a scientific discipline is identified by the community of scholars, a kind of 'forum' acting as umpire in the competition of new ideas and methods (de Groot, 1971).

An approach like this does not take into consideration the typical setting of the discipline, the roles of the social actors involved and the constraints confronting them, however. If we look at sociology as a social system from the viewpoint of organisational sociology and from economics we can get a broader perspective and a more adequate explanation of the developments that led to the present situation in the discipline. In the broader perspective, sociology as a discipline can be seen as an open social system. It is a network of direct and indirect social relationships between sociologists and their institutes and other work organisations, and this network has been integrated into more-encompassing social networks. The more-encompassing social networks put constraints on the developments within sociology, and therefore also on its achievements. Like all social systems of this kind sociology is not an absolutely 'open' system, however, but a relatively open one only.

What are the principal characteristics of today's sociology? We can give an answer to this question by looking at the mechanisms that co-ordinate and control the communication and interaction within the system. In some respects it looks like a complex organisation, a hierarchical structure of a bureaucracy. Most of all, however, it looks like a market. Clan, bureaucracy and market are ideal types (Ouchi, 1980).

In the 1950s the dominating school in sociology was functionalism. The upmarket part of sociology approached in those years the ideal type of a monopoly. Downmarket there were some dissenting approaches practised, but these marginal activities did not operate as effective competitors to the dominating school.

In the 1960s and the early 1970s a tendency towards extreme market segregation developed. The different schools, paradigms, perspectives, etc. in those years constituted independent segments of the sociological market. The segregation was so severe that not only social mobility but also interaction and communication between market segments was low. The different schools developed as non-competing groups. Without much exaggeration we can say that in those years we witnessed a 'balkanisation' of sociology.

In the middle of the 1970s the situation in the sociological market changed again. Maybe the end of the Cultural Revolution documented by Gadourek (1982) is responsible for this shift. The segmentation of the market decreased, but without, as this volume bears witness, giving way to complete integration.

Since the beginning of the 1980s in a number of countries the situation of sociology has changed as a result of an increasing demand for applied knowledge. In The Federal Republic of Germany and in the Netherlands, for example, the 'no nonsense' policy has ultimately had as a side effect an increasing demand for sociological research into practical problems related to deregulation, privatisation, and reorganisation in sectors like health care, labour markets, income distribution and education. As a result of this improved market position the discipline has been able to defend itself better than before against severe budget cuts and other restrictive measures.

Each of the three traditions in sociology appearing in this book more or less occupies a market segment of its own. Maybe the historico-institutional tradition in sociology has a market that lies nearer to the market of the historical sciences in general than to the market of the analytical tradition in the discipline. In turn the analytical tradition has a market that lies close to that of the empirical sciences searching for explanations and law-like statements in general. The market segments involved do not exist in complete isolation, however. They partly overlap, for instance because the 'readerships' for their 'products' (books, articles, etc.) overlap to some extent.

In today's sociology we not only detect split markets but also a split scientific community. In an abstract sense there is such a thing as an overall community of sociological scholars. Sociologists all over the world have been socialised with regard to a number of concepts, approaches and values. They share a number of major and minor classics. If they are members of an international association of sociologists, it is the same one (the International Sociological Association). But to a certain extent this 'common culture' is window-dressing only. If historical developments had taken a different course, the three traditions in contemporary sociology might have developed into three different disciplines, or each might have become part of another discipline, without much difference from the present situation with regard to research, theory formation and application.

This does not imply that the traditions in sociology have remained unchanged since the 1950s. In the analytical tradition the search for 'covering laws' has been reformulated (see Chapter 2). In the hermeneutical tradition the methodology for the interpretation of documents has changed, and the plea for 'grounded theory' by Glaser and Strauss (1967) has initiated a major innovation. The historico-institutional tradition has changed its preferences as well, taking developments in the historical sciences in general into consideration.

Since the 1960s sociology has grown from 'little science' towards 'big science' (de Solla Price, 1963). Large numbers of 'invisible colleges' have emerged (Crane, 1972), especially in interdisciplinary areas of study related to practical problems. These processes of growth have undermined the identity of the discipline. They have blurred the boundaries between traditional sociology and neighbouring disciplines. On the other hand these tendencies of growth are related to external demands for the services of sociologists, and therefore they have to be taken into consideration when explanations are sought for the continuing existence of the discipline.

The external 'pull' has been mainly directed at the applied part of sociology. The pure part of sociology has had to stay alive more or less on its own, prospering on a 'push' coming from the inside of the discipline. Financially, pure sociology has been at the mercy of parliament and other central budgetary forces almost completely.

The foregoing characterisation of today's sociology requires differentiation with regard to national situations, however. In the United States, sociology is highly market-oriented, showing a lot of competition going together with voluntary evaluation mainly by peer review, without a central authority. In Sweden, sociology has been oriented towards state bureaucracy more and more during the last few decades. State officials and allied interest groups have developed a strong capacity of overriding the traditional privileges and the autonomy of university professors. In Italy we find a strong scientific community in sociology, oriented towards a powerful national academic oligarchy (Clark, 1983). In Figure 13.1 the situation of sociology (including education of students in sociology) is sketched.

Searching for an optimal organisation of sociology as a social system we have to keep three points in mind. First, that disciplines with a strong internal organisation (like the physical sciences) profit from this situation, but have also to pay a price for it: new ideas often have to struggle for a very long time before they get recognition. Second, that because of the strong quest for applied knowledge sociology will always display the dual characteristics of a specific academic community, on the one hand, and 'producer' of services for society at large, on the other. Last, but not least, that in an optimal scientific discipline we want to find both creativity and a fair discussion of new ideas.

3 SOCIAL ACTORS AND THE CONSTRAINTS CONFRONTING THEM

In the relatively open market situation in sociology *individual sociological scholars* have played their part. According to popular

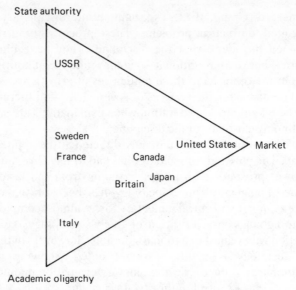

Figure 13.1   The triangle of co-ordination
Source: Burton R. Clark, *The Higher Education System*, 1983, p. 143.

belief, disciplines are ruled by scientific 'giants'. Sometimes this is true. In recent decades there has, however, been no Keynes or Chomsky in sociology, dominating the discipline for a long period or causing a one-man shift in paradigms. Sociology has hosted some 'little giants', like Parsons, and still hosts 'little giants' like Habermas or Boudon, but those have not been able 'to lay down the law' in sociology. The same applies to each of the three traditions. None of these traditions has hosted a sociologist who could dominate the whole tradition. Maybe the frequent changes in sociology and its traditions outlined above have acted as constraints against the domination by specific individual members of the discipline and of its subdivisions.

Universities and their (national or international) associations, university departments and related organisational units – none of these has seen fit to act as a major force in the development of the discipline. In sociology no rich faculties have 'bought' enough major scientists to be able to dominate the whole market or a significant part of it. Some activities by actors like these may carry some weight in the long run, however. In Britain, for instance, the heads of university sociology departments have decided to contradict collectively in public any serious attack directed at sociology as a discipline. Budgetary cuts since the mid–1970s have curtailed in general the power of universities and faculties to influence developments in disciplines.

Professional associations acting as moral entrepreneurs (both national and international) have had some impact on sociology. By publishing refereed yearbooks and journals they have contributed to 'peer review' and to the communication of ideas. But professional associations in disciplines like sociology are not in a position to specify and enforce standards of professional quality. They would lose too many members doing so. A number of competing professional associations might lead to a specification of professional standards and to their enforcement. But a system like this requires a discipline that is vital enough to demand quality control. Often external pressure is required to induce a discipline to organise some kind of quality control.

National and international science councils have been active in stimulating achievement in sociology. If they are in a monopolistic position there is a real possibility that they will exert a conservative influence. Scientists trying to get funding for their research projects then have no choice but to comply with the requests from the monopolistic science council. If there are two or more science councils competing with each other, achievement may be stimulated in an effective and progressive way.

Governmental departments and international organisations (like UNESCO) have also tried to stimulate achievement in sociology. If intervention by government agencies is directed by the preferences of individual bureaucrats and without independent peer review, the results may be disastrous. But sometimes government intervention is restricted to providing funds for stimulation of disciplines or specific subject areas, and the allocation of funds is put into the hands of independent evaluating bodies. In this case government intervention can turn out to be effective, for instance, if 'preferential support' is provided.

The Max Planck Institutes in the German Federal Republic are an example of 'preferential support'. Distinguished scholars are given an opportunity to establish a research centre of high quality. The future of the institute is linked to the duration of the working life of the founder(s). If they cannot guarantee quality any more, the continuation of the institute may be questioned and eventually it will be closed down. Another way of stimulating quality is practised by bodies like the World Health Organisation who select research institutes and appoint them as 'affiliated research centres'.

Editorial boards of scientific journals or book series can also exert influence, but on a limited scale only. They can act as 'trend setters' in a specific area. If the trend turns stale, editorial boards are often slow in changing their policy with respect to which contributions are acceptable and which not.

Last, but not least, *all the members of the discipline*, from senior scientists to young assistants, are contributing to one or more strategies in the discipline involved. Acting as individuals or in work organisations they apply for research funds, do research, publish, apply the results of their work and contribute to the utilisation of knowledge. As long as there is some general idea behind their activities, or as long as competing ideas do not contradict each other too much, the market system may function acceptably. If a scientific discipline like sociology is structurally in a vulnerable position, however, reliance on some kind of spontaneous order in the market system becomes too much of a gamble. Because sociology lacks an overall public or bureaucratic support, it has a heavy price to pay for the 'liberal anarchy' it tolerates in its market system.

4 STRATEGIES AND THEIR CONSEQUENCES

Next we shall elaborate a number of *strategies* that could be used by one or more of the actors involved. In the first place we have to specify the *objectives*. The principal objective of each of the strategies would be stimulation of achievement in sociology (maybe combined with stimulation of achievement in related disciplines). Auxiliary objectives would have to be improvement of the internal and external relationships of sociology as a social system. These auxiliary objectives require an explanation. A sound disciplinary social system is a necessary precondition for achievement on more than an incidental basis.

Second, the *instruments* have to be specified that could be used to accomplish the objectives. Let us assume that the actors involved could utilise:

1. low-budget activities: improving peer review, stimulating affiliation with organisations practising quality control; identification of landmarks among the results obtained in the discipline;
2. medium-budget activities: stimulation and support of publications (yearbooks, journals); stimulation and support of conferences,

etc; stimulation and support of international exchange programmes; selective budget cuts with regard to academic departments;
3. high-budget activities: preferential support (on a temporary basis) of high-quality individuals and research institutes; training programmes for gifted young scientists; other activities involving substantial financial resources (more research grants, etc.).

Third, the *strategies* themselves demand our attention. We shall specify three strategies. Strategy A will be called 'voluntary co-operation and quality control', where sociologists hold the initiative. Strategy B is called 'governmental control', showing central government as the dominant actor. Strategy C carries the name 'consumer sovereignty and disciplinary autonomy', and in this case the 'clients' of sociology take the initiative. Each of the three strategies will be elaborated a little bit further now.

In strategy A, the most important actors would have to be the professional associations, the science councils and groups of sociologists, with government agencies and international organisations operating as mediators. In this strategy voluntary quality control (by peer review mainly) would lend power to the research centres in specific areas relying partly or mainly on sociology. Strategy A is especially appropriate in a period of expanding financial resources for social research in general and for sociological research in particular. This strategy leads to a quite differentiated picture of sociology as a discipline, and people outside sociology might find it difficult to get an overview of the discipline and of achievement in it. In the triangle of co-ordination present earlier in this chapter Strategy A is nearest to the corner called 'academic oligarchy'.

Strategy B introduces a strong emphasis on central control by government agencies. University departments would be forced to prove that their research activities meet the standards specified by government. Selective budget cuts would provide enough margin for central government to finance the whole operation. By using preferential support decided upon by government, the direction of developments in the discipline would be dictated. Because analytical sociologists can meet crude quantitative standards best, they would have a headstart under this strategy, leaving the members of the two other traditions in relatively unfavourable positions. Under strategy B a considerable number of university departments would by-pass the activities of central government by increasing their volume of contract research, thereby earning enough money to avoid part of the hardships of central governmental control. Strategy B is to be expected in times of severe cutbacks by central government combined with strong central regulation. Strategy B may lead to a distinct image of the discipline. Central control in general has a tendency to crush new initiatives and to evoke rigid structures. In the triangle of co-ordination, strategy B lies near 'state authority'.

Strategy C is directed at the 'market' position in the triangle. Now sociologists adopt a 'two-hands strategy'. With one hand they serve their consumers, accepting the demands of consumers without much discussion. They provide research projects and provide consultancy on request. The second hand in this strategy is a more or less autonomous one: distributing money and other resources towards fundamental research, advanced training and detached social criticism. Strategy C is appropriate as an escape in times of cutbacks and privatisation. In the short term it might give sociology a bad reputation in 'academe' and in progressive circles. In some countries, such as the USA, strategy C has been followed for so long that it has become generally accepted. The image of sociology might become fuzzy were this strategy to be followed.

These strategies cannot be utilised without taking the situation in the country concerned into consideration. In a country with a favourable economic development and a liberal political climate, strategy A might be optimal. A harsh economic development and a centralised govern-mental system may lead to strategy B, with ultimately strategy C as an escape. The three strategies are sketched with a number of assump-tions in mind. We have to make these assumptions explicit in order to avoid misunderstandings. The first assumption involved is that sociology will continue as a specific academic discipline. The second assumption is made that the different traditions in sociology will stay with us for a long time and maybe forever (cf. Lammers, 1974). As a third assumption we mentioned that sociology will co-operate with other disciplines without losing its own identity. Assumption number four states the conviction that there will be a demand for sociological contributions to the solution of social problems in future years.

References

*Clark, B. R. (1983) *The Higher Education System* (Berkeley: University of California Press).
Crane, D. (1972) *Invisible Colleges: Diffusion of Knowledge in Scientific Communities* (Chicago: University of Chicago Press).

Gadourek, I. (1982) *Social Change as Redefinitions of Roles* (Assen: van Gorkum).

Glaser, B. G. and Strauss, A. L. (1967) *The Discovery of Grounded Theory* (Chicago: Aldine).

Groot, A. D. de (1971) *Een Minimale Methodologie* (The Hague: Mouton).

Lammers, C. J. (1974) 'Mono- and Poly-Paradigmatic Developments in Natural and Social Sciences', in R. Whitley (ed.), *Social Processes of Scientific Development* (London: Routledge & Kegan Paul) pp. 123–47.

Ouchi, W. G. (1980) 'Markets, Bureaucracies and Clans', *Adminstrative Science Quarterly*, vol. 25, pp. 129–41.

Solla Price, D. J. de (1963) *Little Science, Big Science* (New York: Columbia University Press).

Ultee, W. C. (1980) *Fortschritt und Stagnation in der Soziologie* (Darmstadt/ Neuwied: Enke Verlag).

14 Conclusions
Henk A. Becker and
Christopher G. A. Bryant

1 ACHIEVEMENT IN SOCIOLOGY: A SECOND LOOK

In our introductory chapter we said of 'achievements' that they 'have a presence which cannot be ignored and they help others to orient their work. They give form to what otherwise might be amorphous and they point the way where otherwise there might have been aimlessness.' We also said we would return to the issues of achievement and progress in the Conclusions. Helped by material drawn from our contributors we are now in a position to do so. With one exception we shall continue to treat achievement as that which the sociological community recognises as such; the exception concerns achievement in applied sociology for which recognition outside the academy is also relevant. Put another way, claims for achievement are redeemed when those to whom they are addressed agree to them. Claims may be made within a particular research programme, or more broadly within one of our three research traditions, or within sociology as a whole, or with a view to endorsement outside sociology (by other social scientists) and outside the academy (by various interests and publics). We shall also acknowledge that the enhancement of sociological knowledge, the application of sociological knowledge and the development of sociology as a social system, pose different requirements.

1.1 The Enhancement of Sociological Knowledge

In his introduction to the history of sociology, Laeyendecker (1981) reconstructs three criteria – systematicity, verifiability and relevance – that have been used by sociologists to decide which contributions are worthy of inclusion in the history of their discipline.

Of systematicity Laeyendecker writes:

Precisely formulated this criterion says that phenomena must be

248

described in an orderly way – that the relationships between phenomena must be ascertained and that these relationships must be explained . . . Insights into relationships, formulated as propositions, are yielded by explanations. Explanation constitutes the objective of the search for knowledge in all scientific disciplines. Alternatively we can describe science as a specific method for answering 'why' questions. (Laeyendecker, 1981, pp. 52–3).

Systematicity, it seems to us, is about ordering, about making connections. Here, as with each of Laeyendecker's criteria, one might posit the use by the sociological community of a narrow and broad interpretation. The narrow interpretation allows only causal analysis related to law-like statements a place in the 'body of knowledge' of the discipline. The broad interpretation admits other ways of making connections, such as the contextualisations of the hermeneutic tradition and the figurations of the historical-institutional tradition.

Verifiability he specifies as follows:

A systematic approach needs a foundation. Description and explanation must be reliable and valid. They must be neither haphazard nor accidental. This is possible only if the propositions are verifiable, that is to say it must be possible to ascertain their truth value . . . The criterion of verifiability presupposes a reliable research methodology. What we consider to be reliable depends on our convictions with regard to the characteristics of knowledge and knowledge acquisition. In other words we need an epistemological theory to guide the selection of methods. (ibid, p. 53)

Here the narrow interpretation requires adherence to strict methodological rules such as those formulated by Popper (notwithstanding his ontological anti-foundationalism). By contrast the broad interpretation argues that there are no sure foundations for our knowledge, no privileged methods that guarantee truth, but that there are rules of argument and evidence that may be said to work in that they yield explanations and understandings which are adequate for the purposes in hand, academic and practical.

The third criterion, relevance

has been described as being useful in one way or another. This criterion is relatively vague unless we specify the senses in which science has to be useful. As a rule theoretical and practical relevance are distinguished. The first implies that the outcomes of science have to contribute to our insights into the world. This is seen as an objective in its own right. Practical relevance has to do with the applicability of the outcomes. There are, however, no strict border lines between these two types of relevance. Insights into connections between phenomena almost always have a practical utility, although the latter is not always evident in the short term. (ibid, p. 54)

The narrow interpretation separates verifiability and relevance. Verified knowledge is useful theoretically if it connects with other knowledge and adds to our insight into the world, and is useful practically if it has applications (such as empirically traceable impacts on decisions). The broad interpretation treats relevance as an extension of verifiability in so far as the latter is only intelligible in the context of whatever it is sociologists are trying to do. Although none of them wrote with Laeyendecker in mind, contributors to Fiske and Shweder (1983) not only take up positions similar to the thin and broad interpretations we have sketched out, but also extend their reasoning beyond anything we have space for here.

The criteria that Laeyendecker has reconstructed bear some resemblance to those used by Deutsch (1986) in his essay 'What Do We Mean by Advances in the Social Sciences?' Deutsch also refers to criteria-in-use in characterising advances in terms of impact, frequency of citation, etc. His 'rationality' (in operational terms 'retraceability'), 'confirmability' (by way of empirical methods based on standardised operations) and 'limited validity' (in time and space) also do much the same job as Laeyendecker's systematicity, verifiability and relevance. We prefer our elaboration of Laeyendecker, however, because the broad interpretation of his criteria does not require us to defend some version of the unity of the natural and social sciences, something to which Deutsch explicitly subscribes. In addition we think Laeyendecker's criterion of 'relevance' for which Deutsch has no analogue, is an important one.

Laeyendecker does not try to identify 'progress'. To do so involves the claim that achievements are greater or more numerous compared with some earlier time. We like Deutsch's suggestion that progress consists of an increase in the range of understanding and control – 'an increase in what people can recognize, what they can predict, and what they can do' (Deutsch, 1986, p. 10). But we would change the emphasis in two ways. First, recognition is a bigger issue than Deutsch supposes in so far as it shades into the constitution and reconstitution of society; we do not just discover or uncover, explain or account for, our world –

we make it and remake it. Second, there are ways, some of them long ago identified by Weber, in which sociology would seem destined to remain eternally young. In particular, what there is to be recognised and controlled, and what we choose to attend to out of what there is, are forever open to change. The questions thereby raised, however, are beyond the scope of this volume.

Adherents to the narrow approach, reviewing the achievements suggested by our contributors, will find little which meets their requirements. Even the analytical tradition has not a great deal to offer. Subscribers to the broad approach within the analytical tradition, on the other hand, have less difficulty in coping with open systems and what Boudon calls disorder; and Becker has been able to identify achievements. Participants in the other two traditions almost always take the broad approach; and again Williams and Mennell have been able to identify achievements without difficulty. In addition Bryant has pointed out that achievements in theory extend beyond the explanatory theory with which Becker is concerned to such fields as the history of social thought and the philosophy of social science; and Abell has identified solutions to technical problems in research methods. Both Becker and Abell, however, have also noted weaknesses in the linkage of theory and research.

All in all, what we have assembled here are circumspect appreciations. Much has been achieved – but no one wants to make exaggerated claims which, when exposed as such, leave sociology worse off than it was before.

1.2 The Application of Sociological Knowledge

Those who take a thin perspective will only talk of achievement where impacts from the application of sociology are measured by quantitative research, and where requirements are met which were stated by the parties concerned prior to the start of the research project or innovation process at issue. Examples are few. If a broad outlook is adopted, the picture changes. In particular Bulmer has indicated that more examples of applied sociology conform to the enlightenment and interactive models than to the social engineering model of applied research. Either way, sound methodology is a prerequisite of success.

1.3 The Development of Sociology as a Social System

Do we have criteria for evaluating what goes on in sociology as a social system? The Dutch Ministry of Science Policy (1978) has provided criteria for all the social sciences in the Netherlands; these are worth considering. The first criterion lays down that the social sciences in the Netherlands should monitor and review developments elsewhere so as to ensure that the Dutch Goverment has available to it knowledge that is already available to governments in other societies. Second, social scientists in the Netherlands are expected to make enough contributions to their disciplines to be accepted as partners in the international scientific community. Third, Dutch social scientists should develop theories, approaches and data-sets about the situation in the Netherlands relevant to policy formation with an expertise comparable to that at the disposal of other governments. The fourth criterion pertains to social scientists as social critics. The Dutch government expects the social sciences to alert it in good time about developments which might acquire problematic characteristics. The fifth criterion demands that the social sciences assemble, maintain and refine the humanpower, organisational structures, equipment and documentation necessary to meet the first four criteria. Becker (1986) has assessed social research in the Netherlands using these criteria as a starting-point. Arts and Becker's chapter on Strategy also addresses some of these issues at the national and international levels, and further points arise in the next section on the five national chapters.

2 STRENGTHENING SOCIOLOGY: LESSONS FROM FIVE SOCIETIES

The authors of our five 'national' chapters all had the same brief, reprinted with only minor amendment as the Introduction to this volume. They have interpreted it in different ways and there have been practical limits to the degree of consistency which we could subsequently impose. In particular Mullins writes about the institutional base and social context of American sociology but eschews any mention of substantive achievements. However, so many of the references in Chapters 2 to 7 are to American works that this matters less than might have been expected.

In none of the five societies with which we have been principally concerned can sociologists feel confident that the institutional structure of teaching and research in sociology, and the wider cultural and political context in which they take place, are entirely satisfactory. But if each has its particular configuration of problems, each also offers lessons about one or more of the components which would seem to be needed if sociology is to be both securely established and highly productive.

2.1 Diversity of Provision and Funding for Teaching and Research

First, there is virtue in diversity of funding for teaching and research and diversity of control of the institutions which deliver them. Mullins has emphasised that President Reagan's major cutbacks in federal support for social science research did less damage than might have been expected – and not just because social scientists fought back through the Consortium of Social Science Associations (COSSA). There were too many federal providers for President Reagan to control them all easily, there were alternative public providers at the state level and there were also many private supporters of teaching and research who did not share President Reagan's hostility towards social science. It is important to note, particularly in Britain where Mrs Thatcher's governments are applying the twin policies of privatisation *and* the centralisation of public authority, that the American experience points up the virtue not only of mixed public and private support but also of diversified support within the public sector. In America and Germany, states and *Länder* respectively maintain their own university systems; in Britain, central financial control of formally self-governing universites has from 1989 been extended to polytechnics which hitherto had been owned, and ultimately run, by local authorities. The American experience also points up the need for public research foundations to retain some independence of judgement. The American National Science Foundation, for example, has more discretion than the British Economic and Social Research Council (ESRC) which, ever fearful of abolition, cannot afford to offend its mistress.

2.2 The Advantages of Size and Scale

Second, there is virtue in size in the conduct of major empirical research programmes. Here, as Weymann makes clear, Germany has shown the way in quickly setting up large research institutes, and large joint research programmes of the universities and the Deutsche Forschungsgemeinschaft (DFG), to investigate topics of major social importance at a time when sociology numbers at the Centre National de Recherches Scientifiques (CNRS) in France have, according to Bernoux, ceased to grow and ESRC support for sociological research has declined. Six of these German institutes each had between 40 and 130 full-time social scientists working for them in the mid-1980s (Weymann, 1988). It is probably premature to ask whether they represent value for money – for they are formidably expensive – but it is immediately evident that British conceptions of the concentrations of human and other resources necessary to make a significant impact on a cluster of related problems are puny by comparison. The sole big British sociology programme in recent years – ESRC's new economic life initiative conducted by teams in fourteen centres under the overall supervision of Duncan Gallie at Oxford – has involved at various times a total of thirty-two holders of teaching appointments and twenty-six research officers (Gallie, 1989). The first phase, beginning in May 1985, had an initial budget of £1 370 000; the second, beginning in October 1988, has a budget of £262 000. The German example, and also that of the long-established CNRS, which, in Bernoux's estimate, employs around 500 sociologists, are also a reminder that some countries provide career structures for large numbers of full-time researchers, whilst other, like Britain, do not. The British may well be right in believing that teaching at the highest level benefits from the involvement, in contrast to French university practice, of most teachers in research. But that is not to say that large centres of social research, both connected to and separate from teaching departments, and with large staffs, some of whom will remain full-time researchers throughout their careers, should not also be established. The small size of most teaching departments in Britain compared with those in North America and on the Continent, and the range of courses they are obliged to teach, also make it harder for British sociologists to develop specialist expertise at the highest level. Then, too, coping with cutbacks and reorganisation has taken its toll in both Britain and the Netherlands.

2.3 Placement of Graduates in a Range of Employments

Third, there is virtue in preparing graduates for employment in a wide range of occupations in both the private and public sectors. Here the Dutch experience is instructive. Dutch social science departments grew large on the provision of graduates for employment in public administration. Laeyendecker claimed at Noordwijk that 70 per cent of Dutch graduates in sociology work for the government in some capacity or other. It is, of course, highly desirable that all public bureaucracies should have respect for the skills in social research and analysis which social science graduates (should) possess. Mullins has commented that it exists in America, and Laeyendecker acknowledges it in the Netherlands. But the Dutch relationship was too cosy. When the public sector was cut back, student demand for social science courses, and government funding for social science teaching, fell because both prospective students and the government over-associated the employment of social science graduates with public administration. The prime example of the placement of sociology graduates in a very wide range of employments is, of course, the American, but it is increasingly supported by British experience too.

2.4 A Balanced Age Structure

Fourth, there is virtue in a balanced age structure of sociology teachers and researchers. At Noordwijk, Bryant expressed doubt about Abell's argument that metatheory has occupied far too many young sociologists by questioning whether, in Britain at least, there has actually been much of a young generation who could have been corrupted by it. Many departments have no staff under the age of 35 and theorists seem to be greying just as surely as everyone else. What is less contentious is that those in mid-career have been less challenged by younger colleagues keen to embrace new ideas and new activities than they ought to have been. There are comparable problems in other societies too. According to Stephen Turner:

> The demographic structure of American sociology differs from that of British sociology, in that a large cohort entered the field after the Second World War. This group has reached retirement age, but because of the effective abolition of mandatory retirement, many who should have retired have not. So the 'graying' of Sociology is, if anything, more visible in the US. (S. Turner, 1988, pp. 6–7)

Mullins, too, claims that lack of openings for sociology PhDs has had a lot to do with the crisis some American sociologists feel. Failure to renew through fresh recruitment is especially harmful where those in post got their first jobs against comparatively little competition and include some who have had difficulty both in keeping up with subsequent developments and in rethinking their old positions on theoretical, methodological and substantive issues. Laeyendecker has explicitly referred to this problem in the Netherlands, but there are variations on it in all the societies we have considered. It should also be noted that unbalanced age structures have impeded the cause of equal opportunities in academic life in so far as the reduction in the volume of appointments has coincided with attempts by women to end their historic underrepresentation.

2.5 Lobbying

Fifth, sociologists have got to learn to promote themselves better. COSSA, described here by Mullins, has shown what lobbying can achieve. The Reagan administration may have intensely disliked the social sciences but it has proved less able to damage them than might have been expected because social science expertise is widely respected in government agencies and the business world and COSSA was able to appeal to their interest in its maintenance. As Eldridge notes, the Association of Learned Societies in the Social Sciences (ALSISS) in Britain would like to do something similar to COSSA but has had first to raise the cash. There is also no comparable tradition of respect for social science expertise in Britain, and there is a special scorn reserved from sociology that has no parallel in other societies. Lobbying is thus more difficult and will have to be done with particular skill and persistence. Lobbyists might well have more receptive audiences to appeal to in the Netherlands, France and Germany. Increased attention to the interactional model of applied sociology discussed by Bulmer would also help in so far as it brings home to would-be applied sociologists that their task is not over when they publish but is rather only just beginning. There might also be one trend running in favour of sociology in a number of societies. The great expansion of sociology degree courses took place in the 1960s. Graduates from that era are now in mid-career; some of them can be expected to go on to senior positions in public and social administration and in industrial and commercial management. They might well prove more supportive of sociology than those now retiring, many of whom, in Britain at least, are not even graduates – let alone former students of sociology.

2.6 Intellectual Vitality and Intellectual Breadth

Sixth, the intellectual vitality of the sociology of the future is best assured by making provision for all the tradition of sociology discussed at Noordwijk. Mullins has commented that in America research in the analytical tradition is very much better founded than theoretical research as most Europeans would understand it; and Eldridge asked at Noordwijk whether there was a future in America for the critical tradition of Veblen, Lynd, Mills and Gouldner. Similarly Weymann has indicated that in Germany work in the analytical tradition enjoys much more of an institutional infrastructure than work in the hermeneutic and historic-institutional traditions. In discussion at Noordwijk he also argued that the split between the big applied social research centres and academic sociology is too great; the former have not yet contributed significantly to the theoretical development of the discipline and the two camps do not always show much respect for one another.

If Bryant is right about the circumspection which has followed the war of the schools, the renewed interest in theoretical synthesis and integration and the increasing influence of post-empiricist philosophy of science, the theoretical climate is changing in favour of more balanced provision. The key here may prove to be the readiness of analytical sociologists to come to terms with post-empiricist philosophy of science. Becker, for example, is readier to do so than Jonathan Turner in another recent review of analytical sociology (Turner, 1987; Bryant, 1989). Balanced provision also requires a sophisticated understanding of what Abell has called variable-centred and account-centred research methods and of research designs which incorporate elements of both. This is not easy to obtain. On the one hand Alexander has deplored 'the technocratic fetishism of empirical sociology' which prevails in the United States whilst on the other a recent report from ESRC in Britain has complained that sociologists and political scientists are insufficiently numerate (Alexander, 1982, p. xiv; ESRC, 1987). Certainly quantitative analysis, computing and the use of video should be part of every undergraduate degree course; in some societies, such as Britain, provision of the appropriate facilities on the scale necessary is held back by the classification of sociology as an arts discipline for purposes of funding. Notwithstanding this shortcoming, plus the need for better understanding of some of the achievements in research methodology which Abell outlines, and the continuing poverty of research funding, it could well be that British sociology has come as near as any to getting the balance right between the different traditions of sociology. Open to both the empirical and statistical traditions of American sociology and the theoretical and philosophical traditions of European sociology, it has had the singular fortune to be a meeting point for the sociologies of the world.

References

Alexander, J. C. (1982) *Theoretical Logic in Sociology*. vol. *1 Positivism, Presuppositions, and Current Controversies* (London: Routledge & Kegan Paul).

Becker, H. A. (1986) *Social Research and Policymaking* (Utrecht: van Arkel).

Bryant, C. G. A. (1989) 'Towards Post-Empiricist Sociological Theorising', *British Journal of Sociology*, vol. 40, pp. 319–27.

*Deutsch, K. W. (1985) 'What Do We Mean by Advances in the Social Sciences?', in *K. W. Deutsch, A. S. Markowits and J. Platt (eds), *Advances in the Social Sciences, 1900–1980* (Lanham and Cambridge/Mass.: Abt Books and University Press of America).

Economic and Social Research Council (1987) *Horizons and Opportunities* (London: ESRC).

Fiske, D. W. and Schweder (eds) (1986) *Metatheory in Social Science: Pluralisms and Subjectivities* (Chicago: University of Chicago Press).

Gallie, D. (1989), Letter to C. G. A. B., 26 January 1989.

Laeyendecker, L. (1981) *Orde, Verandering, Ongelijkheid: een Inleiding tot de Geschiedenis van de Sociologie* (Meppel: Boom).

Ministry of Science Policy (Netherlands) (1978) *Memorandum on the Five-Year Plan Regarding Social Research and Policymaking* (The Hague: Government Printing Office).

Turner, J. H. (1987) 'Analytical Sociology', in A. Giddens and J. H. Turner (eds), *Social Theory Today* (Cambridge: Polity Press).

Turner, S. (1988) Letter to the editor, *Network: Newsletter of the British Sociological Association*, no. 40, January 1988, pp. 6–7.

Weymann, A. (1988), Letter to C. G. A. B., 12 December 1988.

Index

Note: page numbers in *italics* indicate references.

259